LEADING *the* CO-TEACHING

Dance :

Leadership Strategies to Enhance Team Outcomes

Council for Exceptional Children

Wendy Murawski

Lisa Dieker

Leading the Co-Teaching Dance: Leadership Strategies to Enhance Team Outcomes

ISBN 0-86586-474-8

Copyright © 2013 by the Council for Exceptional Children, 2900 Crystal Drive, Suite 1000, Arlington, VA 22202-3557

Stock No. P6067

Book Design and Layout: Carol L. Williams
Managing Editor: Kathleen McLane

Printed in the United States of America

10 9 8 7 6 5 4

Acknowledgements/Dedication

Wendy Murawski would like to acknowledge the following individuals: Christien and Kiernan Murawski, for their never-ending support, love, and encouragement; Amy Sheldon & Marcia Rea, for being the perfect combination of competence, efficiency, and snarkiness; Nino Belfortti, for bailing me out when I left my money at home while working at a restaurant (Nino, you told me thanking you in the acknowledgements would make us even. Done.); and finally, the ACME Book Club for being my place to laugh, share, vent, and generally get in some great girl-time with some amazing women (and occasionally even read some fantastic literature).

Lisa Dieker would like to acknowledge the following individuals: Richard and Joshua Dieker, for putting up with my love of doing "one" more thing to try and improve the field of education. You both are the definition of love and patience. To my dear friend Dianne Evans Kelley, who passed away this year way too early and who provided me with, as you said, "Eight years of different hairstyles" and what I said were the best co-teaching videos that have ever been created and that as of today have prepared thousands of co-teachers. You were the best co-teacher I have ever observed. Your passion to share thoughts and images of co-teaching will continue to change the field forever. To all of those wonderful co-teachers and leaders who have allowed me to learn from you, thank you.

This book is dedicated to the educational leaders who truly encourage and inspire collaboration and inclusion in their schools. We look up to you.

Table of Contents

Preface: **Meet Your Dance Instructors** ix

Chapter 1:   **Learning the Basic Moves**. 1

Defining Co-Teaching 1
Clarifying Inclusion 2
Identifying the Menu of Options 3
Benefits of Co-Teaching 7
What Co-Teaching Is Not. 8
The Essential Question of Co-Teaching. 9
Five Keys to Co-Teaching 11

Chapter 2:   **Setting the Stage** 15

Developing a Culture to Support Co-Teaching 15
Improving Schoolwide Communication About Co-Teaching 18
Determining Who Should Participate. 20
Strategic and Differentiated Professional Development 23
First Steps With New Teams 24
Building on Success 26

Chapter 3:   Beginning Choreography 33

                Avoiding Common Scheduling Mistakes 34
                General Scheduling Guidelines 40
                Beginning Stages Versus Veteran Schools 41

Chapter 4:   Advanced Choreography 49

                Small Schools Versus Large Schools 49
                Models of Elementary and Secondary Schedules 51
                Steps for Getting Started in Scheduling .68

Chapter 5:   Planning for the Dance 71

                The Need for Planning Time 71
                Creating Time for Co-Planning 73
                Strategies for Building In Time for Co-Planning 74
                Tools to Support Co-Planning 80
                Helping Teachers Use Co-Planning Time Efficiently 82
                When Co-Planning Goes Wrong 86

Chapter 6:   Creating Your Own Moves 91

                Understanding the Various Approaches to Co-Instruction 91
                Taking Co-Instruction to a Deeper Level 103

Chapter 7:   So You Think You Can Dance 105

                Observation and Feedback for Co-Teaching 105
                Co-Teaching Solutions System Observation Tables 107
                Other Co-Teaching Observation Tools 108
                Identifying Potential Problem Areas 110
                Providing Feedback for Improvement 120
                Addressing Conflict 124

Chapter 8:   **Getting Your Dance Scores** **127**

     The importance of Data Collection 127
     Co-Assessing Strategies 132
     Co-Teaching and Grading 135
     Data Collection by Administrators 138

Chapter 9:   **Becoming a Dance Pro** **139**

     Lessons Learned 139
     Institutionalizing Co-Teaching Through Goal-Setting 147
     Creating an Individualized Education Program
      for Co-Teaching 148
     Creating Co-Teaching Leadership Teams 149
     Mentoring Others 150
     Disseminating Success 151

Chapter 10:   **Performing for Others** **155**

     Creating a Movement 155
     Continuing Your Research 156

References **165**

Appendices 1 through 11 . . . . **175**

Preface

Meet Your Dance Instructors

If students are the nucleus of a school, administrators are the cell membrane. They help decide what programs, teachers, curriculum, policies, and philosophies are allowed to permeate into a school and which need to be kept out. Part of the administrator's job is to thoroughly scrutinize new initiatives in order to determine which are valid, viable, and worthy of the limited time and resources of faculty and staff, and which will have the most positive impact on student success. As the leader in your building, district, county, or state, we assume you are leading the dance toward change, higher outcomes, and any other initiatives that emerge to move students toward increased academic, behavioral, or social achievement. As the authors of this book, we want to provide you with steps we have learned to instruct you in the dance called "co-teaching." Therefore, this preface is devoted to quickly sharing the expertise and backgrounds of the authors, our work in co-teaching with school districts nationally and internationally, and the research that we use as a basis for the rest of the book. We know that if you are going to allow us to lead, you want to know that the materials and strategies we are sharing are practical and, most importantly, applicable to your specific role as an educational leader.

Not that this announcement will be news to you, but typically school leaders are more pressed for time than most educators — so we kept in mind that your time is precious as we wrote this book. We use an informal tone that is quick to read and easy to digest; we offer multiple tables and visuals that can be duplicated and shared with faculty, staff, and parents; we provide references to additional hard-copy articles and books, as well as online resources that can be obtained at your convenience and viewed at home in your comfy clothes. Because of the informal tone and light-hearted nature that we both often use with schools in our presentations and consultations, we sometimes get questions about our research base or the serious nature of our work.

This preface will help to lay those questions aside. After sharing our backgrounds, we'll then focus on providing you with the strategies and examples for improving co-teaching in your state, district, or school that we have gleaned from our own work and that of other wonderful researchers in the field of collaboration and co-teaching. In this next section, we share our personal and professional backgrounds. For many of you, this will be pertinent information, as you want to know who is communicating with you and what validity we may have. For those of you who really don't care about our backgrounds or may already know us and want to move straight to the book's content, feel free to skip this next part. That's going to be how we envision our readers using this book. You read the parts you need and you skim or skip the parts you don't need or have already mastered.

Authors' Professional Backgrounds

Dr. Wendy Murawski

Wendy Murawski has teaching credentials in learning disabilities, emotional disturbance, and German. She received her B.A. with a double-major in German and comparative literature from the College of William and Mary in Virginia. She followed it with a Master's in Special Education, also from William and Mary. Her first teaching job was at a high school in Virginia as a half-time German teacher (levels 1–5) and half-time special education teacher. That first job allowed Wendy to experience both sides of the table, as it were. She was a general educator with large class sizes and college-bound students, and she was a special educator with a life skills class, as well as students included in multiple general education classes. She co-taught that very first year, and her positive experiences continued from there. Working as department chair, Wendy then received her Ed.S. degree and certification in Educational Administration, but decided to pursue a career in higher education rather than school administration. After moving to California with her husband (actor/writer Christien Murawski), she completed her Ph.D. in Special Education with an emphasis on co-teaching and research, while teaching as a full-time special educator in Burbank. Wendy was hired at California State University, Northridge (CSUN) and was inspired to work with her mentor, co-teaching innovator Dr. Lynne Cook.

Over her 14 years at CSUN, Wendy has become a Professor in Special Education and the Eisner Endowed Chair of the Center for Teaching and Learning, in addition to Faculty President for the Michael D. Eisner College of Education and grant director of two federal grants focusing on transdisciplinary and collaborative teacher development. Though very active at her own institution, she also stays active in her field. Wendy is the Vice-President of the Teacher Education Division (TED) of the Council for Exceptional Children (CEC). She owns her own consulting company called 2 TEACH LLC (www.2TeachLLC.com) and has provided ongoing consultation to many districts across the country, including Paramount, CA; Baltimore County,

MD; Fayetteville, AR; San Angelo, TX; the Indiana State IEP Resource Center; and throughout the state of West Virginia.

Wendy has established herself as a national expert in the area of collaboration and co-teaching. She has authored numerous journal articles in both general and special education journals as well as multiple book chapters and an instructor's manual. She has three books on co-teaching published with Corwin Press and a best-selling resource handbook on co-teaching. She is an award-winning researcher (receiving the 2002 Dissertation Award from CEC's Division of Learning Disabilities), author (receiving the 2004 Publication Award from CEC's Division of Research), and teacher educator (receiving the 2004 California Teacher Educator of the Year Award from the California Council of Teacher Educators). Her meta-analysis on co-teaching research with Dr. Lee Swanson is often cited in the literature. She has presented nationally and internationally, is a frequent keynote speaker at conferences, is on multiple speakers' bureaus, and is often requested to consult and present to schools, districts, state departments, and at conferences. She has focused often on the administrators' role in co-teaching and has been a keynote speaker on the topic for multiple state-level principal's academies and conferences.

Wendy's crowning glory, however, is her 7 year-old son, Kiernan, who attends a fully inclusive charter K–8 school and has been in a co-taught classroom since he was in kindergarten. Obviously driven and passionate about co-teaching, only her dear friend, Lisa Dieker, rivals Wendy's high level of energy in her presentations and work!

Dr. Lisa Dieker

Lisa Dieker also is certified in general and special education with a degree in elementary education (K–8) and special education (K–12) in the areas of learning disabilities, behavior disorders, and intellectual disabilities. She received her undergraduate and master's degrees from Eastern Illinois University and her doctorate, which focused on both special education and curriculum and instruction, from the University of Illinois. Very early in her career she realized a passion for working with middle school and high school students. She co-taught throughout her career in the K–12 classroom in social studies, science, mathematics, English, culinary arts, and industrial arts. In higher education, she co-taught her special education methods courses in science, mathematics, and English. During her first sabbatical in Milwaukee, Wisconsin, she spent a semester substitute teaching in K–12 classrooms in urban schools, reminding herself of the challenges teachers face daily, and ensuring she could still walk the walk. During a more recent sabbatical, she spent her time visiting over 100 schools across seven states to look at what is working related to collaborative settings.

Lisa's first position in higher education was at the University of Wisconsin-Milwaukee, where she gained a passion for working in urban schools, and where she learned to embrace the unique opportunities available in urban schools, classrooms and communities. In Milwaukee, she co-founded and co-directed the University of Wisconsin (Madison)/Milwaukee Public Schools Special Education Internship Program in the high-need local education agency of Milwaukee Public Schools and received over $2.1 million in funding. Lisa is currently at the University of Central Florida (UCF) as Professor and Lockheed Martin Eminent Scholar. At UCF she works across general and speciation education. In special education, she coordinates the Ph.D. program and is proud to have had nine students with disclosed disabilities graduate from the program. She has received more than $3 million in funding for doctoral preparation from the U.S. Office of Special Education Programs. She is proud that she just received the UCF Doctoral Mentor of the Year Award. On the general education side, Lisa serves as the Director of the UCF/Lockheed Martin Mathematics and Science Academy, where she brings together doctoral students and teachers in collaborative structures across special education, mathematics, and science. In this role, she directs a K–8 teacher leadership program and a career-change program in mathematics and science. Lisa was instrumental in bringing together three colleges at UCF to collaborate on and create a simulated classroom environment called TeachLivE (http://www.ucf.edu/teachlive) to prepare teachers for urban settings. This virtual classroom simulator is currently being used by over 20 universities across the country, and the team at UCF, led by Lisa, just received the American Colleges of Teacher Education Innovative Technology of the Year Award and Honorable Mention from the National Consortium for Continuous Improvement in Higher Education. She was recently selected as CEC's Child Advocacy Network Coordinator of the year for her work related to policy. In addition, Lisa's research agenda focuses on high-need local education agencies, she has ongoing relationships with Alexandria, VA; Colorado Springs, CO; Omaha, NE; Putnam County, WV; Boston Public Schools; and the state of Arkansas. Annually, she is the lead faculty for a Secondary Urban Inclusion Institute for Dr. David Riley and the Urban Special Education Collaborative. Lisa has produced four books and two DVDs on effective strategies for inclusion, and she provides keynote presentations both in the United States and internationally. She has published numerous articles and serves on multiple editorial boards. She served as Co-Editor of *Journal of International Special Needs Education* and is the current Associate Editor for *TEACHING Exceptional Children*. One of Lisa's favorite activities is finding a way to connect with her friend Wendy to write together, shop, eat, sightsee, and spend time with family.

Speaking of families, one of the unique perspectives Lisa brings to the book is that of a parent and sibling of individuals with disabilities. Lisa and her supportive husband, Rich, live in Orlando, Florida with their 16 year-old son, Josh. Lisa and Josh recently keynoted the Learning Disabilities Association conference, where they shared Josh's experiences as a student with Tourette's syndrome and learning disability (not to mention his experiences as a regional gold medalist in men's gymnastics and as a competitor at the Junior Olympics) and Lisa's experiences as his mother.

Experiences With School Districts

As you can see from our background (and if you skipped that part, that's okay with us too), we've both co-taught across K–12, we've both taught teachers about co-teaching from preservice to inservice, and we've both completed extensive consulting, presenting, research, and writing on the topic of co-teaching. All of that would be just ivory tower, though, if we could not demonstrate application with school districts and actual classrooms. In Table 1-1, we identify some of the school districts with whom we have established long-term consulting relationships. With some of these districts, we started co-teaching from scratch and doing workshop after workshop on "Co-Teaching 101"; with others, we were or are continuing to help them develop long-term institutionalization of co-teaching practices. We completely agree with McLeskey and Waldron's (2002c) assessment that each school is going to have its own culture related to inclusion; there is no one-size-fits-all in terms of co-teaching or inclusive practices. We take our cues from the school leaders; although we know co-teaching, they know their teachers, their students, their community and families, and their own issues. Working with them, however, has helped us learn what is happening globally related to co-teaching. We have been able to glean best practice strategies that work, as well as observe practices that time and again result in frustration, fear, and failure. We promise to share those potholes we have seen along the way, but not perseverate on what is not working. Instead, the purpose of this book is to share how to move past those bumps in the road to what we have seen as successful outcomes for leaders who support teachers in their efforts to serve students. We thank these many school districts for allowing us to learn from them so that we can pass those insights on to you through this book.

> *Critical Connections*
>
> There is no "one-size-fits-all" for developing inclusive practices. Each school has its own culture that needs to be respected.

Research Base for this Book

This book is based on our personal research as well as the research in the field on co-teaching and education in general. Feedback from the hundreds of administrators we have worked with has informed us that although educational leaders want to be assured that the information they are getting is research-based and best practice, they do not need to be inundated with details, and they prefer to receive their information in quick-to-digest formats to match their busy schedules. Thus, although we have an extensive literature and research base from which we are pulling, we have written this book to conform to those preferences. We will synthesize research in the chapters themselves and provide an extensive reference list for those who wish to delve deeper into particular areas. Our goal is to give you access to the pieces of information relevant to an issue you might need to address in your school while allowing you to move past or revisit points not relevant to you at this time.

Table 1-1. Examples of national work by Murawski & Dieker		
State	**Districts**	**Years of Engagement**
Alabama	Baldwin County	5
Arizona	Deer Valley, Chandler, Kyrene, Glendale	5, 3, 2, 3
Arkansas	State Dept, Fayetteville	8, 2
California	Paramount Unified, Montebello Unified, Oxnard, Centinela Valley HS District, Los Angeles Unified, CHIME Institute, Granada Hills Charter, Ventura SELPA	4, 3, 4, 1, 7, 9, 4, 3
Colorado	Colorado Springs, Grand Junction	3, 2
Florida	Orange County, Seminole County	6, 3
Hawaii	Honolulu	1
Indiana	State Dept LRE Resource Center, Decatur Township	2, Beginning
Maryland	Baltimore County	5
Massachusetts	Everett, Boston Public Schools	3, 1
Nebraska	Omaha Public Schools	7
Ohio	Region 8, Canton Public Schools, Madison County, Electronic Classroom of Tomorrow	3, 3, 1, Beginning
South Carolina	Horry County	Beginning
Texas	San Angelo, Midway, El Paso, Corpus Christi, Amarillo	5, 2, 2, 2, 2
Virginia	Alexandria, Virginia Beach	4, 2
West Virginia	State Dept, RESA VIII, Putnam County	3, 4, 4
Wisconsin	Sun Prairie, Madison, Milwaukee	7, 3, 8

However, there is a relative dearth of research specific to the role of administrators in co-teaching. There are numerous factors involved when looking at educational research, and the variables are increased when dealing with interactions, collaboration, and communication. We will be referencing research conducted directly with co-teachers, but we have also garnered our information from related areas, such as educational administration, policy studies, and communication. In addition, our own work with schools and districts is quite broad and has led to research and practical findings we will be sharing throughout the book. Let us give you two prime examples.

Wendy worked with the West Virginia State Department for several years to help increase and improve their use of co-teaching statewide. After presenting to many elementary administrators and at least one administrator from every secondary school in the state, Wendy served as the Primary Investigator on a statewide research grant on co-teaching. In collaboration with the Department of Special Programs and the eight coordinators of the Regional Education Service Agencies, a survey was sent out across the state to all general and special education teachers identified as co-teaching. A total of 2,700 co-teachers responded to the survey. In analyzing the results, certain factors were revealed to be statistically significant. One of the items of particular importance was that 80% of the respondents stated they had administrative support at their schools; this finding is critical because most prior research gleaned from the teacher perspective identifies administrative support as typically lacking. The fact that 80% of the state's co-teachers stated that their administrators were indeed supportive of the practice speaks volumes about the focus placed on providing professional development at the statewide level to this population. It doesn't mean the co-teaching was immediately successful in that state, but what it does mean is that focusing on administrators made a difference in the perception of support by co-teachers themselves. Other pertinent results of that research will be shared at appropriate places in this text.

Another example of personal research that has impacted our knowledge base regarding co-teaching is the work Lisa has done with the Arkansas state department of education. In collaboration with a strong leader in the state, Rose Merry Kirkpatrick, and ongoing research with a colleague from UCF, Cynthia Pearl, Lisa and her colleagues continue each year to impact the number of students with disabilities included in general education, as well as to help schools see increased positive outcomes from co-teaching. Since 2010, they have trained over 789 co-teachers from 208 schools, representing 143 Arkansas school districts. These teams are then supported by ongoing webinars, which focus on developing co-teaching teams and building leadership teams. These leadership teams were charged with monitoring and supporting co-teaching within their schools and districts. These teams have provided the foundation for

> **Plugged In**
>
> Share your own thoughts, ideas, & concerns with our online co-teaching community on Twitter at @coteachingdance.
>
>

statewide systemic change in Arkansas and will provide the foundation for one of many examples in this book.

Overall, our intent is to provide you with the perfect blend of research and practice. Too many times higher education is criticized for looking only at research, and school-based leaders are criticized for not keeping up with current research. This book is unique in that we are grounded in cutting-edge developments in education (through the CSUN Eisner Center for Teaching and Learning, the Lockheed Martin Academy, and virtual teacher preparation such as TeachLivE); we conduct our own research that is both experimental and classroom-based; and we are also entrenched in the daily challenges of today's schools, leaders, and teachers across the country. We hope you will add to our knowledge as you read this material by sharing your thoughts with us at @coteachingdance on Twitter.

The Dance Metaphor Explained

We've clarified our backgrounds and offered a bit of our research, but we also should explain our dance metaphor before moving into the more substantive content of our text. Although Wendy has used a marriage metaphor in her co-teaching books for teachers (Murawski, 2009; Murawski, 2010; Murawski & Spencer, 2011), Lisa coined the dance metaphor in explaining co-teaching with her audiences. We used this metaphor in our preconvention workshop for the international CEC convention in Baltimore, Maryland in 2011, and it was received enthusiastically. Attendees appreciated the metaphor of novice co-teachers as akin to elementary school students at a dance, boys on one side and girls on the other, unsure of how to approach one another and even unsure if they want to do so (with the fear they might get cooties). Co-teachers with a bit more experience mimic middle school students dancing, hands on shoulders and much space between them, but beginning to learn one another's rhythm. Veteran co-teachers are similar to high school students; at times, it is hard to tell where one begins and the other ends! They know one another's moves and they are even ready to make up their own moves. Last, we also have professional dancers: those who not only are able to create their own award-winning routines, but are also able to teach and mentor others as they learn to dance.

This book is designed to help you lead this co-teaching dance. Don't get unnecessarily worried; even if you yourself are not a "dancer" or have never done the "co-teaching dance," you can be a strong leader in this regard. This book is designed to give you the tools to do so. We want you to feel comfortable enough to use the right terminology, to give feedback to your "dancers," and to help them develop from novice to veteran co-teachers. We will use this analogy throughout the book. Most importantly, however, our goal is to help you develop collaborative, communicative partners who work seamlessly to deliver the kind of differentiated, inspiring, and challenging curriculum that students in today's schools deserve, but often do not receive. Let the dance begin!

Chapter 1

Learning the Basic Moves

Defining Co-Teaching

Regardless of your interest in dance, we're pretty sure you know that there is a difference between the cha-cha, the bump, hip-hop, and ballet. You don't need to be able to do any of these dances (remember, this is only a metaphor), but you do need to recognize the differences that exist within each genre. If you walked into a dance studio and began to discuss the waltz, only to discover the dancers were doing a samba, you would have lost all credibility with those dancers. Why would they listen to your critique, seek your feedback, or value your input? You don't even know what they are doing.

That is why when Wendy identified the five keys to successful co-teaching in The School Administrator (2008), the number one key was "Know what co-teaching is and when it is needed." Let's deal with the first part of that statement first: Know

---

For Your Bookshelf

Go directly to the source and get a copy of this to-the-point, one-page article to share with other administrators.

Murawski, W. W. (2008, September). Five keys to co-teaching in inclusive classrooms. *The School Administrator*, 27.

Critical Connections

Help your teachers understand the components of co-teaching by connecting it to their prior knowledge. Every teacher needs to plan, instruct, and assess; thus it is clear that co-teachers need to do these things too, but together.

Need to Know

Inclusion — a philosophy that all students can have their individual needs met in the general education setting, with supports and services provided there rather than through pull-out; depending on needs of the child, this can look very different in different settings.

what co-teaching is. We are constantly astounded by how many administrators and other educational leaders have been told by those on high that they need to ensure that co-teaching is occurring in their school or district, without ever getting any personal instruction on what co-teaching actually entails. In turn, they task their own teachers to co-teach, but are unable to provide clear details on how that would look and how it would differ in the range of grades and students being supported in the school or district. We are emphatic that co-teaching is not merely putting two adults in the same classroom; likewise we are emphatic that, as with any new instructional technique, to be successful in co-teaching, teachers need instruction and professional development in order to know how to work together to help students be successful.

What is co-teaching? Cook and Friend (1995) first defined co-teaching as "two or more professionals delivering substantive instruction to a diverse, or blended, group of students in a single physical space" (p. 1). Wendy got more specific by stating that co-teaching requires three specific things: co-planning, co-instructing, and co-assessing (Murawski, 2003, p. 10). If your co-teachers are not doing those three things, we believe they are not truly co-teaching. They may be collaborating. They may be teaming. They may be communicating, consulting, monitoring, or supporting, but they are not truly co-teaching. The rest of this book will provide you with strategies for helping your teachers to do those three things: co-plan, co-instruct, and co-assess.

Clarifying Inclusion

Is co-teaching necessary for all children with disabilities? No. In fact, it is just one of many options for serving students with special needs. Lisa, in her book *Demystifying Secondary Inclusion* (2006), noted that inclusion is not something you do but something you believe. It is a philosophy that drives your resources, professional development practices, and schedules. Co-teaching is considered a "service delivery option" because it is indeed an option, but it is one typically found in a school with an inclusive philosophy. We think co-teaching is an excellent option because it allows two experienced, licensed experts to work with a group of students with various needs. We are open-minded and honest enough, however, to recognize that it is not the only option, nor is it always the most appropriate option.

Inclusion is a term that is often bandied about these days. The main point of inclusion is that the necessary adaptations or assistance that any student needs is provided in the general education setting when appropriate, rather than through a pull-out or segregated model as it was done in the past (and as it continues to be done in many schools nationally). In no scenario is "dumping" a child in a general education class without meeting his or her individual needs an acceptable option. But that is exactly what has happened in many instances in the name of mainstreaming or, more recently, inclusion. In fact, students with mild to moderate disabilities typically receive at least 80% of their instruction in general education classrooms (Annual Report to Congress, 2006; The American Youth Policy Forum, 2002), and those numbers just keep rising. Co-teaching is one way to help ensure students are getting their legally mandated services, are having their educational needs met, and, more importantly, are getting education of the same quality as their peers without disabilities.

Many parents and professionals support the most inclusive programs for students with special needs and fight for the right for students to be included in general education classrooms with whatever modifications or accommodations they need. Although philosophically many administrators may agree with an inclusive paradigm, logistics and pragmatics often create barriers to inclusion. We will go into those barriers and provide suggestions for addressing them later in this text.

For now, however, we think it is important to clarify that federal law does require a continuum of options for meeting the needs of students with identified disabilities. For some, their least restrictive environment (LRE) may be an institution or hospital setting, for others it may be a special school or room, while for others the general education classroom is indeed the most appropriate setting. Our focus for this book will be the general education classroom, though it is certainly possible for individuals to co-teach in different settings as well. The location in which services are provided to a student is still a decision to be made by the IEP team, driven by collaboration between the school, the parents, and the student.

Identifying the Menu of Options

Monitoring

Prior to jumping right into co-teaching, it is imperative that educational leaders know what the other options are for meeting students' needs in an inclusive setting (see box, "At-a-Glance: Menu of Service Options From Most Supportive to Least Supportive"). For some, monitoring may be sufficient. Monitoring involves a

> **Need to Know**
>
> Least Restrictive Environment (LRE) — a term used in the Individuals With Disabilities Education Act (IDEA) that requires children with disabilities to be educated with children who do not have disabilities, to the maximum extent appropriate. The LRE for a child is determined by the individualized education plan (IEP).

special service professional (e.g., special education teacher, speech pathologist, school psychologist, occupational therapist) who merely keeps in contact with a child's teacher, is informed when the child is having difficulty, and tracks grades and overall progress. It is never acceptable for a special service provider who has a child on her caseload to state that she doesn't know how the child is doing because she "never sees her." If monitoring was the selected service delivery option, the service provider must be active in ensuring that she is indeed monitoring the child's progress, even if she doesn't have an opportunity to see the child in person. That same service provider is often responsible for keeping parents apprised of the situation as the child progresses. This service delivery option is considered an indirect service to the student, but it is still a service requiring time and support from the special service provider. A move from monitoring to consultation or another service delivery option might be required if a student is faltering without additional services.

Consultation

Another similar option is consultation. In this scenario, a special service provider would consult with the general education teachers regarding the student's progress and provide strategies for differentiation, suggestions for changes in instruction, and modified materials for use in the classroom. The consultant is typically not a regular participant in the classroom, but may at times model the strategies or suggestions provided. Service providers may find it helpful to observe in a class and give the teacher strategies later to help with behavior or classroom management, instructional strategies, or specific methods to emphasize a child's strengths. This option is also considered an indirect support model and might at times include minimal direct intervention with the student.

Facilitated Support

Facilitated support is when a special service provider collaborates with a general education teacher in order to co-plan, co-instruct, or co-assess (Dieker & Hines, 2012). Notice that the operative word is "or." In some cases, there may not be sufficient time or the requisite schedule to allow teachers to co-teach. However, if they share students, they need to be sure that those students are having their needs met. In the case of facilitated support, teachers would jointly decide what makes the most sense in meeting those particular needs. For example, in one situation a speech language pathologist (SLP) and a third-grade teacher may decide it makes the most sense to plan together because the third-grade teacher has multiple children receiving speech services. Instead of coming to the classroom, the SLP meets weekly with the teacher and provides him with strategies for addressing speech goals through the third-grade curriculum. In another scenario, a reading coach comes into the classroom to facilitate a center in a sixth-grade language arts class. Through this co-instruction, she is better able to provide differentiated support for students and see what real needs they have in the classroom; because she plans and runs her own center regularly, there is limited co-planning, and thus it is not actual co-teaching. In the final example, a gifted education specialist may meet with a high school science teacher to work on co-assessment. During these meetings, the gifted education specialist will help the science teacher come up with assignments and assessments that will enrich the curriculum and challenge students appropriately; together they can look at the products of students and determine if they are meeting the standards and if additional higher-order thinking questions need to be included. In each of these examples, educators are collaborating and communicating in the best interest of students. These are valid options for service delivery, though they don't provide the daily, consistent, and thorough support that co-teaching may provide.

In-Class Support

In-class support occurs when a special service provider, most often a special education teacher, is in the general education setting directly interacting with the students. The difference between in-class support and co-teaching, however, is that most of the involvement in the classroom is reactive in nature, rather than proactive. This is also different from the co-instructing aspect of facilitated support in that the special service provider does not have a regular role that has been identified proactively to meet a particular need. Special educators often find themselves going into classes where there has been no co-planning or prior discussion regarding what will be occurring that day; instead they show up and ask, "What are we doing today?" If it is a topic they know, they may be able to walk around and help with instruction; if not, they are relegated to managing behavior through circulating and using proximity control. Even the most confident teacher thrown into this situation finds herself feeling similar to a glorified aide when no co-planning or prior discussion has occurred (Weiss & Lloyd, 2002; Wischnowski, Salmon, & Eaton, 2004).

Paraprofessional Support

Paraprofessional support comes in a variety of forms. For some students, a one-on-one paraprofessional is required, often due to needs so severe that behaviorally, physically, or academically the child cannot function without continuous adult support. Giangreco

---

For Your Bookshelf

We recommend this handy reference booklet for helping understand how to best utilize paraprofessionals: Gerlach, K. (2010). *Let's team up! A checklist for paraeducators, teachers, and principals (7th ed.).* Washington, DC: NEA Checklist Series.

(e.g., Giangreco & Broer, 2005) has described numerous research studies that promote the avoidance of an overreliance on a 1:1 paraprofessional to student ratio in the classroom, as it may lead to an increase in learned helplessness and a decrease in independence. Other paraprofessionals might be assigned to a classroom or a teacher to help with the larger needs of a class or caseload. Although these individuals (also known as aides, paraeducators, and assistants) can be a boon to teachers, so too can they be additional burdens if teachers don't know how to supervise, train, or utilize their roles effectively. When well supported, trained, and monitored, however, a paraprofessional can be considered another option for providing student support in the general education inclusive classroom.

Co-Teaching

We now come full circle back to co-teaching. Although co-teaching is not specifically identified by name in federal law, many schools have adopted its use in response to both the No Child Left Behind Act of 2001 (NCLB, 2001) and the Individuals With Disabilities Education Improvement Act (IDEA, 2004). NCLB calls for highly qualified content teachers, increased standardized and high-stakes assessments, and more uniformity in instructional practices; on the contrary, IDEA calls for individualization, differentiation, and specificity in meeting the particular needs of students with disabilities. These seemingly opposite laws can be met through the collaboration of the general education teacher, who typically focuses on the content standards (and today is the one who will probably be first to engage in professional development on the new common core standards) and overall class needs, and the special service provider, who typically focuses on the individual's needs and strategies for learning content. Voilá! A clear rationale for co-teaching emerges.

As stated, co-teaching requires co-planning, co-instructing, and co-assessing between two or more professional educators (Murawski, 2009). A history teacher and a school psychologist can co-teach a lesson, as can a special educator and a speech-language pathologist. A teacher of the gifted may co-teach with the librarian, and the technology integration specialist may co-teach with the reading specialist and the teacher of English language learners. A pair of second grade teachers can co-teach, as can high school English, drama, and history teachers. As long as two or more professionals are co-planning what they are going to do, doing it together collaboratively with a group of students, and then assessing the results together, they are co-teaching. The focus of this book will be on the interactions between special education teachers and general education classroom teachers, but feel free to apply our strategies to your own situations, whatever they may be. The concepts will be relevant, as will the majority of the strategies.

At-A-Glance: Menu of Service Options
From Most Supportive to Least Supportive

Self-contained — Services are provided primarily by a highly qualified special education teacher in a separate classroom reserved for students with identified disabilities.

Co-teaching — In this model, support is provided to students with and without disabilities in the general education setting. This support is provided by both the special and general education teachers. The special educator is in the classroom on a regular basis. The two teachers are expected to co-plan, co-instruct, and co-assess together.

Facilitated support — In this model, the special education teacher provides support directly to the general education teacher. Support is provided to the general education teacher and the students through either co-planning, co-instructing, or co-assessing.

In-class support — In this model, the special service provider gives support directly to the students in the general education classroom. The special educator may be in the classroom for all or part of the instructional period, every day or just for a few days a week. They provide support to the students through on-the-spot accommodations or modifications. In-class support may be provided through special education teachers or trained paraprofessionals.

No support — Students with disabilities are included in the general education setting with no direct services from a special education teacher. They may still be monitored or provided indirect support through consultative services to their general education teachers.

Benefits of Co-Teaching

Co-teaching is a strong way to encourage collaboration between teachers in order to support the diverse array of students and student needs in today's schools. We realize, however, that is too pat a response for the stakeholders who are going to ask you why they need to have co-teaching as a service delivery option in schools at all. However, research has found that co-teaching can be effective in serving a variety of learners in a plethora of capacities. For example, students with specific needs, such as those with hearing impairments (Luckner, 1999) or learning disabilities (Rice & Zigmond, 1999; Weichel, 2001; Welch, 2000), or those who are gifted (Hughes & Murawski, 2001) or are English language learners (Bahamonde & Friend, 1999; Mahoney, 1997) can have their needs addressed. Students learning specific subject matter, such as language (Miller, Valasky, & Molloy, 1998), social studies (Dieker, 1998), or English (Murawski, 2006) classes, can be better served through co-teaching. Co-teaching has also been found to be beneficial for instituting school change and systemic change (Villa, Thousand, & Nevin, 2004). For these and other reasons, schools are embracing co-teaching now more than ever before. As they do so, however, many schools are "rushing the goal line" (Beninghof, 2003) and trying to do too much without a clear vision as to where they are going. For co-teaching to be implemented effectively, it is necessary that administrators know what it should be as well as what it is not.

True co-teaching occurs between two individuals who have parity, or equality. One does not assume that he or she has more power or credibility or importance than the other. Co-teaching requires respect and trust. To give up control in a classroom is difficult; to do so, a teacher has to feel comfortable that his or her partner is able to instruct students competently. Co-teaching requires a division of labor and a sharing of responsibilities and accountability. Teachers need to know that when they co-plan, their partner will indeed follow through with whatever was decided. Co-teaching requires flexibility. Plans fall through, students don't always react in the ways we expect, and instruction with two teachers is different from instruction with one teacher. All of these things require change, which can be scary for teachers. A leader's job is to alleviate that fear and help teachers embrace positive change.

What Co-Teaching Is Not

Co-teaching is not easy, nor is it what we see in many classes that are calling what they are doing co-teaching. Nationally, schools have been good about meeting four of the six criteria for co-teaching first established by Cook and Friend (1995).

- ☑ Two or more adults in the room

- ☑ Both are professionals

- ☐ Both are collaborating

- ☐ Both are delivering substantive instruction

- ☑ Students are heterogeneously grouped

- ☑ The class is in a single space.

It appears easy to put two or more professionals in the same class together with a group of diverse learners. Less easy, though, is to ensure that those professionals are equipped to collaborate in such a way that both are providing substantive instruction to the students. Instead, what we often see in schools are two teachers who co-exist in a classroom, and that's all.

We see many situations in which one teacher is unwilling to give up control or one teacher is unwilling to step up and share control. We see situations in which a special educator with 27 years of teaching experience is relegated to the role of instructional aide, walking around and merely providing proximity control. We see situations in which teachers have avoided the need to collaborate or co-plan by immediately dividing students into "your" students and "my" students (or your group and my group) despite the fact that they are physically in the same room, thus essentially doing the pull-out model in a one-room situation. Last, we also see teachers who truly believe they are co-teaching, but all they are really doing is conducting the same whole-group instruction one teacher would, except that they are "swapping the chalk" (or, more likely, the dry erase marker or the interactive whiteboard marker). They take turns getting face time with students, but there is no differentiation, varied teaching strategies, regrouping, or other benefits to students. For a quick reference to these guidelines, see box, "At-a-Glance: Dos and Don'ts of Co-Teaching."

The Essential Question of Co-Teaching

We are finally ready to address the second part of the first key to co-teaching: Know when co-teaching is needed. You can do that by answering the essential question of co-teaching (we have provided you with one here, but feel free to create your own). Essential questions in teaching (Wiggins & McTighe, 2005) are those that relate to the big idea of the lesson. They are formed in such a way that students should be able to leave the lesson and answer the question to demonstrate a comprehension of those big ideas. The question should be formed in such a way that there is no ceiling to the response; it is not a true/false or lower level question. Students who are high-achieving or gifted should be able to answer the question in depth and with detail, and those students with cognitive issues should still be able to answer with the main message of the lesson.

Administrators and other educational leaders need to be aware of the essential question of co-teaching. You need to be able to ask your teachers a question that will demonstrate whether or not those teachers are effective in their collaborative interactions. You need to be able to observe co-teachers in action and ask this question of yourself with a degree of satisfaction. If there is no degree of satisfaction in the response (by administrators or the teachers themselves), the way in which co-teaching is being implemented must be questioned.

The essential question for co-teaching that we pose is:

> **How is what co-teachers are doing together**
> **<u>substantively different and better for kids</u>**
> **than what one teacher would do alone?**
>
> (Murawski & Spencer, 2011, p. 96).

At -A-Glance: Do's and Don'ts of Co-Teaching	
Co-Teaching is . . .	*Co-Teaching is not . . .*
Two or more co-equal (preferably credentialed) faculty working together.	A teacher and an assistant, teacher's aide, or paraprofessional.
Conducted in the same classroom at the same time.	When a few students are pulled out of the classroom on a regular basis to work with the special educator. It is also not job-sharing, where teachers teach different days.
Conducted with heterogeneous groups.	Pulling a group of students with disabilities to the back of the general education class.
When both teachers plan for instruction together. The general education teacher (GET) is the content specialist while the special education teacher (SET) is the expert on individualizing and delivery to various learning modalities.	When the general education teacher (GET) plans all lessons and the special education teacher (SET) walks in to the room and says, "What are we doing today and what would you like me to do?"
When both teachers provide substantive instruction together — having planned together, the SET can grade homework, teach content, facilitate activities, etc.	When the special education teacher walks around the room all period as the general education teaches the content. Also, not when the SET sits in the class and takes notes.
When both teachers assess and evaluate student progress. IEP goals are kept in mind, as are the curricular goals and standards for that grade level.	When the GET grades "his" kids and the SET grades "her" kids — or when the GET grades all students and the SET surreptitiously changes the grades and calls it "modifying after the fact."
When teachers maximize the benefits of having two teachers in the room by having both teachers actively engaged with students. Examples of different co-teaching models include team-teaching, station teaching, parallel teaching, alternative teaching, and One Teach-One Support (see Friend and Cook 2000).	When teachers take turns being "in charge" of the class so that the other teacher can get caught up in grading, photocopying, making phone calls, creating IEPs, etc. — or when students remain in the large group setting in lecture-format as teachers rotate who gets to "talk at them."
When teachers reflect on the progress and process, offering one another feedback on teaching styles, content, activities, and other items pertinent to improving the teaching situation.	When teachers get frustrated with one another and tell the rest of the faculty in the teachers' lounge or when one teacher simply tells the other teacher what to do and how to do it.

Note. Adapted from *Demystifying Co-Teaching*, by W. W. Murawski, 2002, *CARS + Newsletter, 22*(3), p. 19. Copyright 2002 by *CARS+*. Adapted with permission.

If the lesson could have been presented equally well by one teacher, why are the resources of two teachers being wasted? If the outcomes of the lesson (either academic, behavioral, or social) are not improved, what was the point of having the lesson co-taught? What did it accomplish, other than perhaps being more fun for the teachers themselves? As an instructional leader in the school, consider posting this essential question somewhere you can refer to it frequently when observing co-teachers or talking to them about their interactions in the classroom. This question helps you answer the second part of the first key to co-teaching related to determining when co-teaching is needed. If a general education teacher is already using strategies that a special educator might suggest, and thus adding a second teacher in the classroom doesn't substantively improve the situation for students, is co-teaching in that class really needed? Instead, that might be a good class for students with disabilities who can be more independent, thus freeing the special educator to go and collaborate or co-teach with a different general educator.

Five Keys to Co-Teaching

We have already stated the first key for administrators to consider when supporting co-teaching (i.e., Know what co-teaching is and when it is needed.). The box, "At-a-Glance: Five Keys to Leading Co-Teaching" shares that key as well as the remaining four, with a brief description of each. Feel free to print a handy copy for easy reference.

The second key is to "Recognize that co-teaching is a marriage and you are the matchmaker." In Chapter 2, we share strategies for identifying potential partners for co-teaching. We urge you to consider a variety of ways to get teacher input in creating partnerships. We have worked with many administrators who have said they selected co-teaching teams based on who they thought would work well together. Although it is true that strong educational leaders really know their staff, it is equally true that teachers do not always share everything with their administrators. You may not know the personal gripes, outside friendships, or common interests that would cement a strong co-teaching partnership (or conversely, tear it apart). A variety of research and literature has emphasized the importance of teacher voice in volunteering for co-teaching and/or for identifying their co-teaching partner (Kohler-Evans, 2006; Murawski, Boyer, Atwill, & Melchiorre, 2009; Sileo & van Garderen, 2010). We recognize that as the administrative leader you are often the matchmaker, and that comes with a lot of responsibility as well as with a caveat: We strongly recommend you get frequent feedback from the teachers themselves related to their prospective dance partners. (Please allow us our mixed metaphors.)

The third key is to "Make scheduling a priority." If you are a school leader, you already know the importance of scheduling. You likely also know the headaches of scheduling. Although we respect that every school has its own culture and that we cannot provide a lock-step approach to scheduling, we do have tips for helping to make this more manageable. In Chapter 3, we provide general tips for scheduling,

At-A-Glance: 5 Keys to Leading Co-Teaching	
Keys to Leading Co-Teaching	*Brief Description*
#1. Know what co-teaching is and when it is needed.	Co-teaching involves co-planning, co-instructing and co-assessing. If co-teachers are not doing all three, they are not co-teaching. To determine if co-teaching is needed, the essential question must be answered: How is what these two teachers are doing together substantively different and better for kids than what one of them would do alone?
#2. Recognize that co-teaching is a marriage and you are the matchmaker.	As a professional marriage, administrators need to provide opportunities for co-teachers to select their partners. "Voluntariness" and choice are helpful for positive outcomes. Recognize that educational leaders often end up playing the role of "marriage counselor" also.
#3. Make scheduling a priority.	Put students with special needs in the master schedule first, prior to the computer sorting students into classes. Avoid having more than 30% of any general education class be students with special needs, otherwise the class begins to resemble a self-contained class.
#4. Planning is critical.	Without strong co-planning, there will be no successful co-teaching. Teachers need time to plan together and administrators and other instructional leaders need to use a variety of options to ensure they can do so.
#5. Monitor success, give feedback and ensure evidence-based practice.	Work with co-teachers to provide supportive feedback for co-teaching improvement. Identify mentors, peer observers, & co-teaching coordinators. Collect data on student outcomes & teacher perspectives. Identify areas of strength & build on them; identify barriers and work around them.

Note. Adapted from Murawski, W. W. (2008, September). Five keys to co-teaching in inclusive classrooms. *The School Administrator, 27*.

and in Chapter 4 we offer more suggestions for scheduling co-teaching in a variety of schools (e.g., elementary and secondary schools, small and large schools, and schools in which co-teaching is a new concept versus those that have engaged in co-teaching for a while).

The fourth key states that "Planning is critical." We know this seems to be a no-brainer, yet we have experienced thousands of teachers who come to us lamenting that although they are co-teaching, they never have time to plan with their partner. We would argue that if they never plan together, they are not really co-teaching. Instead, one of the teachers is perhaps providing some in-class support while the other teacher is running his or her own show. Even if those teachers do share some of the instruction, it typically lacks the uniqueness of what would have existed if the teachers had truly planned together. Remember to come back to the essential question of co-teaching: How is what they are doing together substantively different and better for students than what one of them would be doing alone? If teachers haven't co-planned, it is not likely that the special educator has had much input in the lesson itself. The "special" aspect of special education will be lost; instead, classes will resemble a typical general education classroom with an additional adult support in the room. We don't know many school districts that can afford that, either financially or logistically. In Chapter 5, we address a variety of strategies for helping to lead effective co-planning between educators, including the incorporation of technology and differentiation into those plans. Chapter 6 provides the language needed to know which instructional approaches co-teachers are using in the classroom.

Finally, the fifth key to co-teaching states that administrators need to "monitor success, give feedback, and ensure evidence-based practice." Again, this statement may seem obvious, but it reflects a real need in the field. Hundreds of administrators have worked with us and admitted that, although they are being told to include co-teaching as a service delivery option in their schools, they don't know what it really is; that they are in the position to support co-teaching teams but just don't know how to do that; and that they are willing to go in to observe co-teachers in action, but don't know what they are looking for or what would constitute success. School-based administrators are not the only ones creating the need for monitoring and data collection; the field of special education in general has called for more concrete research on co-teaching impact, especially as it relates to student outcomes (Damore & Murray, 2009; Hang & Rabren, 2009; Murawski & Swanson, 2001; Scruggs, Mastropieri, & McDuffie, 2007). Co-teachers report frustration with administrators who come in to observe and question the fact that the special educator is leading content instruction, or administrators who lack the right terminology to acknowledge co-teachers' use of parallel teaching at the beginning of the period and alternative teaching at the end. These are just a few examples of why it is so important that educational leaders are not only aware of what co-teaching is, but also are well-versed enough in the topic to provide their teachers with instructional strategies and suggestions to enhance and improve the team outcomes with one another, and especially with the students. Chapter 7 relates to the observation and feedback strategies helpful when observing and/or evaluating co-teachers in action. Chapter 8 provides additional information on ways for co-teachers to collect data on student outcomes, and for instructional leaders to collect data on students, teachers, and even school districts.

Our final chapters (9 and 10) relate to institutionalizing co-teaching by building on successes, creating mentor teams, setting goals for improvement, collaborating with other entities, and disseminating findings. But we are getting ahead of ourselves here. Now that we know what co-teaching is (the first key), we may need to take a step back in order to ensure we have the collaborative culture necessary to make co-teaching a viable option for teachers and students. As part of your role in leading the dance, you can ensure that you are prepared to address the five keys by building a strong foundation (i.e., a "stage") for your teachers to become strong co-teaching dance teams. Chapter 2 addresses creating collaborative cultures to enable schools to be ready to embrace co-teaching as a viable option for meeting students' needs.

Chapter 2

Setting the Stage

Developing a Culture to Support Co-Teaching

We often see schools trying to make co-teaching work in a situation that simply is not ready for it. In a school that has dysfunctional inclusive practices but is trying to incorporate co-teaching as a service delivery option, we find one of two things: (1) dysfunctional co-teaching, or (2) exhausted co-teachers who have to work twice as hard due to the lack of structure in the school. As we stated in the preface, Lisa has visited over 100 schools and collected data on what made them successful or not. During these visits, two primary themes emerged that led to a successful collaborative culture and ultimately made co-teaching easier for teachers and more effective for students. Although these two themes may appear simple, they were also clearly evident in the schools that embraced change and inclusive practices (Dieker, 2006).

The first theme that emerged from these visits to schools where students with disabilities were successfully served in the general education settings was the "no whining" theme. What Lisa saw consistently in these schools was a basic philosophy of finding a solution or multiple solutions to any problem that a student might bring to the inclusive setting. It was that simple. "There's a problem?" led to "What can we do to solve it?" Keep in mind that most of these schools had the same issues other schools are facing: too many students, insufficient materials, outdated technology, and not enough teachers. The difference was that these schools focused on what they could do to solve any issue that arose, rather than perseverating on what was wrong. Teachers felt a true team spirit, and they were not isolated or working alone on any issue that arose. The schools in which students successfully participated in the general education setting had at their core the ability to look at any challenge a student presented as an opportunity to find a solution, rather than an opportunity to whine and complain. In these schools, teachers' lounges and conference rooms were not filled with grumbles of protest, but with heartfelt discussions about how to help students and how to work together more effectively.

The second theme that emerged was that all of the practices across the school (from co-teaching to grading to behavior to use of technology) were "consistent but flexible." These two terms may appear to be in contrast with each other, but in schools that embraced all learners, the administrators identified and supported practices that could be used by all classes and all teachers, regardless of label. Putting consistent practices in place (such as those provided in the box "At-a-Glance: Necessary Structures for Successful Inclusive Settings") helps make working collaboratively with a multitude of teachers more manageable. This type of culture is also supportive for students because they know what to expect related to technology, grading, classroom management, assessment, and behavior. On the other hand, flexibility within this common structure is important as well. Too often, the pendulum swings too far one way or another in education. Teachers feel they must adhere to a particular policy even when it goes against what is good for students, or else they are all going their own way with no regard for students' need for consistency. Those schools that managed to find the happy medium and do it with aplomb were the most successful in their implementation of inclusive strategies. Therefore, they had an easier time implementing co-teaching structures.

> ### Critical Connections
>
> Imagine the school in which all educators avoided whining in favor of problem-solving and engaged in consistent but flexible practices. Co-teaching would just be one of many positive initiatives that could be implemented for students!

Let us return to our dancing metaphor. A collaborative school culture creates the stage required for co-teachers to perform. We have our dancers and we're asking them to dance on that stage. We know that this is a stage that is filled with positive energy and no whining, and we know that we have dancers who are committed to being flexible within the structured routine. We are the judges who are going to score their dancing and judge them accordingly. Sounds fair, right? Not so fast.

You may have the best co-teachers in the world, who are ready to impress you with their co-teaching prowess, but if the stage on which they are expected to dance is flimsy, falling apart, full of holes, or just plain wobbly, they will never be successful. In this metaphor, the stage is the foundation for inclusive practices created at your school. Great school leaders make sure the stage that co-teachers will dance on has a firm foundation so they can focus on building their relationships and skills and not defending inclusion, figuring out the rules for behavior, or even talking about their

---

At-A-Glance: Necessary Structures for Successful Inclusive Settings

Want to develop appropriate structures for your inclusive setting? Take notes from those schools that were able to develop consistent, but flexible, practices related to these important areas:

- **Technology use and adoption:** Schools provided students with disabilities with technological tools and taught teachers and students how to use those tools to meet their unique needs so that they could become successful independent learners.

- **Self-advocacy preparation:** Schools had procedures and policies in place to help students with disabilities become aware of their own strengths and disability areas, and to learn how to advocate for their personal needs.

- **Grading:** Grading was discussed across schools and teams as a way to report student progress to parents. These were authentic processes (e.g., standard-based report cards, portfolios), not just twice a year letter–grade report cards.

- **Homework:** Teachers coordinated efforts across the school to provide a logical structure to when homework assignments were due and how much would be expected.

- **Teams:** Teachers (both general and special education) were aligned by content teams, grade level teams, or Professional Learning Communities to work together toward the success of all students. This provided a solid, thoughtful structure for collaboration, rather than the typical "chicken with their heads cut off" syndrome that many special educators experience by trying to collaborate with too many partners or in too many subject areas.

- **Collaborative teaching:** Schools with strong consistent inclusive practices embraced co-teaching as a service delivery model for more than just special education. Teachers in classrooms working together included special educators, general educators, English as a Second Language (ESL) teachers, reading specialists, math and reading coaches, and speech therapists. Co-teaching was accepted and implemented consistently.

- **Behavior:** Successful inclusive schools discussed with their entire faculty and staff the need for similar rules and consequences. The majority of them implemented many Positive Behavioral Intervention Support (PBIS) approaches.

- **Active Learning:** Active learning strategies were embraced consistently in all classes, not relying just on teacher personality or whim. It was common to see students actively engaged in cooperative learning or peer support groups, rather than sitting in rows listening to a lecturer.

Note. Dieker & Hines, 2012

differences in philosophy related to homework. The smoother the stage is, the better the dance steps. We encourage you as leaders not only to assess your teachers, but also to take a good look at the stage on which you are asking them to dance. Is there a foundation that is positive and not full of complaining or negative focus on issues? Is the foundation consistent but flexible? Communication and careful partnerships are structures needed to develop the collaborative culture that will allow the best dance possible.

Improving Schoolwide Communication About Co-Teaching

Once a collaborative culture is in place to promote inclusive practices and collaborative service delivery options, other structures can be more easily created to facilitate these practices. Four specific components that will help ensure strong co-teaching are: communication, thoughtful partnerships, strategic professional development, and planning. Because planning is such a major aspect of effective collaboration not only for co-teaching teams but for all educators, an entire chapter (Chapter 5) is devoted to developing strong planning practices. Thus, here we address establishing communication strategies, determining who to include, professional development strategies, and what to do with your new co-teaching teams.

Plugged In

Go to www.Edmodo.com to learn a new, secure social networking site that can be used by classes, schools, and districts to communicate internally. This is an amazing reference for administrators to use and share with their community.

In all schools, teachers talk. In truly collaborative schools, however, teachers talk about strategies to promote success. Educational leaders can create structures by which the sharing of ideas and collaborating around problem solving is encouraged and easier for busy teachers. Communication should not occur only between teachers who teach the same grade or subject, but needs to be open and inclusive of teachers, staff, support personnel, families, community members, and even students. The box "At-a-Glance: Ideas for Increasing Communication" provides a variety of strategies for creating structures for ongoing communication. Clearly, open dialogue and increased communication are important to helping establish a collaborative culture, and administrators interested in seeing co-teaching succeed can use many of these strategies to share information on co-teaching and inclusive education.

At-A-Glance: Ideas for Increasing Communication		
People involved	**Mode of Communication**	**Description**
All teachers, general and special *TO* All teachers, general and special	Wiki on a particular topic related to inclusive education	Different topic each month for teachers to discuss and upload info
Special service providers *TO* Gen Ed teachers	Create a "resource" newsletter	Give strategies and ideas for accommodating; shows how valuable a resource special service providers can be
Teachers/Students/ Parents *TO* Teachers/Students/ Parents	Book study on topics related to inclusive ed; see book ideas in "For Your Bookshelf" on page 21	Get different folks together to read books of common interest; develop rapport; identify areas of concern, disagreement, and confusion
Administrators *TO* Parents	Polleverywhere.com at Back to School night	Have parents text in their answers about what they are pleased with, or what concerns they have, or what they want more info on
Administrators *TO* Community	E-newsletters; Kaffee Klatsch (coffee morning talks); evening chats	Electronic method to share the school's progress and needs; way to invite community members to come talk to teachers & kids
Teachers *TO* Parents	Class websites; Edmodo	A closed social network for parents to collaborate with each other and the teacher; teachers can upload class lectures, handouts, etc.
Teachers/Students/ Parents *TO* Teachers/Students/ Parents	Class websites; blogs; interactive journals; Twitter; Edmodo; glogster; instagram	Create ways to get information to students as a group or individually; find ways for students to communicate with teachers

Determining Who Should Participate

Garner Enthusiasm

The second key to co-teaching success for administrators is to "recognize that co-teaching is a marriage, and you are the matchmaker" (Murawski, 2008, p. 27). We are mixing metaphors here (so stick with us), but we want to emphasize how important the right partnerships are. Using the dance metaphor, we still maintain that as the dance leader, it is truly important with whom you pair your teachers. Co-teaching requires collaboration, which requires an aspect of "voluntariness" (Friend & Cook, 2007), but throwing teachers together and hoping it will all work out is a primitive and often ineffective strategy. Instead, strong administrative leaders create ways in which they can select team members strategically and thoughtfully. These ways include:

- Presenting information about co-teaching and then allowing teachers to volunteer to participate. Try to find a few people who are dynamic presenters and have experienced successful co-teaching themselves. These are the kinds of folks who can introduce the concept to the whole school staff in a way that generates energy and interest. Make sure you do not trust just any faculty member to do the initial introduction or you will have shot yourself in the foot before even starting.

- Providing surveys for teachers and paraprofessionals to complete regarding their teaching preferences and using those surveys to help align complementary pairs. (See Figure 2-1, Figure 2-2, and Figure 2-3 at the end of this chapter for examples.)

- Asking specific teachers if they would be willing to partner with one another. Have a one-on-one discussion with teachers to find out their preferences.

- Putting a group of teachers in a room with some snacks and the information they need about students (e.g., "We have 15 children who need to be in a co-taught English class"); have them figure out who will co-teach with whom and how often.

- Continuing with the marriage metaphor, consider this the "dating phase" (Murawski, 2010). Encourage introductions and possible connections by having special service providers meet more of the general education teachers through a quick "speed dating" process. Make it fun by calling it a co-teaching party and see who attends.

Regardless of which method is used to identify teams, it is important that teachers feel some ownership in the process. Teachers who feel that they were thrown into an arranged situation and don't have any rapport with their partner going into co-teaching are far less willing to embrace the approach initially. Irrespective of the level of professionalism, training, or expertise of both co-teachers, experts have found time and again that a primary factor in the success of co-teaching is the personality match of the teachers (Murawski et al., 2009; Wischnowski et al., 2004; Scruggs, Mastropieri, & McDuffie, 2007). The more teachers respect and trust one another, the more willing they are to collaborate and try new teaching strategies.

For Your Bookshelf

Starting a book study to initiate more communication about inclusive practices? Consider these texts.

Brownell, M. T., Smith, S., Crockett, J., & Griffin, C. (2012). *Inclusive instruction: Evidence-based practices for teaching students with disabilities*. New York, NY: Guilford Press.

Dieker, L. A. (2013). *Demystifying secondary inclusion (2nd ed.)*. Port Chester, NY: National Professional Resources, Inc.

Downing, J. A. (2008). *Including students with severe and multiple disabilities in typical classrooms: Practical strategies for teachers (3rd ed.)*. Baltimore, MD: Paul H. Brookes.

Levine, M. (2002). *A mind at a time*. New York: Simon & Schuster.

Murawski, W. W. (2010). *Collaborative teaching in elementary schools: Making the co-teaching marriage work!* Thousand Oaks, CA: Corwin Press.

Murawski, W. W. (2009). *Collaborative teaching in secondary schools: Making the co-teaching marriage work!* Thousand Oaks, CA: Corwin Press.

Murawski, W.W. & Spencer, S. (2011). *Collaborate, communicate, and differentiate!* How to increase student learning in today's diverse classrooms. Thousand Oaks, CA: Corwin Press.

Avoid Resistors.

The other mistake we often see is trying to force those who don't want to co-teach. We have that found creating a core team of those who want to participate is much easier and more effective than forcing those who are resistant. Then as teams are more and more successful and others hear about their successes, it is easier to continue adding other names to the dance card slowly. Remember what we said at the beginning of this section about the dance party. Not everyone should be invited right away. The box "In Action 2-1" demonstrates typical human behavior.

In Action 2-1

Typical Human Behavior

Situation 1: John hears there is a dance party starting at 8 p.m. tonight. It is mandatory for everyone. He thinks, "I don't want to go. They can't make me. I'll tell them I'm sick."

Situation 2: John hears there is a dance party starting at 8 p.m. tonight. It's open to everyone. He thinks, "Hmm. Maybe I'll go. Maybe I won't. We'll see. I wonder who else is going and if it's worth my time."

Situation 3: John hears there is a dance party starting at 8 p.m. tonight. It's by invitation only and he didn't get an invitation. He thinks, "Why didn't I get invited? I want to go! How can I wangle myself an invitation?"

Notice John's immediate reaction in Situation 1. When something feels forced, our inclination is to resist, even if it is a good idea. In Situation 2, there is an option. Although John is weighing his options and may attend, he also is looking to see what's in it for him and who else is part of the equation. In Situation 3, however, he is immediately intrigued because of the exclusivity of the event. We know what you are thinking, by the way. You are thinking, "Wait a minute. Isn't this about inclusion? Why are these authors advocating exclusion?" We aren't, really. What we are advocating is a standard. We are suggesting that when you raise the standard for who is invited and announce that only those who are truly interested and committed can be part of the co-teaching community, you will raise the interests and expectations of other educators. You start small, find success, publicize that success, and then begin to grow your program with other committed individuals. Your teachers who want to dance together will make the extra effort needed and your public praise of their efforts will be rewarding. Those who do not participate in the beginning will eventually get tired of being left out or not praised for their work and want to be invited to the party. So let the dance begin.

Strategic and Differentiated Professional Development

As you start the dance, consider the group or groups collectively and individually that you are addressing. We suggest you decide whether the group or an individual educator may need a change of heart or a change in behavior. There is a difference that we have observed. may merely be naïve about the concept of working with students with disabilities. They may have had a bad experience with co-teaching, or they may have some unrecognized bias against students with disabilities. These are individuals who are resistant to the concept of inclusion and co-teaching and are the ones who can sabotage the dance before it even begins.

These individuals need to be provided with opportunities to hear motivational speakers discuss the equal rights of students with disabilities to have access to the general education curriculum. This group is one that will require a great deal of patience; as a leader, you will need to listen to their concerns and probe to see what is causing their resistance. Prior to ever gaining skills in co-teaching, they first need to embrace the notion of having students with learning and behavioral differences in the same classroom as students without disabilities. When they do share the philosophy that all students have the right to the general education classroom, they will be much more likely to want a colleague with whom to work in order to address those varied needs in the classroom. Remember the importance of having a solid stage upon which to dance. These individuals are still dealing with rocky and unstable footing; your leadership can help move them forward and strengthen their overall foundation for co-teaching and inclusion.

For the quick win in building and strengthening your co-teaching initiative, focus on those teachers who need a change of behavior, not a change of heart. Start with those you supervise who want to include students and show an interest in co-teaching, but simply don't know how, don't have the time to set up the structure, or don't know the dance steps. These teachers are the ones who show up at the party, but stand on the side and wait for someone to ask them to dance. They are the teachers who are willing, but do not know where to start. They are the teachers who are trying but may have no planning time, training, or support. Similar to the first group, these teachers need patience and for you to listen to their needs. The difference here is that this group can change more quickly and more easily. They will learn to dance more quickly, as they have the interest, motivation, and flexibility; all they need are the steps. Strong suggestions for helping to make their co-taught experience more successful include:

- Providing them with the opportunity to talk with an administrator about scheduling.

- Encouraging them to watch another co-teaching team at the same grade level or in the same content area; make a visit to another district on a professional development day so they can see the behaviors in action.

- Providing them with a coach to help with communication difficulties.

- Giving them paid planning time monthly to meet.

- Sending both teachers to professional development in an area in which they are struggling.

Great leaders see the differences in what they need to provide to their teams. One group is reluctant to even get onto the dance floor, while the other is prime to learn some new moves. You clearly want both groups to move forward, but the mistake too many leaders make is trying to adopt a "one-size-fits-all" approach. Picture this: all teachers in a school are expected to attend a basic, mandated inservice on "Co-teaching 101." Although this sounds reasonable, the result is often that those who need a change of heart are angry throughout the training and don't engage, while those already dancing need to be provided more complex steps than are taught in this one-size-fits-all group situation. Just as we try to individualize learning for students, the same has to be true for your faculty and administration in order to move this initiative forward.

First Steps With New Teams

Another important consideration regarding the development of teaming structures relates to timing. Putting partners together the day before school starts (or after school has already begun) doesn't allow teachers to coalesce and develop into a true team. Co-teachers need time to learn one another's preferences, pet peeves, curricular considerations, concerns, methods of communicating, and so on. In the marriage metaphor, this would be considered the "Engagement" phase (Murawski, 2009); in the dance metaphor, this would be when partners have a chance to get to know one another's moves and practice a bit together before going on stage in front of an audience!

In 2004, we published an article entitled "Tips and strategies for co-teaching at the secondary level" in the journal *TEACHING Exceptional Children.* In that article, we provided a form called the "S.H.A.R.E. worksheet" designed to help teachers communicate their various teaching and classroom management preferences. Having used this form with schools for years, we have learned how helpful it is for teachers to have time to share this information with one another prior to having students in the room. In fact, although the S.H.A.R.E. worksheet was designed with co-teachers in mind, many teachers and administrators have told us that they now use the worksheet with all of their teachers and paraprofessionals at the beginning of the school year in an effort to improve communication across all team members. We have even seen the S.H.A.R.E. worksheet being used with student teachers and master teachers at the university level. Certainly some aspects of the worksheet would be figured out as the teachers worked together, but do you really want one of your teachers to stop in the middle of instruction and say to her partner, "Hey, remember when we were talking about pet peeves? What you just did is one of *my* pet peeves!" Better that they talk things out before they are in front of the students. To that end, we have provided a blank copy of the S.H.A.R.E. worksheet for you at the end of this chapter.

Last, once you have a team that works, stick with that team. Too often we see administrators changing up dance partners just as teams are really beginning to perfect their practice. Remember that learning to dance solo is much easier than with a partner. Yet each time a new partnership is developed, those dancers essentially have to start over. New teams have to spend precious time focusing on developing their relationships rather than being able to focus on the learning outcomes of the students. We are very consistent regarding our advice to administrators in this regard. Here it is: If you have a team that is dancing together beautifully, leave them alone! If you have a team in their first year, stepping on one another's toes but still growing in the process, leave them alone! On the other hand, if you have a team that fights in front of students, refuses to work together, or otherwise clearly jeopardizes the learning of students, do not leave them alone. Instead, use other options:

- Meet with partners individually and then together to see if you can effectively counsel them to a more effective partnership.

- Work with co-teachers to identify each of their strengths and how to maximize them in the classroom.

- See if there are other possible partners who would work more effectively with each individual. Sometimes it's just the partnerships, not co-teaching itself.

- Ensure that teachers understand the vision and purpose of co-teaching. Have them identify alternative ways to meet the needs of all students if they feel co-teaching is an ineffective option for them.

Regardless of what is done, it is most important to meet the needs of students, not just to meet the needs of teachers. We don't want to allow teachers to be rewarded for choosing not to collaborate or work to include students with special needs. We don't want teachers to feel they can opt out of how you see the vision of your school moving forward. It is simply unacceptable for teachers to be allowed to demand their own domain and stick to past practices if those practices are not working for all students. Certainly, working together is more effort, but the outcomes of any kind of collaboration have been documented repeatedly as worth the time and effort.

Building on Success

Now that you have several dance teams you are leading, how do you keep up the momentum? One of the first things to remember is to continue to praise successes publically but keep issues of conflict between the teams in your office. One of the best techniques we observed was in a school district that implemented a rule of "open and fair communication" between its teams. What did that rule mean exactly? Basically it meant that co-teaching teams were encouraged to talk about one another and their situations, including both successes and struggles (the open part), but only if the whole team was present (the fair part). As the school leader, this would mean that if one teacher came to you to share a concern that involved her co-teaching relationship, you would listen politely but then remind the teacher of this rule. You would ask her to return with the rest of her team for further discussion and problem-solving with you. This rule seemed to make a huge impact on that school moving forward successfully in co-teaching practices because teams felt safe in their relationships as well as in their support structures.

We also recommend the art of patience in making co-teaching work from the classroom level to the district and state levels. Too often, schools want co-teachers to enter the classroom and instantly perform as a professional dance team. However, have you ever watched *Dancing With the Stars* on TV? If not, go online right now (www.youtube.com) and watch a clip from a show early in the season. Now think about what you saw. That show clearly demonstrates that, even if one dancer is a seasoned veteran, when that person is paired with someone new it takes significant time for the team to develop a professional look. Too often, time is exactly what we do not give.

Plugged In

You can check out clips of Dancing With the Stars at www.youtube.com but you may find that typing in "co-teaching" will provide you with a plethora of more pertinent videos.

We especially enjoy this spoof of our "50 Ways to Keep Your Co-Teacher" article (2008). http://www.youtube.com/watch?v=WVffcgVuANM&feature=colike

Figure 2-1. Co-Teaching and Collaboration Preparation Survey for General Education Faculty

Name: _____

Classes I typically teach: _____

Grades I typically teach: _____

Complete the following questions:

	Least				Most
My experience working with students with special needs	1	2	3	4	5
My comfort level in having students w/special needs in class	1	2	3	4	5
My experience working with special educators	1	2	3	4	5
My comfort level in collaborating with special educators	1	2	3	4	5
My experience co-teaching with special educators	1	2	3	4	5
My comfort level in co-teaching with special educators	1	2	3	4	5
My willingness to co-teach this year	1	2	3	4	5

My concerns about co-teaching or having students with disabilities in my class are

_____

_____

Working closely with a special educator could help me in the following ways:

_____

_____

If I were to co-teach next year, I would prefer to co-teach with:

_____

_____

Other comments we should know:

_____

_____

Note. Adapted from *Collaborative Teaching in Elementary Schools: Making the Co-Teaching Marriage Work!* (p.113) by W. W. Murawski, 2010, Thousand Oaks, CA: Corwin Press. Copyright 2010 by Corwin Press. Adapted with permission

Figure 2-2. Co-Teaching and Collaboration Preparation Survey for Special Education Faculty

Name: _____

Subjects and classes I prefer to teach::_____

Grades I prefer to teach: _____

Complete the following questions:

	Least				Most
My experience working with students with special needs	1	2	3	4	5
My comfort level in having students with special needs in a general education class	1	2	3	4	5
My experience working with general educators	1	2	3	4	5
My comfort level in collaborating with general educators	1	2	3	4	5
My experience co-teaching with general educators	1	2	3	4	5
My comfort level in co-teaching withgeneral educators	1	2	3	4	5
My willingness to co-teach this year	1	2	3	4	5

My concerns about co-teaching and collaborating with general educators are

_____

_____

Working closely with a general educator could help me in the following ways:

_____

_____

If I were to co-teach next year, I would prefer to co-teach with:

_____

_____

Other comments we should know:

_____

Note. Adapted from *Collaborative Teaching in Elementary Schools: Making the Co-Teaching Marriage Work!* (p.114) by W. W. Murawski, 2010, Thousand Oaks, CA: Corwin Press. Copyright 2010 by Corwin Press. Adapted with permission

---

Figure 2-3. Co-Teaching and Collaboration Preparation Survey for Support Staff

Name: _____

Subjects I feel most comfortable supporting _____

Grades I feel most comfortable supporting _____

Students I feel most comfortable supporting: (Can be names of students or types of disabilities, like students with autism, students with behavioral or attentional needs, students with learning disabilities, etc.)

Complete the following questions:

	Least				Most
My experience working with students with special needs	1	2	3	4	5
My comfort level in having students w/special needs in class	1	2	3	4	5

My concerns about supporting students with disabilities in a general education class are

_____

_____

Working closely with both general and special educators could help me in the following ways:

_____

_____

Other comments we should know:

_____

_____

_____

_____

Note. Adapted from *Collaborative Teaching in Elementary Schools: Making the Co-Teaching Marriage Work!* (p.115) by W. W. Murawski, 2010, Thousand Oaks, CA: Corwin Press. Copyright 2010 by Corwin Press. Adapted with permission

S.H.A.R.E.
Sharing Hopes, Attitudes, Responsibilities, and Expectations

Directions: Take a few minutes to individually complete this worksheet. Be honest in your responses. After completing it individually, share the responses with your co-teaching partner by taking turns reading the responses. Do not use this time to comment on your partner's responses – merely read. After reading through the responses, take a moment or two to jot down any thoughts you have regarding what your partner has said. Then, come back together and begin to share reactions to the responses. Your goal is to either (a) Agree, (b) Compromise, or (c) Agree to Disagree.

1. Right now, the main **hope** I have regarding this co-teaching situation is:

   _____

   _____

2. My **attitude**/philosophy regarding teaching students with disabilities in a general education classroom is:

   _____

   _____

3. I would like to have the following **responsibilities** in a co-taught classroom:

   _____

   _____

4. I would like my co-teacher to have the following **responsibilities**:

   _____

   _____

   _____

Note. Adapted from *Co-Teaching in the Inclusive Classroom* (p. 40–41), by W. W. Murawski, 2003, Bellevue, WA: Bureau of Education and Research. Copyright 2003 by W. W. Murawski. Adapted with permission.

S.H.A.R.E.
Sharing Hopes, Attitudes, Responsibilities, and Expectations *(cont'd)*

5. I have the following expectations in a classroom:

(a) regarding discipline —

_____

(b) regarding classwork —

_____

(c) regarding materials —

_____

(d) regarding homework —

_____

(e) regarding planning —

_____

(f) regarding adaptations for individual students —

_____

(g) regarding grading —

_____

(h) regarding noise level —

_____

(i) regarding cooperative learning —

_____

(j) regarding giving/receiving feedback —

_____

(k) other important expectations I have —

Note. Adapted from *Co-Teaching in the Inclusive Classroom* (p. 40–41), by W. W. Murawski, 2003, Bellevue, WA: Bureau of Education and Research. Copyright 2003 by W. W. Murawski. Adapted with permission.

Teachers need both planning time and time together to develop as a strong team. What we see in practice, however, is that just as teams get comfortable and begin to develop real skills together, someone comes along and decides they are so good together that they should be separated to go train other teachers. It is not that easy. There are two components of development that all relationships must have to create a great team: maintenance and task. We are sure you have seen two people dance together, both of whom are very talented individually, but together are simply awful. They are missing the chemistry (or maintenance time) that allows them to work together as a team. They need maintenance time to learn each other's moves, preferences, and dislikes. Once the chemistry is in place, your teams are ready to identify and address the tasks they are to complete. In this relationship, we are clearly talking about improving student learning. Your successful teams are not just ones in which the teachers enjoy working with one another but are the teams who can actually share with you data to prove that their students' academic and social skills are improving.

When you have a team that can do both, what should you do? You know what we're going to say by this time: Leave them alone! Let them continue to build on their successes. A great leader knows what great performance is and not to interfere with it. If you can identify those who have good chemistry but need to work on their tasks or skills, work with them in that area. If you notice a team who understands the co-teaching approaches and individually are strong with students, but together they struggle to work as a unit, work with them in the maintenance of their relationship. One of our favorite models for promoting success is to let your teachers watch one another. Work with your teams to have them identify their own strengths and areas of weakness. Then have teams observe other teams who have strengths in areas in which they need support. It's called collaboration!

In the next two chapters, we focus on creating schedules that will enable more effective, efficient, and (let's face it) sane co-teachers. We emphasize again that co-teaching is designed to meet the needs of students, not teachers. However, we also recognize that when teachers feel uncomfortable, unsupported, or inefficient due to external factors, they are simply not able to do their jobs to the best of their abilities. In Chapter 3, we provide more general strategies for scheduling. We call them general strategies, but we have found that without these basic guidelines, many schools are guilty of very common mistakes in setting up for co-teaching. In Chapter 4, we offer additional strategies for different types of schools, settings, and co-teaching teams. In conjunction with this chapter, we also have provided numerous examples of co-teaching schedules. Use these examples as primers for developing your own co-teaching schedules.

Chapter 3

Beginning Choreography

No dance team is successful without a strong choreographer, that is, someone with the vision to see how the dance should look, the power to provide sufficient time for the teams to practice in advance, and the leadership skills to teach others the moves. If every person dancing wants to be a prima donna and run his or her own show, there will be no effective group routine. A successful choreographer knows how to insert solos for those who need attention, how to highlight the strengths of particular dancers, and, most importantly, how to bring it all together into one seamless performance. Creating a school schedule that incorporates inclusive practices (among them co-teaching) as well as time for teachers to plan together is the daunting choreographical job of the school administrator.

We couldn't have a book focused on leadership in co-teaching and not talk at length about scheduling. Scheduling is that necessary evil most of us have dealt with way more often than we'd prefer. Ultimately, scheduling can make or break co-teaching practices. The schedule has that much impact! As a leader, you probably hold the power to create or at least influence the schedule. In order to address the various issues related to schedules as well as respect the fact that different schools and districts have different scheduling issues and cultures, this topic is broken into multiple sections within two chapters. In this chapter, we first provide common mistakes that should be avoided in scheduling. Second, we offer general guidelines for scheduling. Third, we provide examples for schools that are just starting to co-teach versus those that have been co-teaching for years.

Avoiding Common Scheduling Mistakes

Prior to telling you what you should incorporate into your co-teaching schedule, we need to be specific about what should be adamantly avoided. (In the dance world, this may be akin to never including the chicken dance in a performance of *The Nutcracker.*) There are three specific mistakes we see frequently in schools, which lead to ineffective practices in co-teaching. These include a lack of consistency in schedules, a lack of purposeful selection, and an unreasonable number of partnerships. Let us clarify each of these so you can avoid these mistakes.

Lack of Consistency

The importance of consistency in a schedule cannot be overrated. Many of the teachers with whom we work complain that they are not able to efficiently co-teach because of the lack of a consistent schedule. This issue may occur for several reasons: the special education teacher is called out of the co-taught class to substitute for another class, an "emergency" IEP meeting is called, a parent is on the phone and needs to discuss important issues, the special education teacher is asked to help with one of "her" students who is having difficulties in another class, the schedule dictates that the special educator be in more than one place at once, or there is simply a backlog of paperwork and the special educator finds herself needing the extra time to catch up or assess students. Although all of these reasons frequently occur across the nation, we need to emphasize that they are not acceptable reasons for a special education teacher to leave a class that has been designated as a co-taught class.

The more consistency co-teachers have, the better. The co-teachers will be able to depend on one another, and they will be more likely to engage in different co-instructional approaches. The students will see the co-teachers as equals, and there will be a stronger chance at true parity between the teachers. Having a consistent schedule for the special education teacher will also help with accountability. For some teachers, a schedule that varies on a daily basis is a temptation to disappear and take extended breaks, which makes it difficult for administrators and others to find them. For others, their internal work ethic is strong, but the lack of a consistent schedule is frustrating and results in a lack of productivity. A consistent schedule will also help teachers identify when they can get together for common planning time. When one teacher's schedule is always up in the air and changes frequently, co-teachers may find it difficult to identify a regular time to meet and plan.

Substitute teachers

A few of the more common issues taking teachers away from the co-taught classroom deserve a bit more explanation: removing teachers for class coverage, last minute IEP meetings, and the different forces driving teachers' actions. First, administrators need to be keenly aware that although it may make intuitive sense to take a class with two teachers in it and remove one of those teachers in order to provide coverage for a class in which there is no teacher or available substitute, this practice can put you in legal hot water. Students with disabilities have legal documents (called individualized education programs or IEPs) that state how they will be supported. For many students, this support is in the inclusive, co-taught class, in which a special educator is present to ensure students' needs will be met. To remove that teacher means, simply put, removing those services. Further, the special education teacher is a teacher, not a substitute. If you think this practice is not happening at your school, please ask some teachers or counselors; often we find that when administrators assure us this is not occurring at their school, their teachers are sitting right behind them rolling their eyes and telling us nonverbally, "Oh, yes it is!"

Last minute IEP meetings

Some of the other practices mentioned require a change in frame of reference for the special education staff, administrators, counselors, and office staff. If a true emergency IEP meeting is required, then of course the caseload manager or teacher of record for that student needs to be in attendance. If that teacher co-teaches, it may be appropriate to get a substitute teacher to enable both teachers (the general educator and the special educator) to attend the meeting. What we often see, however, is a lot of last minute IEP meetings that occur not because of an emergency, but because of a lack of planning. It is simply unacceptable for a special educator to remove herself from a co-taught class in order to hold an IEP meeting that wasn't scheduled in advance. IEP meetings are held once a year; there is plenty of time to identify when they need to occur and to work backward in scheduling them. Strong administrative leaders will work with the special education department to create a system by which these meetings can be proactively scheduled so that they do not occur during times in which the special educator is teaching or co-teaching. This structure will also assist those teachers who frequently find themselves with a backlog of paperwork or assessment requirements. Being a successful special educator requires an immense amount of organization; when some individuals do not possess that trait, it may fall to the administrator to help create structures and processes in order to help facilitate that organization.

Different driving forces

Due process refers to the legal requirement that states must ensure that everyone has his or her rights respected and protected. In the context of this book, due process would relate to a parent taking the school district to court, claiming that the rights of the child, as governed by IDEA, have been abused. Because much of special education has resulted from due process cases, most special education teachers and administrators are acutely aware of the power of due process. However, most general education teachers do not share that awareness or concern. That is not to say that they want to do anything that is illegal or would in any way negatively impact a child with special needs, merely that they may not be fully aware of the implications of due process, as others may be. What we are advocating is that educators do what is best for the child and class in the long run because it is the right thing to do, rather than responding immediately to individual situations in an effort to merely avoid dispute with parents. Let us give an example (see box "In Action 3-1").

In Action 3-1

Mrs. Rich, the special education teacher, is on her way to co-teach fifth grade with Mr. Stanford when the phone in her room rings. She answers it out of habit and hears Matthew's mom, Ms. Silverman, on the phone. Ms. Silverman begins to explain why she called, why she's upset about Matthew's progress, and what she wants done about it. Worried about the possibility of Ms. Silverman going due process, Mrs. Rich looks at the clock, sighs, and sits down to listen to Ms. Silverman and allay her concerns. Mrs. Rich frowns, thinking about how Mr. Stanford will react when he realizes she will be late . . . again.

Although teachers certainly need to ensure that they follow legal procedures, we suggest that administrators share strategies with teachers for addressing this type of situation. For example, in the "In Action 3-1" situation with Mrs. Rich, an administrator could suggest that (a) Mrs. Rich doesn't answer the phone right before heading to a class, (b) she send parents a proactive schedule of when she is available to talk, in addition to her e-mail address, and (c) she feel comfortable saying to this parent, "Ms. Silverman, I would definitely enjoy talking to you about Matthew and what we can do to better meet his needs, but my class starts in two minutes. May I call you back during my planning period, or would you prefer to e-mail me?"

Again, much of this is about frame of reference. If special educators are used to answering phones, responding to parents' immediate needs, and using class time to get work done, that is what they will continue to do. If office staff were taught years ago that they needed to notify the case manager of a child with an IEP and have that case manager come work directly with the student when the student was sent to the office or having issues in class, then that is what would happen. Instead, administrators need to share with the entire faculty and staff that they need to work collaboratively to address students' needs, but not at the sacrifice of every other student (e.g., leaving a co-taught class to work with one student so five others are not served). Use the reminder that there will be times when a special education teacher is absent; what is the back-up plan on those days? Use the reminder that, in life, students with disabilities need supportive environments, but not only one specific person upon whom to rely. Use the reminder that collaborative cultures support all children, regardless of ability or disability. Encourage your special educators and other special service providers to be resources to the other school personnel; have them teach skills and strategies for working with specific children. We'll discuss shortly the concept of role release in education. Ultimately, however, our goal is to help meet students' needs; it doesn't matter who does it.

Lack of Purposeful Selection

We call this error the "chicken-with-its-head-cut-off-syndrome." Rolls right off the tongue, doesn't it? (The special educators in us really want to make that an acronym — CWIHCOS.) Although there are always a few individuals who may be the bad apples in the bunch, we want to take this time to say how impressed we are with our field in general. Teachers work so very hard and are obviously not compensated financially for their hard work. In fact, they work so hard that the burnout rate for special education teachers in general has been estimated to be between 8% and 13% (Boe, Cook, Bobbitt, & Terhanian, 1998; Whitaker, 2000; Wasburn-Moses, 2006). Approximately 30% of teachers flee the profession after just three years, and more than 45% leave after five years (Grazzinio, 2005). Boe and colleagues (1998) reported that the attrition rate of special educators is the highest among any other teacher group. Why is this?

We have a theory — grounded in research — that, although most individuals who go into traditional teaching know what they are signing up for, not everyone is as familiar with the role and job responsibilities of a special educator. In addition to the planning, teaching, and grading of the typical classroom teacher, special education teachers also have to assess students, write IEPs, communicate daily with parents, conduct functional behavioral assessments, design modifications and accommodations, share strategies, lead professional development, and communicate and collaborate with a wide range of individuals. They work with students who are typically struggling academically, behaviorally, socially, or all of the above,, and they do it with a smile, patience, and positive attitude. In fact, one study found that 68% of special educators simply did not have enough time to do their work (Morvant, Gersten, Gillman, Keating, & Blake, 1995). Although we can't solve this problem, we can offer strategies for at least helping to manage the situation and minimize the damage.

> **Need to Know**
>
> *Frame of Reference* — everything an individual brings to an interaction colors his or her frame of reference. This includes experiences, upbringing, opinions, biases, culture, and even current mood. By being aware of and open to different frames of reference, administrators can communicate and work with others more effectively.

You've probably heard of the maxim, "Work smarter, not harder." We enjoy this one and think it is very appropriate when considering scheduling for co-teaching. Too many special educators have the CWIHCOS (see the beginning of this section if you've forgotten the acronym. Hint: it relates to beheaded poultry). Many administrators, counselors, or even department chairs who do not understand the impact of scheduling on special educators may randomly identify who will co-teach with whom, when, and for what content areas or grades. Thus, the result is special educators who are expected to co-teach with six different teachers at all different grade levels and subjects. This CWIHCOS approach is simply unreasonable and infeasible. Again, let us give you an applicable scenario (see box "In Action 3-2").

In Action 3-2

Mr. Jefferson teaches science at the high school level. His principal, Dr. Smartz, has just come to him with an "opportunity" for the next school year. Dr. Smartz lets Mr. Jefferson know that he will be teaching one period of earth science, one period of intro to the scientific method, one period of biology, one period of chemistry, and one period of physics. He would, of course, still have his one planning period as well. As Mr. Jefferson sits there stunned, his friend, special education teacher Ms. Alina, says, "Welcome to my world." He looks up, confused. Ms. Alina explains, "I have a different class every period, in fact sometimes two or three I'm supposed to be in. In addition, at least yours are all science. I'm expected to work in English, math, science, and social studies at different grade levels. And don't forget, all the students on my caseload have identified disabilities of a variety of types." Mr. Jefferson frowns and asks, "How in the world do you do it all? How are you effective?" Ms. Alina responds, "I don't and I'm not. I do everything I possibly can, but even with a Master's degree in Special Education and tons of expertise in strategies and differentiation, when the schedule has me spread in too many directions I can't possibly be as effective as I would be if there was more consolidation and rhyme or reason to my schedule." Mr. Jefferson nods, "I understand. I'm a great science teacher, and I have the ability to teach each of those classes effectively. I just know I won't be able to be as effective with so many different preps. Maybe we should go in together to Dr. Smartz and see if we can discuss our shared need for a schedule that would help us help the students. What do you say?" Ms. Alina grins and agrees. "I would love to be able to help our administrators see from a general education perspective what this is like for special education teachers. Maybe then they'll understand how much more effective I can be with our students with disabilities if I just didn't have CWIHCOS." Mr. Jefferson looks confused as Ms. Alina just laughs and says, "It's a special education thing."

An Unreasonable Number of Partnerships

In keeping with our dance metaphor, this may be akin to trying to perform Swan Lake in a mosh pit at a Def Leppard concert. The more partners you throw in the mix, the less likely true planning is to occur. Although a few members may have the best of intentions, after a while the end result is a "free for all" or an "each man for himself" mentality. We often see this in schools where there are multiple service providers who are in many of the same classes.

Let's set the stage. We were recently in a situation where the support services department included three counselors, four resource support (special education) teachers, four teachers of English language learners, two speech and language support teachers, and twelve paraprofessionals, all of whom worked in general education classes. As we observed classes, we would sometimes see two adults in the room, sometimes three, sometimes four, and once six. We asked one of the classroom teachers (let's call him Mr. Ogle) who he worked with during the day and if he co-taught. Mr. Ogle's response was, "Well, there is always someone who comes in the room during the day, but it varies. I'm not sure if what we are doing is called co-teaching or not." When asked the roles of the folks who joined him throughout the day, he replied, "I'm not sure. I mean, I know they are here to help the kids who struggle, so I guess they are special education teachers, but I don't really know." With a little pressuring from us, Mr. Ogle admitted that he didn't really know the difference between a resource support teacher, an English language learner teacher, a speech and language support teacher, or an assistant. If that's the case, how can we possibly assume he would be willing (much less eager) to share any responsibility with these folks?

> **Need to Know**
>
> **Transdisciplinary Approach to Education** — an approach that advocates the sharing of roles across disciplinary boundaries. Coordinated services help the child and family by reducing miscommunication and fragmentation of services while increasing and improving communication and collaboration among stake-holders. Requires team members to share their expertise.

What we are advocating here is for the administrator to pay close attention to the various supports that are available in the school and to work collaboratively with those individuals to ensure more structure and sense to those supports. This helps ensure the consistency we were advocating earlier. Rather than having a special educator and an English language learner teacher work at different times with the same teachers, it would make much more sense to have those two individuals communicate and collaborate to teach each other their strategies using a transdisciplinary approach. Transdisciplinary approaches require role release, wherein experts are able to share their knowledge with one another in order to increase the consistency with which students get services (Davies, 2007; King et al., 2009; Klein et al., 2001; Limbrick, 2005; Rainforth, 1997). If these two teachers were able to do that, only one of them would need to go into Mr. Ogle's class, and during that time, all students with disabilities and/or English language needs would have their needs met. By reducing the number of people Mr. Ogle sees in a day, it is more likely he will be motivated to actually co-plan and co-instruct with that other individual.

Not only do you now have another teacher available to potentially support another general education teacher, at the same time you are reducing the number of individuals our special service providers are supporting. We have found this more focused approach key to their sanity and effectiveness. Too many schools are emphasizing quantity over quality. Special service providers are spread so thin among so many different classes that they are unable to truly serve anyone. Remember that to truly co-teach, teachers need to co-plan, co-instruct, and co-assess; we don't believe that is possible with more than two (or max, three) partners. We'll discuss the rationale for this statement in more detail later. Suffice it to say that strong administrators provide leadership that enables special educators to focus on particular grades, subjects, or students so that they can actually make an impact, rather than having them running around with the CWIHCO problem (remember that one?).

General Scheduling Guidelines

Just as we have keys to ensuring successful co-teaching, here we offer the keys for successful scheduling. However, before you read these guidelines, we need you to keep an open mind. Too often, the complaint we hear is "That wouldn't work in our school" or "We couldn't do that in our school." Why not? Because the current schedule doesn't allow for it. Remember, this isn't the time for whining. This is about re-creating a schedule that will support inclusive practices. That may very well entail doing what one administrator in Baldwin County, Alabama told us she had to do: "I realized I had a lot of 'sacred cows' in our current schedule — things no one was willing to give up. So, I just took those cows out back, shot 'em dead, and they made the best BBQ! And then I was able to re-create a schedule from scratch that met the needs of almost everyone and, more importantly, was better for kids!" You are probably able to think of your own sacred cows right now (e.g., band needs to be before school; Mrs. Lothum always wants her prep right after lunch and she's had it that way for 35 years; football needs to be during fifth and sixth period; kindergartners need an earlier recess than the fifth graders). Regardless of how sacred you think they may be, hear us out. Go into this scheduling conversation with an open mind and a willingness to consider change, especially if it results in improved outcomes for students.

Plugged In

Use technology to help your teachers communicate with one another more efficiently. Check out Creative InPerson for video conferencing and even to let special educators "see into" a classroom if they are somewhere else! http://inperson.creative.com

Rather than provide you with a lot of narrative about major scheduling guidelines, we opted to put this information into a handy format (see box, "At-a-Glance: Important Guidelines for Scheduling") for easier access and reference. Bring them with you to the next administrative meeting you have. Some of the recommendations may warrant a philosophical conversation with your colleagues to make sure you are all on the same page in terms of the direction of your school. Some of the guidelines will require you to work closely with department chairs and with the individual or individuals who typically create the schedule. Please consider carefully who needs to be in on this scheduling conversation. We have worked with many schools that have crafted new, strong schedules only to have issues arise when vice principals or school counselors begin overscheduling students with disabilities into the co-taught classes because they were not in on the conversation. For example, in one school, teachers got angry and felt they were being "dumped on" as the percentage of kids with disabilities in the class rose from 30% to 65%. They felt their administrators promised them a situation they weren't getting and they wanted out of co-teaching. Once we worked with the school and discovered that the counselors thought they were supposed to put all students with IEPs into the co-taught sections, the situation was ameliorated. It was merely an issue of a lack of communication.

Beginning Stages Versus Veteran Schools

There is obviously a difference between schools that are just getting into co-teaching versus those that have been doing it for a while. One of the major concepts we try to repeat with all schools and districts with whom we consult is to take baby steps (Murawski, 2005). Although it is commendable that some of the folks who bring us in are excited for major change and are ready to embrace co-teaching whole-heartedly, we caution that doing too much too soon will end up backfiring. On the other hand, we also need to emphasize that we aren't in any way excusing those schools that embrace the status quo without taking any steps toward change at all. We encourage change so long as we are also preparing the teachers, staff, parents, students, and community at the same time. Please remember that we also promote consistency, so don't change for the sake of change. Instead, make changes based on student needs and student data; we find that teachers rarely argue when the change is really about the students.

When beginning co-teaching in a school, we recommend you start small. Having everyone in the school learn about co-teaching is a great strategy; asking all of them to immediately then implement it is not. A stronger action is to identify those teachers who are truly interested and begin with a pilot group. Be sure to select those teachers who are also well respected within your school. Your goal is to have so much success in the first year that other faculty are clamoring to be a part of this movement.

At-A-Glance: Important Guidelines for Scheduling	
Scheduling Guideline	**Description**
Put students with disabilities in the master schedule first.	All the administrators who have been successful in scheduling co-teaching & inclusion report that this is mandatory. Trying to retrofit students with disabilities into an already created schedule simply will not work. By putting them in the master schedule first, the rest of the schedule can fall into place. It is important to do this correctly right from the beginning and that starts with the Master Schedule.
Resist the urge to increase the student-teacher ratio.	Part of the benefit of co-teaching is that it reduces the student-teacher ratio. Having two credentialed teachers in the room is not license to double the number of students. However, if the typical class size is 30, the co-taught class might be capped at 32, just slightly higher than the typical class. Remember though that this class has a number of students with identified disabilities in it. That alone warrants keeping the numbers low.
Recognize that general education teachers should only have one co-teaching "dance partner".	Content area teachers are less likely to truly co-teach (co-plan, co-instruct, co-assess) if they have multiple partners across the day. To encourage real planning together, general educators should have just one partner with whom they collaborate for co-teaching, even if they have multiple preps or if that partner comes in at different times throughout the day.
Recognize that special education teachers can only have 2-3 "dance partners" for co-teaching.	While best-case scenario would have a general and special education teacher able to co-teach all day long, this is not typically an option. Special service providers work with multiple teachers. Be aware, however, that they will not be able to truly co-teach (co-plan, co-instruct, co-assess) with more than two new co-teachers at a time (a third can be added over time). They may assist in classes through in-class support in addition to their co-teaching, but it won't be at the same level of involvement as true co-teaching.

At-A-Glance: Important Guidelines for Scheduling *(Cont'd)*	
Scheduling Guideline	**Description**
Limit the class proportion of students with special needs to no more than 30% of the class.	When those who create the master schedule see two credentialed teachers in one room, especially when one of them is credentialed in special education, the tendency is often to place all students with special needs in those classes. Even those schedulers who are aware of the need to avoid going over the 30% rule will sometimes rationalize that only 30% of the class has IEPs and identified disabilities, the others are students who are on 504 plans, are English Language learners, are struggling students with no label, or have other needs. This results in a class that resembles a de facto special education class, not the inclusive heterogeneous class it was designed to be. Co-teachers in this type of scenario often report feeling like they are being "dumped on" and are not able to be effective with the range of needs.
Ensure that those who schedule also know the guidelines and will continue to follow them throughout the year.	Make sure that anyone who has access to scheduling students is aware of the need for heterogeneity in the class. Often, we find that while those administrators who have been trained in co-teaching assure us that no classes have more than 30% of students with special needs, the co-teachers show us rosters with 60-80% of the class with IEPs or other special needs. In researching the issue, we find that other individuals, such as counselors who weren't in on the co-teaching training, have inadvertently been scheduling new students into these classes.

At-A-Glance: Important Guidelines for Scheduling *(Cont'd)*	
Scheduling Guideline	**Description**
Incorporate the proactive feedback of teachers, especially special education teachers.	Special education teachers typically know the students on their caseload and can help to determine what types of classes (self-contained, co-taught, monitor only) they need to have. They can also provide insight into what types of teachers may work best with particular children. But in addition, ask for teachers' feedback on what classes or grades they may prefer. Many special educators are given their schedules without being consulted, and learn belatedly that they are to co-teach in a math class when their strength is in language arts, while a colleague who majored in math is being assigned to the language arts classes! Input from teachers can help assure that they are best able to support students and keep up with the general education content.
Avoid over-scheduling special educators to the point that they cannot be effective. Select one of four strategies for focus: by subject matter, by grade, by professional learning community (PLC), or by caseload.	Ask any general education content teacher if he is interested in having 5 different preps and he'll respond that, while he may be qualified to teach those different classes, if he had to do so, he would be spread too thin to be effective. Yet, that is exactly what is regularly done to special educators. Instead, provide some structure by allowing special educators to specialize by subject matter (e.g., I support the Math teachers while you support in English), by grade (e.g., I support K-2, while you support 3-5), by professional learning community (e.g., I support the Tigers cluster, while you support the Eagles), or by caseload (e.g., I "loop" with one group of students for 5th, 6th and 7th grades over the next three years, while you "loop" with your own caseload).

At-A-Glance: Important Guidelines for Scheduling *(Cont'd)*	
Scheduling Guideline	**Description**
Keep in mind the additional job responsibilities of special educators and build them into the schedule (assessing, IEP meetings, monitoring, adapting materials).	While all teachers need planning time, special educators need planning time and a separate time for activities that cannot be done at home. We strongly advocate for special educators to have both a planning time (for individual planning, as well as planning with co-teaching partners), as well as an additional time when they are not scheduled with students. Don't call it planning as other teachers will be upset to think that special educators get two planning periods. Instead, use another term, e.g., Monitoring/ Facilitative Support/ Consultation /IEP /Assessment, etc. This additional time will ensure that special educators are able to assess students, have IEP meetings, make curricular adaptations, and so forth, which will ensure that students get their needs met. Though it may seem antithetical to take teachers away from students in order to meet their needs, we feel in this case the students will benefit more by teachers having the time to prepare their supports than if they were merely running between classes.
Consider the physical placement of co-teachers and their respective classrooms.	The closer co-teachers' actual classrooms are, the more easily and often they can communicate. This proximity will also increase their ability to do small group instruction during their co-taught lessons. Consider giving them a webcam to chat virtually if they are not in close proximity. (See the "Plugged In" box on page 40 for another tech option called "Creative InPerson".)
Create time for co-planning into the schedule.	This is nonnegotiable if you want co-teaching to work (yes, it's our "sacred cow"). In Chapter 5, we offer a variety of options for building in planning time, but without a doubt our # 1 option is that teachers have a common planning time or period built into the schedule from the beginning. As you build your schedules, have this need at the forefront. As you determine when each co-teaching team will be teaching kids together, also figure out when they will be planning together. Please do not try to squeeze in planning time as an afterthought; it will never happen and when it gets lost in the shuffle, the result will be ineffective co-teaching. You've worked this hard to make it successful; don't stop now!

The other benefit to starting small is that you can do things right. You can ensure teachers are well matched and have had input regarding the person with whom they will co-teach. You can ensure there is common planning time built into the schedule. You can ensure teachers have had proactive training on what co-teaching is and is not and that they have time prior to beginning to co-teach in order to make decisions regarding classroom management, homework policies, instructional procedures, and so on. (Don't forget to give them the S.H.A.R.E. worksheet we provided in Chapter 2.) You can put two teachers' desks in the room and order two teacher's manuals. You can fix the computer system to recognize both names and put them on the students' schedules and the report cards; you can make sure both of the teachers' names are on the classroom door and materials that go home or are posted on the web site. If you tried to do this with your whole school, you would face barrier after barrier. Doing it with a few teams is far more manageable and helps you work out the kinks before going schoolwide.

For those of you who have had co-teaching at your schools for a while, your next step is to identify your strengths and weaknesses. These are team-specific as well as schoolwide. For example, you may have a team who is incredible at classroom management while another team excels at using different co-teaching approaches. Proactively identify those teams so that new teams you've just created to start next school year are able to go and observe the veteran teams in action. One of the major issues teachers have (and it is hugely due to scheduling) is that they don't know what their schedules will be or who they will be working with until right before the school year begins (and in many cases, even after that). Although it is a major inconvenience, administrators need to work to identify their co-teaching pairs well in advance.

In order to identify schoolwide strengths and issues, survey your teachers. Include those who are currently co-teaching, those who have co-taught in the past, and those who have never co-taught (yes, essentially everyone). Find out what the perceptions are about co-teaching. Different issues call for different solutions. In one school, teachers may state that they love the idea of co-teaching but they are reluctant because there isn't sufficient planning time. The resulting action would be to create more co-teaching teams, but to make common planning time a promised addition. In another school, teachers may state that they are not supportive of co-teaching at all because they don't want children with disabilities in their room or they don't want the extra work. In that situation, rather than spending a year creating more co-teaching partnerships, administrators should instead schedule time for professional development so that teachers have a better understanding of what co-teaching is, who children with disabilities are, and what strategies can be used in the inclusive classroom to help all students. Other schoolwide issues we've seen come up frequently include (a) the need for both names in the computer system so that both teachers have access to grades and are put on the report cards, (b) inconsistent IEP meetings (which result in pulling teachers out of co-taught classes), and (c) frequent changes in partnerships. Each of these is a different scheduling issue; the first is technological, the second is organizational, and the third is philosophical.

Both Names in Computer

For the first issue, we have a simple solution. To ensure compliance with NCLB, schools need to demonstrate that the teacher of record is a highly qualified content teacher. In co-taught classes, simply create a new name that hyphenates that of the general educator with that of the special educator. For example, when the computer sees "Murawski" it knows there is a highly qualified teacher present; it will accept "Murawski-Dieker" as an alternative. If this doesn't work for you, go to your technical specialist and ask him or her to work it out. Both names should be represented so the parity is present.

Inconsistent IEP Meetings

For the second issue, we have to admit to our pet peeves. It is frustrating to us how many schools still are having IEP meetings at irregular times and days with no thought of teachers' schedules and the disruption this inconsistency causes. We recommend consistent IEP schedules to combat this problem. Identify a day (or days if you are a large school with many students) and have that be the day for IEPs. For example, if you select a Tuesday, there can be a sign-up sheet, a Google document, or another electronic scheduling system that will allow teachers to schedule their IEP meetings. Options can be available for before school and after school, but typically if parents are given sufficient notice, most meetings can happen during the school day and teachers can be sure not to schedule them during their co-teaching or teaching periods. Knowing what day IEPs are held on will also help administrative designees and any other designated service personnel know what day to hold for meetings. The box, "In Action 3-3" demonstrates how this would work.

In Action 3-3

Sitting at his computer in the classroom, Juan looked at the schoolwide IEP schedule in front of him. He picked up the phone and called Mrs. Jackson. "Hi, Mrs. Jackson? It's Juan Garcia, Hakim's teacher. I was calling to schedule his upcoming IEP meeting with you. We usually hold our IEP meetings on Tuesdays and I was hoping we could do Hakim's meeting in the afternoon around 1 p.m. I'm looking at three weeks from now. Would 1 p.m. on Tuesday the 30th work for you?" Juan listened and then said, "Okay, no problem. How about the following week, on Tuesday the seventh? Perfect. Alright, the school will send you a reminder notice and I'll be sending home a packet of information and then calling you to discuss what will be going on in the next week or so, okay? Great. Thanks! Talk to you soon." As soon as Juan hung up, he typed in Mrs. Jackson's name, her phone number, and Hakim's name into the space provided for 1 p.m. to 2 p.m. on the 7th. He then put it in his own phone calendar and began to move on to another task.

Frequent Changes in Partnerships

The third common issue is one that drives us insane. (We admit to having lots of pet peeves.) Please, administrators and school leaders, we implore you, when you have a great co-teaching team, leave them alone! Too often teams are changed each year due to scheduling issues, new philosophies, or just a lack of insight. We know we've stated this already, but it warrants repeating. The biggest bang for your buck is when you have teams who are able to remain together for multiple years. Those veteran teams are the ones who have worked out the kinks, who have identified strategies that work for them and for the students, and who are often the ones you can use to mentor others. Work to develop those types of veteran teams.

In the next chapter, we offer helpful guidelines for scheduling in schools that are very small and have fewer teachers versus large schools with numerous teachers. Then we share numerous concrete examples of schedules from successful elementary and secondary schools. Last, we respond to a variety of commonly asked questions related to scheduling.

Chapter 4

Advanced Choreography

Small Schools Versus Large Schools

Schools with 15 special education teachers or support professionals obviously have a different dynamic and more options for scheduling than schools with only one special educator. We understand that in the latter, in some respects, many hands are tied. However, we also want to point out that, for the most part, caseload sizes don't change based on the room in which you are teaching. What we mean by that is that if a teacher would typically have 20 students with disabilities on her caseload, she has those students whether she is pulling them out to a resource room or co-teaching in a general education classroom. Thus, in both situations, we are really talking about how to support those students in the most inclusive situation possible, given of course the requirements of the students' IEPs. When figuring out co-teaching at a small school, we offer two expressions as guidance. The first is "know what co-teaching is" and the second is "cluster and spread." When working with large schools, we recommend they "divide and conquer."

Know What Co-Teaching Is.

We often hear teachers who are in very small schools bemoaning the fact that they are being expected to "co-teach with eight different teachers." Our first response is to clarify that there is no way in the world that they are truly co-teaching with eight partners, not if you remember that the definition of co-teaching is that they are co-planning, co-instructing, and co-assessing. They agree; they are unable to do all of those things with so many partners. We clarify that they may be collaborating, supporting, monitoring, consulting, or observing in those classes; they may be helping in a variety of ways, but they are not co-teaching. It is amazing to see how relieved teachers look when we help them realize that they can lay their burden down because it is simply unrealistic (indeed, impossible) for them to co-teach with that many teachers. Next, we suggest that they should first try to truly co-teach with one of those partners while clarifying to everyone else that they are doing in-class or facilitated support in the other situations. This discussion on various structures and roles helps take the excessive pressure off of the special educator, and also helps the general education partners understand what they can and cannot reasonably expect from their colleague.

Cluster and Spread

The expression "cluster and spread" is a mantra we often repeat. What we mean by this related to scheduling is that students who are going to be in a co-taught classroom should be "clustered" so that about 30% of the class has identified special needs. That percentage warrants having a special educator co-teach the class, but doesn't result in a class that is a *de facto* special education class, with a majority of students with disabilities. The "spread" part is for those students with disabilities on the teacher's caseload who are not in the co-taught class. Those students should be spread out among many classes so that no one general education teacher faces a large percentage of students with disabilities without a special educator available to help. When possible, we also recommend that any paraprofessionals available in the school be used to support those students who are spread out in the various classes as the special educator co-teaches, rather than being in the same room with the two co-teachers. (In our opinion, unless the students have very profound physical or behavioral needs, two credentialed teachers should be able to manage a class efficiently without additional paraprofessional support, despite the fact that it is easier to run three groups and address behavior with more adults in the room. We simply have to be more judicious in where we schedule our supports.)

Divide and Conquer.

In large schools, we find that the expression that is most appropriate is "divide and conquer." Finding out the strengths of the various special service providers enables administrators to help teachers work with the appropriate departments, grade levels, or professional learning communities. Rather than each teacher being responsible for the variety of grades and subjects for every student on their caseload, teachers

Plugged In

Another great way to help teachers communicate for caseload management, instructional planning, IEP scheduling, or assignment modification is through the use of Google Docs. "Google Docs is a free, easy-to-use online word processor, spreadsheet and presentation editor that enables individuals to create, store and share instantly and securely, and collaborate online in real time." www.google.com/educators

can work together. This allows them to develop stronger relationships with general educators, become more familiar and comfortable with specific content, and advocate for students with disabilities during grade-level or department meetings. Don't forget about the transdisciplinary approach to education we described previously. A major requirement of this approach, however, is that teachers develop a system for communicating with one another to share students' progress and needs. The box "In Action 4-1" demonstrates the "divide and conquer" approach.

In Action 4-1

7:30 a.m.   Brenda logs into Google Docs and quickly checks to see how the students on her caseload are doing in the various classes. She spends 10 minutes updating information on students in the various English classes in which she co-teaches. She logs off and heads to class.

12:45 p.m.   During lunch, Brenda is on the phone with Mrs. Avon. Keeping the Google Doc open in front of her, she is able to update Mrs. Avon on how Raudel is doing in all of his classes, even though she sees him only in his English class. She notes Mrs. Avon's concerns on the Google Doc for the other teachers to see.

3:30 p.m.   During the monthly special education department meeting, teachers share with one another specifics that were not as clear on the Google Doc. They update one another on how students are doing, share units or assignments that are coming up, and communicate strategies and accommodations they are using. Brenda spends a few extra minutes talking to Yesenia, who co-teaches in the math department, to discuss Mrs. Avon's concerns about Raudel's progress.

Models of Elementary and Secondary Schedules

Major differences exist philosophically and logistically between elementary and secondary schools. Elementary schools tend to have students stay in one classroom with one teacher except when they go for "specials" such as art, music, or physical education. Teachers are expected to teach all subjects to all students, and most elementary teachers do not have a scheduled planning period. On the other hand, secondary schools tend to have students change classes each hour in different class periods. Teachers are content experts and usually teach in one subject area all day, though there may be different courses within that subject. Most teachers at the secondary level have a class period designated as a planning period. Much has been written about co-teaching in both elementary and secondary schools, and in the "For your bookshelf" box, we offer articles that focus on the different levels.

Although most elementary and secondary schools vary according to the criteria we mentioned above, we have been in elementary schools in which students change rooms regularly, and we have been in secondary schools which implemented a homeroom approach wherein the students stayed together and the teachers moved around. Although neither of these is common, they demonstrate that schools are different. What we provide here is a multitude of scheduling options for you to consider. One or two of the examples may resonate with you immediately and appear to be exactly what you need, or you may find you need to create a combination of the approaches provided here in order to make your own completely new approach. We understand the need for diversity and the need to respect different school cultures. Our only caveat is that administrators need to work collaboratively with teachers to ensure they are selecting approaches that make the most sense to teachers as well. Major decisions such as this should not be made in a vacuum. The following are different possible approaches to scheduling co-teaching in your schools.

For Your Bookshelf

Dieker, L. A. & Murawski, W. (2003). *Co-teaching at the secondary level: Unique issues, current trends, and suggestions for success.* The High School Journal, 86(4), 1-13.

Keefe, E. B., & Moore, V. (2004). *The challenge of co-teaching in inclusive classrooms at the high school level: What the teachers told us.* American Secondary Education, 32(3), 77-88.

Nevin, A., Cramer, E., Salazar, L., & Voigt, J. (2008). *Instructional modifications, adaptations, and accommodations of co-teachers who loop: A descriptive case study.* Teacher Education and Special Education, 31(4), 283-297.

Full Support Model

In this model, a special education teacher and general education teacher are paired and work together all day long in the same classroom. The benefits of this model are that it allows teachers to develop quickly as a team, it shows that the teachers are equals, and it allows continuity for students. This also makes it much easier for teachers to share roles and responsibilities and find time for planning. The downside of this approach is that most schools find it difficult to allow a special educator to stay in one room for the entire day. A consideration for this approach is that some teachers of small, self-contained classes of fewer students may find that they are able to consolidate their classes into general education classes so that teachers can stay together all day long. This consolidation is more likely to occur at the elementary level than at the secondary level. Figures 4-1 through 4-8 illustrate the elementary and secondary differences.

Grade or Subject Support Model

Grade/subject support model are in Figure 4-3 through 4-4. In this model, a special education teacher co-teaches with two (and sometimes three) general education partners, but there is an emphasis on a particular grade or subject. Keep in mind that to co-teach, these teachers have to have time to plan, instruct, and assess together. Thus, we are not advocating for teachers to be asked to co-teach with more than three partners; fewer is better. They may collaborate, co-plan, consult, monitor, or support other teachers, but they will never truly be able to co-teach with more than three partners (and that is pushing it). The benefits of this model are that the special educator is in multiple classes in which students with disabilities are included; this not only helps the general education teachers and the students, but it also helps the special educator know what curriculum is being taught in those classes. When teachers are able to stay with one subject or grade level, they are better able to add real value. Another major benefit is that although the special educator is only providing direct support to the students in the classes in which she is co-teaching, she is still able to provide indirect support to the students with disabilities in the other classes taught by the same general educator. Through planning with the general educator, the special educator is able to address the needs of students even if she is not going to be present. Adaptations made to assignments, visuals or graphic organizers created, and behavioral management suggestions are available for students in different periods or classes. The box "In Action 4-2" clarifies how this works. The consequences of this model are that teachers can be spread too thin if planning is not allocated in the schedule, and it can sometimes be difficult to find multiple partners who complement one another. A consideration for this approach is to try to minimize the different subjects, grades, or classes within which the special educator is co-teaching.

In Action 4-2

As always, Ms. Weichel and Mrs. Hutchinson met 15 minutes before school started to make sure their ducks were in a row. They didn't co-teach until third period, so Mrs. Hutchinson (the English teacher) always made sure her first and second period classes were one day behind the other classes so she could implement any new strategies she learned from working with Ms. Weichel into those classes as well. Today, Ms. Weichel brought in a poster with a mnemonic on it for remembering the grammar points they were reviewing in class. Mrs. Hutchinson took it and was grateful she would have it to post for all her classes, not just the one in which they co-taught. She also told Ms. Weichel about an issue she was having with Todd in her second period class; Todd was on Ms. Weichel's caseload. Ms. Weichel quickly gave her two great strategies to try with Todd (and she thought they might work with another student, Johanna, too). Ms. Weichel also gave her some additional materials to use with a few of the students in her fifth and sixth periods. Mrs. Hutchinson smiled as she headed off to first period. It was so nice to work with such a professional colleague. Even though they only co-taught for one period, all of her classes benefitted from this collaboration, and so did she!

Figure 4-1: Full Support Model Examples **Sample Elementary Schedule With Two Teachers**		
Time	**Ms. Black – 3rd Grade General Education Teacher**	**Mr. White – 3rd Grade Special Education Teacher**
8:00 a.m.–9:00 a.m.	Morning Meeting–room 3	Morning Meeting–room 3
9:00 a.m.–10:00 a.m.	Social Studies/Science–room 3	Social Studies/Science–room 3
10:00 a.m.–11:30 a.m.	Language Arts–room 3	Language Arts–room 3
11:30 a.m.–12:00 p.m.	Lunch	Lunch
12:00 p.m.–1:00 p.m.	Math–room 3	Math–room 3
1:00 p.m.–2:00 p.m.	Specials–room 3	Specials–room 3
2:00 p.m.–2:30 p.m.	Wrap-Up–room 3	Wrap-Up–room 3

Note. Specials are Art, Physical Education, Music, and Library.

Figure 4-2: Full Support Model Examples **Sample Elementary Schedule With Two Teachers**		
Time	**Ms. Black – Math Education Teacher**	**Mr. White – Special Ed Math Education Teacher**
Period 1	Algebra I–room 24	Algebra I–room 24
Period 2	Algebra I–room 24	Algebra I–room 24
Period 3	Algebra I–room 24	Algebra I–room 24
Period 4	Planning–room 24	Planning–room 24
Lunch	Lunch	Lunch
Period 5	Geometry–room 24	Geometry–room 24
Period 6	Geometry–room 24	Geometry–room 24

Figure 4-3: Grade Level Support Sample Elementary Schedule With Two Teachers			
Time	**Ms. Black – 3rd Grade**	**Mr. White – Special Education**	**Miss Red – 4th Grade**
8:00 a.m.–9:00 a.m.	Morning Meeting	Preparing materials, assessing – sped office	Morning Meeting
9:00 a.m.–10:00 a.m.	Social Studies	Co-teach 4th grade Math	Math
10:00 a.m.–11:00 a.m.	Science	Co-teach 4th grade Language Arts	Language Arts
11:00 a.m.–12:00 p.m.	Language Arts		
	Co-teach 3rd grade Language Arts	Science	
12:00 p.m.–12:30 p.m.	Lunch	Lunch	Lunch
12:30 p.m.–1:30 p.m.	Math	Co-teach 3rd grade Math	Social Studies
1:30 p.m.–2:30 p.m.	Specials[a]		
(Plan w/White M/W; plan solo T/Th/F)	Plan with Black M/W; plan with Red T/Th;		
IEP meetings Fridays	Specials[a]		
(Plan w/White T/Th; plan solo M/W/F)			
2:30 p.m.–3:00 p.m.	Wrap-Up	Adapt materials, assess, write IEPs, etc – sped office	Wrap-Up

Note. M = Monday; T = Tuesday; W = Wednesday; Th = Thursday; F = Friday. IEP = individualized education program.
[a]Specials are art, physical education, music, and library.

Figure 4-4: Subject Specific Model Sample Secondary Schedule With Three Teachers			
Time	**Ms. Black – English 9/10**	**Mr. White – Special Education**	**Miss Red – English 11/12**
Period 1	English 9 (co-taught)	English 9 (co-taught)	English 11
Period 2	Planning w/White T/Th Planning solo M/W/F	Planning w/Black T/Th Planning w/Red M/W Planning solo F	Planning w/White M/W Planning solo T/Th/F
Period 3	English 9	English 11 (co-taught)	English 11 (co-taught)
Period 4	English 10	English 9 (co-taught)	English 12
Lunch	Lunch	Lunch	Lunch
Period 5	English 10	English 10 (co-taught)	English 11
Period 6	English 9	Assessment Period (for IEPs, assessment, adapting materials, etc.)	English 12

Note. M = Monday; T = Tuesday; W = Wednesday; Th = Thursday; F = Friday. IEP = individualized education program.

Cluster or Team Support Model

In this model, a special education teacher co-teaches with two (and sometimes three) general education partners, similar to the model above. Again, we reiterate that, to co-teach, these teachers have to have time to plan, instruct, and assess together. In this model, however, there is built-in collaboration between a group of teachers and the special educator becomes part of that group. If a cluster, team, small learning community, or professional learning community is created so that teachers can share the same group of students, it can become much easier for co-teaching to occur. For example, at the middle school level, you may have a group of teachers who share the same students, even if those students are mixed up every period so they don't move to each class together. Then, during planning, teams of teachers can get together to discuss curriculum, goals, and specific students. Typically, a team would consist of an English teacher, a math teacher, a social studies teacher, and a science teacher. Throw in a special educator and your team is complete. (We are in no way discounting the value of other teachers such as physical education, art, foreign language, drama, and so on, but we find they often work across multiple clusters.) The benefits of this model are that it allows the special educator to be involved in all of the critical decision-making for the cluster and be present at team planning meetings to keep the inclusive philosophy at the forefront. Being part of planning meetings also means the special educator is less likely to have to work as intensely with each individual teacher because she will have been active in the original conversations regarding curriculum, pacing, and goal-setting. The main consequence of this model is that schools often schedule the special education teacher to teach a stand-alone special education class, run a learning center, or otherwise work with students when the cluster of teachers is planning. This works against the special educator being part of the planning team. It is important for that person to meet during the group planning time or the risk is run that students with disabilities will be considered as an afterthought, rather than included proactively in the discussion. Consider carefully building the schedule so that students can attend their electives during planning or staff a learning center with other support personnel (e.g., trained paraprofessionals, speech language pathologists, technology specialists, librarians). Remember to schedule paraprofessionals into the classes in which the special educators are not co-teaching so that the additional support is spread around. Figure 4-5 is the elementary cluster/team model, Figure 4-6 is the secondary cluster/team model.

Time	Mr. White 1st Grade (Special Education)	Ms. Black 1st Grade (Room 3)	Ms. Red 1st Grade (Room 4)	Mr. Blue 1st Grade (Room 5)	Mr. Yellow 1st Grade (Room 6)
7:30 a.m.– 8:00 a.m.	First grade team meeting	First grade team meeting	First grade team meeting	First grade team meeting	First grade team meeting
8:00 a.m.– 9:00 a.m.	Preparing materials, assessing– special education office	Morning Meeting with kids	Morning Meeting with kids	Morning Meeting with kids	Morning Meeting with kids
9:00 a.m.– 10:00 a.m.	Math–room 4 (M/W) Math–room 5 (T/Th) IEPs (F)	Social Studies	Math	Math	Social Studies
10:00 a.m.– 11:00 a.m.	Math–room 3 (M/W) Math–room 6 (T/Th) IEPs (F)	Math	Specials[a]	Social Studies	Math
11:00 a.m.– 12:00 p.m.	Language Arts–room 4	Science (partner w/ Rm 5)	Language Arts (co-taught)	Science (partner w/ Rm 3)	Specials[a]
12:00 p.m.– 12:30 p.m.	Lunch	Lunch	Lunch	Lunch	Lunch
12:30 p.m.– 1:30 p.m.	Language Arts –room 3	Language Arts (co-taught)	Science (partner w/ Rm 6)	Specials[a]	Science (partner w/ Rm 4)
1:30 p.m.– 2:30 p.m.	Language Arts– room 5 (M/W) Language Arts– room 6 (T/Th) IEPs or as needed in Room5 & 6 (F)	Specials[a]	Social Studies	Language Arts	Language Arts
2:30 p.m.– 3:00 p.m.	Adapt materials, assess, write IEPs, meet with paras – special education office	Wrap-up	Wrap-up	Wrap-up	Wrap-up
3:00 p.m. – 3:30 p.m.	Debrief and team planning	Debrief and planning	Debrief and planning	Debrief and planning	Debrief and planning

Figure 4-5: Cluster/Team Model Sample Elementary Schedule With Four Teachers

Note. M = Monday; T = Tuesday, W = Wednesday, Th = Thursday, F = Friday. IEP = individualized education program.
[a]Specials are art, physical education, music, and library.

Period	Mr. White – Ninth Grade (Special Education)	Ms. Black – Ninth Grade (English)	Ms. Red – Ninth Grade (Math)	Mr. Blue – Ninth Grade (Science)	Mr. Yellow – Ninth Grade (Social Studies)
	Figure 4-6: Cluster/Team Model Sample Secondary Schedule With Five Teachers				
1	Co-teach English	English 9 (co-taught)	Calculus	Earth Science	US History
2	Co-teach Algebra I	English 9	Algebra I (co-taught)	Earth Science	US History
3	Support Earth Science	Newspaper	Algebra I	Earth Science (Supported)	World History
4	Support World History	English 9	Calculus	Physics	World History (Supported)
	Lunch	Lunch	Lunch	Lunch	Lunch
5	Team Planning[a]	Team Planning[a]	Team Planning[a]	Team Planning[a]	Team Planning[a]
6	Co-teach English	English 9 (co-taught)	Algebra I	Earth Science	World History
7	Assessment Period (IEPs, assessing, adapting materials, consultation)	English 9	Algebra I	Physics	Yearbook
3-3:30pm	Debrief & Planning (M: Black, T: Red, W: Blue, Th: Yellow)	Debrief & Planning (Monday w/ White)	Debrief & Planning (Tuesday w/ White)	Debrief & Planning (Wednesday w/White)	Debrief & Planning (Thursday w/ White)

Note. M = Monday; T = Tuesday, W = Wednesday, Th = Thursday, F = Friday.

[a]Most ninth-grade students are at electives during the Period 5 planning period. Electives are art, physical education, music, foreign language, drama, woodworking, and learning center.

Hodgepodge Schedule

We just can't come up with a better or more accurate name for the next scheduling examples. They are schedules that special educators at elementary and secondary levels might have as baby steps to better co-teaching schedules. Again, we want to emphasize that we are not advocating these schedules over the ones we have already provided; we are merely adding them here to recognize that some schools are not ready to embrace co-teaching as quickly and may have to "make do" in the meantime. It is important to point out that your teachers (and thus your students) will have more success the more planning, focus, and support you can provide them. Thus, using any of these schedules should be merely a stopgap until you are able to work a more supportive schedule that provides focus and planning.

The main benefit to these schedules, beyond the fact that they may better fit your current schedules, is that they emphasize consistency. Even if teachers have more partners than we recommend or are teaching multiple courses or preps, at the minimum their schedule is consistent. This type of structure is not what we see in a majority of schools that are trying to embrace inclusion. Unfortunately, what we often see are special educators who are expected to be everywhere at once, helping students all over the campus, and they have no specific schedule. Many teachers we meet are expected to work it out for themselves. Although this may work for a few highly organized individuals, the result usually seems to be (you guessed it) CWIHCOS. Special education teachers in these situations are ineffective not because they are inept, but merely because they cannot do it all. This type of scheduling helps identify exactly what they are expected to be doing, when, and with whom. (Do also note in the elementary example that we include pull-out services. We recognize that even in inclusive settings a range of service delivery options will exist based upon students' needs as reflected in their IEPs. In the example below, we show how students would be getting their services based on their level of need, not based on which teacher's caseload they are on. This type of structure requires more collaboration but helps in scheduling.)

Naturally, a consequence of this schedule is that teachers are still asked to do too much with too many partners. What we ask you to consider here is the importance of calling each situation with its appropriate name. Do not call every collaborative situation "co-teaching," because it won't be and doing so will only add to the stress of the teachers attempting to meet that expectation. View the following examples of schedules to see what we mean.

Figure 4-7: Hodgepodge Schedule **Sample Elementary Schedule With Five Teachers**					
Time	**Mr. White – Special Education**	**Ms. Black – Special Education**	**Ms. Red – Special Education**	**Mr. Blue – Special Education**	**Mr. Yellow – Special Education**
7:30 a.m.– 8:00 a.m.	Planning w/1st grade team (M/W/F); Before school reading lab (T/Th)	Planning w/ PreK team (M); Planning w/K team (T); Before school reading lab (W/Th/F)	Planning w/2nd grade team (T/Th); Before school reading lab (M/W/F)	Planning w/3rd grade team (T/W); Planning w/4th grade team (Th/F); Before school reading lab (M)	Planning w/5th grade team (M/F); Planning w/ 6th grade team (W/Th); Before school reading lab (T)
8:00 a.m.– 9:00 a.m.	Co-teach Language Arts 1st grade with Miss Aiken	Pull-out reading (PreK-K level)	Co-teach Math 2nd gr with Mrs. Roberts	Monitoring Support for all 3rd & 4th grade Math classes (paras in the math classes)	Co-teach Language Arts 5th grade with Mr. Zephyr
9:00 a.m.– 10:00 a.m.	In-class support for 1st grade Language Arts (Mon = Mr.B; Tues = Ms. C; Wed = Mr. D; Th = Miss E; Fri = Mr. F)	Co-teach Language Arts in Kinder with Mr. Graves	Co-teach Language Arts 2nd gr with Mrs. Roberts	Pull-out reading (1-2nd grade levels)	Co-teach Math 5th grade with Mr. Zephyr (M/W/F) & Co-teach Math 6th grade with Mrs. One (T/Th)
10:00 a.m.– 11:00 a.m.	Co-teach Math 1st grade M/W/F with Miss Aiken; Co-teach Math 1st grade T/Th with Mr. B	Pull-out reading (PreK-K levels)	In-Class Support for 2nd grade Math with Mr. S (M/T) & Miss T (W/Th); Fri- as needed	Co-teach Language Arts 3rd gr with Mrs. Williams	Monitor all 5th & 6th grade classes (go to classes & check grades, talk to teachers, help paras)

Note. M = Monday; T = Tuesday, W = Wednesday, Th = Thursday, F = Friday. IEP = individualized education program.
[a]Specials are Art, Physical Education, Music, and Library.

Time	Mr. White – Special Education	Ms. Black – Special Education	Ms. Red – Special Education	Mr. Blue – Special Education	Mr. Yellow – Special Education
	Figure 4-7: Hodgepodge Schedule **Sample Elementary Schedule With Five Teachers** *(cont'd)*				
11:00 a.m.–12:00 p.m.	In-class support for 1st grade Math (Mon = plan; Tues = Ms. C; Wed = Mr. D; Th = Miss E; Fri = Mr. F)	In-class support Language Arts in Pre-K (Mon = Mr J; Tues = Ms. K; Wed = Mr. L; Th = Miss M; Fri = plan)	In-Class Support for 2nd grade Science (Mon = Mrs Roberts; Tues = Mr. S; Wed = Miss T; Th = Mr. U; Fri = Mrs. V	Co-teach Language Arts 3rd gr with Mr. Xavier	In-class support (Mon = 5th LA-Mr. Two; Tues = 5th Math – Miss Three; Wed = 6th LA – Mrs. Four; Th = 6th Math – Miss Five; Fri = where needed)
12:00 p.m.–12:30 p.m.	Lunch	1:1 Reading tutorial w/ Ali	Lunch	Lunch	Lunch
12:30 p.m.–1:30 p.m.	In-class support Language Arts in Kinder w/Mrs. H (M/W) & Mr. I (T/Th); Fri – IEPs & planning	Lunch (1/2 hour) 1:1 Reading tutorial w/Bev (1/2 hr)	Training all para-professionals on strategies	Co-teach Language Arts 4th grade with Miss Yoshida	Planning w/ 5th & 6th gr. Teachers (kids at Specials)
1:30 p.m.–2:30 p.m.	In-class support Math in Kinder (Mon = Ms Q; Tues = Mr. P; Wed = Ms. O; Th = Mr. N; Fri = plan)	In-class support Math in Kinder (Mon = Mr N; Tues = Ms. O; Wed = Mr. P; Th = Ms Q;Fri = plan)	Pull-out reading (1-2nd grade levels)	Planning w/ 3rd & 4th gr. Teachers (kids at Specials)	Co-teach Language Arts 6th grade with Mrs. Six
2:30 p.m.–3:00 p.m.	Assessment (IEPs, etc)	Assessment (IEPs, etc)	Assessment (IEPs, etc)	Assessment (IEPs, etc)	Assessment (IEPs, etc)
3:00 p.m.–3:30 p.m.	Special education department meeting 2 times per week	Special education department meeting 2 times per week	Special education department meeting 2 times per week	Special education department meeting 2 times per week	Special education department meeting 2 times per week

Note. M = Monday; T = Tuesday, W = Wednesday, Th = Thursday, F = Friday. IEP = individualized education program.
[a]Specials are Art, Physical Education, Music, and Library.

Period	Mr. White — Special Education	Ms. Black — Special Education	Ms. Red — Special Education
7:00 a.m.– 7:45 a.m. Before school	Para trainings (M); special education department (T); planning with partners (W); IEPs (Th); solo planning (F)	Para trainings (M); special education department (T); planning with partners (W); IEPs (Th); solo planning (F)	Para trainings (M); special education department (T); planning with partners (W); IEPs (Th); solo planning (F)
1	Special education study skills	Co-teach biology with Yu	In-class support for algebra (Jones = M/W; Smith = T/Th; Testing = Fri)
2	Co-teach English 9 (with Zephyr)	Planning (with Yu M/F; solo T/W/Th)	Co-teach English 10 (with Hutchinson)
3	Co-teach English 10 (with Hutchinson)	Special education science	In-class support for health (Brown = M/F)
4	Planning (with Zephyr M; with Hutchinson T/Th; solo W/F)	Co-teach earth science with Snyder	Planning (with Hutchinson T/Th; solo M/W/F)
	Lunch	Lunch	Lunch (eat with Brown and White on M; Jones & Smith on T; Fishman on W; my choice Th/F)
5	IEP Period (for IEPs, monitoring, assessing, adapting work, etc.)	Monitoring (M–W); testing (Th); planning with Snyder (F)	In-class support for biology (with Fishman M–Th; Testing = F)
6	In-class support algebra (M/W/F) with Brown	Special education study skills	Monitoring M = Chalk/Howell/Campbell T = Rodriguez/ Hutchinson W = Farrell/Cook/Ashton Th = Levine/Cox F = Debrief with special education department
3:00 p.m.– 3:30 p.m. After school	M = Math department meeting; T = Health department meeting; W = English department meeting; M-Math dept mtng; T- Social Studies dept mtng; W- English dept mtng; Th – Planning; Fri – SPED dept mtng	M = prep study skills curriculum for department; T = Science department meeting; W = Planning; Th = Planning; Fri = special education department meeting	M = Math department meeting; T = Health department meeting; W = English department meeting; Th = Planning Fri = Special education department meeting

Figure 4-8: Hodgepodge Schedule Sample Secondary Schedule With Three Teachers

Note. M = Monday; T = Tuesday, W = Wednesday, Th = Thursday, F = Friday. IEP = individualized education program

Additional Scheduling Considerations

As we stated at the beginning of Chapter Three, scheduling can be a nightmare, and we recognize that. However, we want to give you as much support as we can. In this section, we provide you with many other tips related to scheduling as we can. Everyone's needs are different, but we hope to cover as many of those needs as possible.

Worried that your special educators won't know their students well enough to support them?
One option is called looping, in which the special education teacher keeps the same group of students on his or her caseload for multiple years (e.g., third, fourth, and fifth grades). The benefits of this structure are that the special educator knows the families and students and can more easily update progress on the IEPs; the consequence is that some teachers, students, or families weren't meant to be together for more than one year. In addition, this approach to scheduling makes it much more difficult for special educators to become familiar with the content and curriculum or to develop strong relationships with other teachers in order to co-teach. Nevin and colleagues (2008) do an excellent job of providing research on co-teachers who were looping with their students and found it to be effective for elementary schools.

Want to encourage baby steps to co-teaching?
Have your teachers co-teach just one lesson or unit with another educator. It doesn't have to be a special education teacher; music teachers, reading coaches, English as a second language teachers, and librarians are also excellent resources for co-teaching. See Murawski (2005) in *Kappa Delta Pi Record* for an article on baby steps to co-teaching.

Concerned that your teachers are not able to plan sufficiently or don't use enough small group strategies?
Make sure their classrooms are next to one another. We have found that teachers whose rooms are adjacent or at least nearby were far more likely to do miniature, ongoing planning and to use both rooms for small group instruction. In addition, less time was wasted by students and teachers running across the campus. If that is not an option, check out the Creative InPerson videoconferencing option discussed previously.

Ready to try a more unique model of co-teaching?
In 2001, Lisa wrote in *Preventing School Failure* about a family support model of co-teaching she saw being used in one school with which she worked. In this situation, the special education teacher actually stayed in her own classroom while the general education teachers brought their classes to her!

In this model, the special educator was able to work with a different subject teacher each day; the change of venue was great for students and teachers and the special educator was able to bring a focus on strategies and behavior support into their co-taught lessons.

Trying to find a way to structure planning in a schedule that doesn't otherwise permit it?

Doing research on a highly successful, fully inclusive school in California, Fabrocini (2012) found that mandated collaborative planning resulted in improved communication and better differentiation. The school in question required teachers to be at the school 45 minutes before school started in order to have grade level teachers meet and co-plan. After school, all teachers, paraprofessionals, and service personnel who worked in a classroom during the day were expected to get together for 15 to 20 minutes at the end of the day to share a success and a challenge. This level of debriefing increased collaboration, improved communication, and ultimately resulted in a smoother day for teachers, paraprofessionals, and students. All participants interviewed in Fabrocini's research reported feeling that although the planning time took work, the outcomes were well worth the effort.

Still trying to figure out the options for scheduling?

Ultimately, it boils down to three options. You can have your special educators organized by grade level (e.g., Wendy does second and third grade while Lisa works with the fourth and fifth grade teachers), by subject area (e.g., Wendy supports in English and social studies while Lisa is with math and science predominantly), or by a caseload of students (known as looping and described earlier). Elementary schools tend to prefer grade level organization or looping (in that order), whereas most secondary schools find that subject matter organization makes the most sense to them, especially given the fact that most department meetings are by subject rather than grade. Schools that implement clusters, teams, or small learning communities can add that as an option as well (e.g., Wendy works with the creative professional learning community while Lisa works with the technical professional learning community). Whatever your selection, try to be consistent and structured. That is the only way co-teaching can be successful, at least at a systemic level.

Trying to figure out the best partnerships?

As discussed in Chapter 2, we think it is always best for teachers to have input in the folks with whom they will be expected to co-teach. In smaller schools, though, we know it is not always possible for teachers to choose their partners (e.g., there is only one third grade teacher or one math teacher). We also know that in these situations there may be multiple dance partners. Although learning to dance with just one partner and being able to dance with that person daily can make for a really strong performance, we recognize that the reality in co-teaching is a need for multiple partners. This work across teachers of course emphasizes the need for all of them to learn the "steps" to co-teaching (e.g., what is co-teaching, what are the characteristics for effective collaboration, etc.). We cannot recommend enough, though, that you limit the number of partners of both teachers as much as possible. Try to have the general education teacher only work with one special educator, even if it is over multiple preps. We'd love to make the same recommendation for the special educator, but we know that is not always possible. On the other hand, please remember that although one and two co-teaching partners are doable, three is a challenge, and more than that may be detrimental rather than beneficial.

Looking for a formula to determine which students should be in co-taught classes?

Sorry. There isn't one. Remember that there need to be options for support. Just because a student has a disability does not necessarily mean he or she needs a co-teacher for every class all day long. We repeat: Just because a student has a disability does not necessarily mean that student needs to be in a co-taught class. We recommend you focus on a range of service delivery options, such as those previously provided. Some students can be in the general education setting with no support, some need facilitative or in-class support, some need co-teaching, and some may need a more restrictive, self-contained setting. No matter the service delivery option, the goal is for the student is to be included in the general education setting as much as possible.

How many students with disabilities should be placed in one class?

A good general guideline is that you follow what are considered natural proportions. This statement means either trying to mimic the proportions of students with disabilities in your school (e.g., your school has 24% students with IEPs, so each class never has more than 24%) or following what are considered natural proportions in life (i.e., 15% to 30% depending on the source) within each classroom. We find that although 20% of the class would be a very appropriate percentage, 30% typically seems more realistic and doable for those who are trying to cluster students for co-teaching (Murawski, 2008). Pearl, Dieker, and Kirkpatrick (2012) also recommended this percentage in their work across the state of Arkansas, which was then reviewed in visits to the districts by the State Department to ensure a more natural balance of students in inclusive settings. This percentage still allows for a balance without the class becoming a de facto special education class. However, do try to remember that all disabilities are not created equal. Avoid scheduling all of the students with severe behavior problems in the same class. You will also need to work with your schedulers to ensure that other students who have special needs but do not have an IEP (e.g., students who are English language learners, have

504 plans, or are at-risk) are not inadvertently scheduled into those co-taught classes without being considered into the 30% guideline. We frequently see administrators who put their best teachers with a class of 30 students, 18 of whom are really struggling, because the administrators think those teachers will fix the issues. We have only rarely (and we want to emphasize rarely) seen this model work. In contrast, when the proportion of students with disabilities is balanced, the outcome is a much more successful experience for all. This type of inclusive class has a balance that enables co-teachers to focus on higher learning gains, rather than having to focus purely on managing behaviors or trying to get a classroom full of reluctant learners motivated to even get started.

How can we watch the 30% guideline when we have a transient student population?

We suggest you use a simple procedure of having four columns for each grade level or content area in which you plan to have co-teaching occur. Refer to the menu of services outlined above. Next, use a process (see box, "At-a-Glance: Sample Scheduling Matrix" for an example) to schedule students by moving a post-it note on the schedule(Dieker & Hines, 2012). We have included three "ghosts" in our schedule to address that possible transient population. Many schools find that if they don't schedule for those possible incoming students, they quickly lose their balance and go over their target of having students with disabilities constituting no more than 30% of the class. Start creating this matrix in January for the following school year and move the post-it notes around as IEP meetings or situations arise. This process will help you, the special education department, and others involved with scheduling identify potential problem areas early on and will provide a more concrete step to what we know is a difficult task.

Steps for Getting Started in Scheduling

Although there is no step-by-step guide we can give you to guarantee perfect co-teaching in your schools, there are some general steps for getting started. Here we provide a step-by-step guide for starting to figure out how many co-teaching classes you may need in your school. Use the forms in Appendix 1 to complete this process (Murawski, 2009; Murawski, 2010).

At-A-Glance: Working Out Your Co-Taught Classes

1. Identify the number of special service providers (teachers and paraprofessionals) you have.

2. Identify the number of students with special needs you have. You can include students in special education, students who are gifted, English language learners, students with 504 plans, and any other students who may need special support.

3. Review each of the students along the continuum and check the appropriate boxes. (This review is often best done by the case manager with the most experience with the student.) Determine the least restrictive environment for each student. From least to most restrictive, these options are: general education only; general education with support; co-taught class; special education only class.

4. Count up the number of courses that need to be taught solely for special education students, as well as those that will be general education classes (monitor only, with support, and co-taught).

5. When possible, go back to the students who are able to be in general education courses (through monitor, in-class support, and co-taught situations) and "weight" them based on academic/behavioral need. This allows you to ensure that no one class will be relegated to all of the students with the most difficult behaviors or academic needs. When weighting, a 1 means the student needs as much support as the typical nondisabled student; a 2 denotes mild/moderate support; and a 3 indicates significant support will be needed. Academic needs are represented by an A, and B stands for behavioral or social needs. Thus, you may have a child who is an A1/B3 (strong behavioral needs only), a child who is an A2/B2 (moderate needs in both academics and behavior), or a child who is an A3/B2 (strong needs academically and moderate behavioral issues as well).

6. Now is the time to apply the cluster and spread strategy we discussed previously. Cluster students for co-taught classes (up to 30%) and spread out the students who will be in in-class support or monitoring situations.

7. Keep the partners limited. Remember that general education teachers should only have one special education teacher with whom they collaborate or co-teach daily. Special educators should have focus in their schedule (e.g., with the same subject, grades or students).

8. Be sure to schedule in planning. Still not sure how to do that? Well then, read on to Chapter 5!

At-A-Glance: Sample Scheduling Matrix			
(Could be Elementary: Fourth Grade or Secondary: Algebra I)			
No Support	Facilitative or In-Class Support	Co-taught Support	Self-Contained
Jason	Sean	Austin	Tim
Matt	Mike	Bill	Elyse
Tanisha	Sam	Star	Kelly
Shawn	Tabitha	Shante	Fred
Sally	Jose	Fred	
Kevin	Angel	Bryn	
Dante	GHOST	Allen	
		GHOST	
		GHOST	

Chapter 5

Planning for the Dance

The Need for Planning Time

Experts assert that successful co-teaching requires common planning time (Dieker, 2001; Friend & Cook, 2007; Scruggs et al., 2007). The lack of time for planning is the number one issue mentioned over and over again by co-taught teams as a barrier to their success (Davis, Dieker, Pearl & Kirkpatrick, 2012; Dieker, 2001; Murawski, 2006). Research has found that without co-planning time, teachers tend to continue to teach as usual, that is, they lack differentiation strategies and resort to a one teach-one support paradigm (Magiera & Zigmond, 2005; Murawski, 2010; Weiss & Lloyd, 2003). The major benefit of co-teaching is *not* in having two adults in the inclusive classroom. (You can manage that by getting an adult volunteer or a paraprofessional.) The rationale for co-teaching is the shared expertise that two professionals with different areas of strength bring to the instruction. "Without time for sharing this expertise, teachers often teach a class the way they have always taught it and there is not 'value added' by the second professional educator" (Murawski, 2012, p. 8).

Commitment to co-teaching is paramount. Teachers who are not truly committed to the concept of co-teaching will certainly use a lack of planning time as their excuse for keeping the status quo. Moorehead (2010) found that in the teams of teachers she observed, those committed to the concept of co-teaching created time to plan by meeting between classes and utilizing various technology resources during their personal time (text messages, e-mails, phone calls, and lesson plans shared on a school database). These teachers' commitment to co-planning was clear; in observations that occurred over the course of the semester, these teachers maintained a consistent positive classroom atmosphere, shared goal-setting responsibilities for behavioral and academic needs, and had role clarity. The teachers on these teams were comfortable with the content delivery and shared instructional time during the co-taught class. On the opposite end of the spectrum, Magiera et al. (2005) reported that many of the co-teachers they observed who lacked planning time taught "on the fly." Their results were teachers who used one teach-one support primarily, who lacked true parity, and who rarely engaged in instruction that demonstrated what was special about special education (i.e., few differentiation strategies).

In our work with teachers across the country, the most common lament we hear is that co-teaching teams don't have sufficient time to plan. There are many reasons we find this issue facing co-taught teams. Too many general educators are scheduled to collaborate or co-teach with the special education teacher, and she is therefore unable to plan with everyone adequately. Teachers are asked to serve as substitutes for absent colleagues, which means they are now unavailable during their planning time. Planning time is provided but is not seen as vital, so there are frequent interruptions as other adults pop in to ask questions of either teacher. Planning time is used for professional development activities rather than for co-planning. Again, because planning time is not seen as critical, teachers keep getting called into various meetings during the co-planning time. Obviously, this list could go on and on and on. These are just a few of the common problems related to ensuring sufficient, quality time for co-teachers to co-plan; but we also know that you, as the instructional leader, need to actively work against these issues.

As you work towards providing common planning time, you may question how much time is needed. In Lisa's research observing teams, she found that veteran co-teaching partners (in their second to fifth years of co-teaching) could plan an effective co-taught lesson in about 10 minutes (Dieker, 2001). It is important again to emphasize that these were not novice teams, but rather partners who had been together for at least one year already. Using that data, it follows that veteran co-teaching teams will need to meet for at least 50 minutes for planning once a week. This amount of time is assuming that they are teaching a similar class to what they taught the year before. If, however, they now have a higher ratio of students with disabilities in their class, they have a new class curriculum or content area to teach, or there have been other substantive changes, they may require more time. Likewise, new teachers will definitely need more than 10 minutes to plan for each class. Too often, new teams are thrown together the day before classes start (or sometimes even after) with no time to work out issues such as grading, attendance, homework, behavior, parent contacts, content, and accommodations for assessment. Without the opportunity to talk out these basic issues, planning will require far more time. In addition, novice teachers need additional time to work out their personalities, preferences, and pet peeves; using the SHARE worksheet provided on pages 30–31 is just one way to start that conversation. These teachers will likely need to meet a few times a week in order to plan their upcoming lessons.

So what is your role with planning? As a school leader, your first job is to provide teachers with time to plan or to work with those who do scheduling to ensure they too understand the strong need for planning time. Second, you need to provide your co-teachers with tools to support their planning. Third, we encourage you to observe their planning process and give them suggestions to use their time most efficiently. Fourth and finally, be aware that there will always be times when co-planning can go wrong. You'll need to listen to your teachers' concerns regarding planning and, if necessary, take action. In this chapter we take each of these four roles and address them so that these seemingly monumental tasks are more concrete and manageable.

Creating Time for Co-Planning

In keeping with our dance metaphor, we want to reiterate the importance of choreography (which for us is scheduling) and practice (for us, planning). Although the best dancers may be able to get out on the floor and get their grove on without much practice when they are dancing solo, a pair of dancers needs to practice their routine together if they want it to be award-winning. When we are talking about students and their instruction, we do indeed want award-winning performances in the classroom. We need leaders to not only understand the rationale for planning time, but also to have the skills to work with the schedule so that time has been created for teachers to collaborate.

There is no one set way to schedule planning for co-teaching teams. Situations, schools, and cultures vary too greatly. Throughout the book, we have provided a variety of options for co-teaching partners to proactively plan for their shared instruction. We caution you not to think that there is only one best way; you may actually find that you will need to use a few of these strategies or perhaps an amalgamation based on the needs of your particular teams. Just as teachers need to differentiate for their students' diverse needs, you too may need to provide options and choice to your teachers.

Before jumping into any of the options provided, don't forget how important scheduling is to the planning issue. Identify who is in charge of scheduling. If it is you, this is easy. If not, however, you may need to work with that person or those people in order to help them understand the rationale and tips for scheduling, especially as it relates to planning time. Emphasize that co-planning needs to take precedence in the schedule. Without a strong advocate who understands that planning results in higher quality lessons and outcomes for students, planning time is often the first thing to go. Work to actively ensure that teachers are provided with planning time in the schedule. Many of our suggestions require the support of leaders who understand both scheduling and co-teaching. In determining how much time to give teachers to co-plan, we always recommend that, whenever possible, as much time as possible is given to any newer teams. As teams gel and become veteran co-teachers, they should be able to require less planning time to accomplish the same tasks and outcomes.

Refer back to Chapters 3 and 4 on scheduling. Remember that students with disabilities need to have their schedules created prior to typical students' schedules. We have often found that in schools in which students' schedules are created after the teachers' master schedule, the special education teachers end up having to support students during what was supposed to be their planning time. We want to avoid chicken-with-its-head-cut-off-syndrome (CWIHCOS); strive to be proactive, not reactive. Strong leaders also make sure that co-planning isn't scheduled during times or days that are notorious for multiple interruptions (e.g., IEP meetings, specialist meetings, inservices, etc.). We have found strong leaders communicate a respect for shared planning time by discouraging phone calls during that time and by not scheduling last minute meetings during those times. Finding ways to build time into a schedule for co-planning is difficult, but not impossible. Many of the successful inclusive schools we have worked with have been quite creative and developed a variety of options. We have provided a multitude of those options here for your consideration.

Strategies for Building In Time for Co-Planning

- *Schedule regular time for planning.*

    o Create common planning periods in the schedule for those who are co-teaching. This structure is hands-down the best option for supporting co-teaching.

    o Arrange for teachers to conduct grade or team level planning one day a week, co-teacher planning two days a week, and independent planning two days a week. This way, teachers know they will have time to plan for their own activities, as well as those that they do as a team or pair.

    o As we discussed in the previous chapter on scheduling, ensure that your special education teachers have two periods (or chunks of time) allocated without direct student instruction. This schedule would enable the special education teacher to have one period for planning (alone, with various teachers, and with teams), as well as one period for modifying work, holding IEP meetings, conducting assessments, visiting classes, and contacting parents. This dual time to plan is especially critical for those special educators with multiple co-teaching partners.

    o When time is at a premium and weekly planning is not possible (at least at first), schedule teacher work days where they are actually able to work and plan (as opposed to being required to attend professional development seminars). Share your expectation with co-teaching teams that they will use that one full day each grading period to co-plan what they will be doing in the upcoming quarter.

- *Use substitute teachers wisely.*

  ○ If a substitute is hired for a teacher who is absent, rather than have the substitute relax during the teacher's typical planning period, have the substitute go in and relieve co-teachers so that they have an additional hour to plan.

  ○ Hire a substitute teacher once a month to substitute for different co-teaching pairs. For example, the substitute can relieve Ms. Specter and Mr. North for the first hour, then Mr. Johns and Mrs. Bell the second hour, and so on. This model provides teachers an extra hour of planning once a month.

  ○ Engage a substitute teacher for your co-teachers for a full day once a grading period. This full day once in a while will ensure your teachers can stay caught up with their planning.

  ○ We know budgets are tight, but we have seen a lot of success with schools that hire a regular substitute teacher to come daily. This "floating sub" is available for any teacher who is absent, but if no one is absent, that person can also be used to lead stations, run hands-on activities, and otherwise take over for co-teachers who need a few extra minutes to plan.

- *Use specialists strategically.*

  ○ Have a regular time for specialists to work in the co-taught classroom. For example, a reading specialist can be invited to work in a social studies class on reading strategies related to the content for 30 minutes once a week. The co-teachers can use this time to plan.

  ○ In the elementary school, when students go to specialists (e.g., art, physical education, music), co-teachers can work together once or twice a week to co-plan. Be sure that the specialists are on board with this strategy. We don't want 60 students left alone with one art teacher.

  ○ Coordinate services so that students are well supported. For example, help create a schedule so that teachers can arrange to have the librarian and technology specialist co-teach a lesson in the library on doing book research online. While those two work with the whole class, the regular co-teachers can plan upcoming instruction.

  ○ Administrators are also specialists. Offer to cover co-teachers' classes once a month. This coverage can occur with different teams so that eight or nine teams in the school benefit from your largesse during the year. Not only does this demonstrate to teachers that you truly support the philosophy of co-teaching, but it also helps build credibility with the teachers and the students regarding your own teaching abilities. You are showing them you are still willing to get your hands dirty (in many cases, quite literally).

- *Provide incentives.*

  o Take away additional duties from those who are co-teaching. Let them know you realize co-planning takes extra time so you are considering that additional planning time as their duty in lieu of hall duty, recess duty, bus duty, coaching, dance supervision, or lunch duty.

  o Recognize that some teachers are reluctant to be out of the classroom and will not appreciate the use of a substitute teacher or specialist. For these individuals, provide them stipends for meeting before school, after school, or on weekends.

  o Consider paying teachers to submit co-taught plans as proof of their additional work time. One school we work with asks for a summary of the "big ideas" for each 9 weeks as well as 2 weeks of lesson plans; for this documented work, teachers are paid for 2 additional hours each 9 weeks.

  o Let those teachers who engage in co-teaching know that because of their additional workload, they will have first choice on special items and activities, such as professional development opportunities, new technology, student teachers, and guest speakers. Teachers who refuse to work with students with disabilities are not provided with these kinds of incentives for additional work, thereby not rewarding their negative behavior.

- *Provide professional development.*

  o Some teachers do not have much rapport or experience with co-teaching; thus, creating lessons together can be onerous and ineffective. Sending them together to professional development will enable them to build those skills and improve their own common language. This will serve to reduce the time involved in co-planning.

  o Some teachers do not have the skills to co-plan efficiently. They know about co-teaching, but they waste time in planning. Have a facilitator help them create effective, universally designed, differentiated co-taught lessons as they work with their own content. The result is a day of learning in which they walk away with the creation of multiple lessons they can actually use. You may also want them to read Wendy's article in TEACHING Exceptional Children (2012) entitled "10 Tips for Using Co-Planning Time More Efficiently."

- ○ Many districts require continuing education or professional development (PD) hours; counting the extra time teachers spend co-planning as time counted toward PD credit for your district will be well-received. We believe that in-depth planning with someone who has different expertise is a true example of PD.

- • *Develop critical partnerships.*

   - ○ Many universities are studying co-teaching and inclusive practices. Contact your local university (the College of Education's Department of Special Education is a good place to start) and see what opportunities they have. Some will have research grants in place and may be able to provide professional development or planning stipends in return for being able to collect research data.

   - ○ Let your state department of education know you are looking to provide co-planning time to your teachers. Ask for minigrants and other supports to do so. Get online to check out the multitude of small grants available for education.

   - ○ See if your school district has a grant writer. Become best friends with that person! Let him or her know you are looking for grants that will support additional collaborative planning time for teachers. Currently, the national focus in education has a great deal of funding in STEM (science, technology, engineering, and mathematics) areas. Consider how you might provide some targeted co-teaching training in these areas.

- • *Organize time differently.*

   - ○ Look into banked time or early release time. Banking time is a way some districts add minutes to the day four times a week in order to have students leave earlier one day a week. By doing so, teachers can have 1.5 to 2 hours once a week for collaborative planning. This is helpful for department meetings, grade level meetings, and co-teacher meetings. However, be careful that you are not scheduling a meeting during each release time. Teachers need to use at least one of those days a month for collaborative planning time.

○ Teacher contracts require teachers to spend time planning. Build in mandated collaborative planning by having teachers come to school 45 minutes early to meet as grade level teams and stay after school for 15 minutes to debrief on what occurred during the day. In Chapter 4, we share the research on a school that used this model successfully in a fully inclusive environment (Fabrocini, 2012). When teachers see how beneficial this is for them and, more importantly, the students, they tend to be less resistant to the time requirement.

○ Move to block scheduling. In block scheduling, students have fewer classes in a day and can go deeper into the content. This model can allow co-teachers more opportunities to build in student-led activities, during which they can be co-planning briefly.

○ Rearrange your schedule altogether. Remember that administrator in Alabama who was tired of all the sacred cows in the schedule? She created a brand new schedule, going from a typical six-period schedule to a new eight-period schedule. Her new schedule might not have kept all the sacred cows, but it did provide each teacher with both an individual planning period and a team planning period.

• *Identify baby steps for planning.*

○ Although the best scenarios involve providing co-teachers with regular daily or weekly co-planning time, that is not always feasible as you begin to move toward a new model. These suggestions are not our favorite ones, but we recognize that they enable teachers to take baby steps toward finding time to plan.

○ Have special education teachers only co-teach four days of the week. Leave one day of the week for the special educator to plan with different teachers. In this scenario, Mrs. Smith might co-teach with Miss White during second period and with Mr. Brown during fifth period Monday through Thursday. However, on Fridays she does not co-teach. That way, during second period she can co-plan with Mr. Brown, and during fifth period she can plan with Miss White. She can also use the other periods for assessments, modifications, parent phone calls, and IEP meetings.

○ A different scenario also calls for co-teaching just four days a week, but this scenario has a different organization. In this case Mrs. Jones has what is called a floating planning period. The box, "In Action 5-1" describes this option. Notice how, though Mrs. Jones co-teaches with three different teachers, the only way she is able to co-plan with them during their planning period is to come out of one of her co-taught classes once a week.

In Action 5-1

Mrs. Jones looks at her schedule. She thinks, "Let's see. It's Wednesday, third period. Time to plan with Miss Smith!" Off she goes, ready to spend a productive period planning.

Period	Monday	Tuesday	Wednesday	Thursday	Friday
1	***Planning w/ Brown***	Co-teach w/ White	Co-teach w/ White	Co-teach w/ White	Co-teach w/ White
2	Teach SPED English	Teach SPED English	Teach SPED English	Teach SPED English	Teach SPED English
3	Co-teach w/ Brown	Co-teach w/ Brown	***Planning w/ Smith***	Co-teach w/ Brown	Co-teach w/ Brown
4	Individual Planning	Individual Planning	Individual Planning	Individual Planning	Individual Planning
5	Teach SPED Math	Teach SPED Math	Teach SPED Math	Teach SPED Math	Teach SPED Math
6	Co-teach w/ Smith	Co-teach w/ Smith	Co-teach w/ Smith	Co-teach w/ Smith	***Planning w/ White***

Note. SPED = special education

○ Consider suggesting to teachers who have limited time to plan that they pick at least one day a week where they know they will have a student-led activity for about 20 minutes. While staying in the classroom and keeping an eye on the students, co-teachers are still able to use those 20 minutes to allow them some time to review the big picture of upcoming curriculum and assignments.

○ Many schools are using double blocks to give students more time with particular subjects. For example, students who are likely to struggle with the common core standards in language arts are given two classes of language arts in a block format. Remember, though, that there is a tradeoff for the student; freeing up this block is often accomplished by removing an elective from the student's schedule. If scheduling simply won't allow for both teachers to co-teach the entire double-block together, the special educator might be in there for the first half of the block before going to another class. Our caution with the special educator leaving at any point in the class is that the students will often see the special educator as a visitor or glorified aide because he or she is not in there the entire class session. Also, although many teachers are more apt to have the second teacher come in during the second block in order to help with activities and application of new content, teachers may want to consider how having the special educator there in the first half of the block instead may actually help to ensure that the original delivery of instruction is done in such a way that it is accessible to all students. Then, a paraprofessional might come in for the second half to help facilitate activities, and the special educator can move to another class.

Tools to Support Co-Planning

Co-planning is hard. The more tools you can provide to your teachers, the more likely they will be to select a method that best suits their personalities, planning preferences, and time options. Here are a variety of resources to offer to your teachers. Many of these have a technological component, so if you are technophobic, get over it and quickly embrace an array of ideas that might just work for your newer generation of teachers. Many teachers have difficulty finding time in the school day to communicate and co-plan. Having an alternative for communicating face-to-face is helpful. Skype provides that option using the computers that you already have. Encourage co-teachers to use Skype to co-plan off-campus if needed, but make sure you provide time for them to learn Skype (e.g., at a faculty meeting).

Social networking sites are important to students, but they can be helpful resources to teachers too when they are secure and used appropriately. Have an inservice to teach the faculty at your school about Edmodo.com. There is actually a co-teaching feature that will allow teachers to link their profiles, students, and classes together to enable a variety of collaborative activities. Teachers can plan to divide the content and materials and take turns uploading information, thereby saving time in planning.

Provide professional development on how to use Google Docs for ongoing planning. Many of the teachers we work with nationally have found this to be an invaluable resource for co-planning, but quite a few mentioned how they were

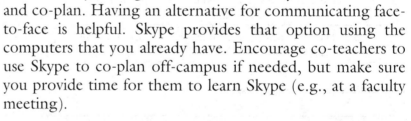

Plugged In

There are free resources online that can help teachers save time in co-planning. Familiarize yourself with these resources and then share them with your teachers.
www.Skype.com
www.drive.google.com (formerly docs.google.com)
www.Edmodo.com and
www.Dropbox.com

reticent to use it until they had training. Once they did, they realized it was easy to use and very helpful and time-saving. Dropbox is another great tool for teachers to share their larger files with one another (http://www.dropbox.com).

Let your faculty know that those teachers who are co-teaching are engaged in practice that takes more time. To support their work and assist them in planning, you could provide each co-teacher with an iPad. Not only would this be of great instructional assistance in the inclusive classroom, but it would also be a way for teachers to use FaceTime, instant messaging, e-mail, and Dropbox to co-plan.

Buy those teachers who are co-teaching an actual lesson plan book that will aid them in their co-planning. Lisa's *Co-Teaching Lesson Plan Book* is a great resource that provides structure for those who want to write their plans. It has questions to guide teachers as they progress from novice to veteran co-teachers. The structure enables general education teachers to take the lead weekly in determining content, pacing, and assessments, while special service providers help determine which co-teaching approaches may be most appropriate and what adaptations may need to be made behaviorally or academically.

For those who love gadgets, gizmos, bells, and whistles, consider purchasing the Co-Teaching Solutions System (CTSS) Teacher's Toolbox, a software program specifically designed to help with co-planning between co-teachers. Wendy helped design the Toolbox with folks at CTSS. The system not only incorporates common core and state-specific standards-based lesson planning tools, but it also provides strategies for differentiation, addressing different learning styles, incorporating response to intervention, and assessment. It can be found at www.coteachsolutions.com or www.2TeachLLC.com.

Plugged In

Encourage your teachers to use the Internet to garner support for buying planning time. This could include going online to university web sites, checking out grants for teachers (such as at http://teacherscount.org or http://www.educationfund.org), or even signing up for tools such as a lesson planner or software to help with planning through www.donorschoose.org

Material purchases don't have to be expensive or fancy. For example, we suggest that you buy your co-teaching teams some type of timer that they can use to share in their instruction and planning. If teachers only have 50 minutes to plan for a week's worth of instruction, they can spend exactly 10 minutes on Monday's overview; when the timer goes off, they need to move to Tuesday. We have found that if teachers do not use a timer, they get caught up in student-specific issues. Both of us (Dieker, 2001; Dieker & Hines, 2012; Murawski, 2012) emphasize repeatedly that if teams start talking about specific students before they plan effective instruction for all learners, time will be gone before the teams accomplish any quality planning. In the next section, we will introduce you to a planning structure that can help teachers use their planning time more efficiently. A timer, however, is a great start.

Helping Teachers Use Co-Planning Time Efficiently

Once you have given teachers time to plan, expect them to use it. Regularly ensure that teachers are having joint planning sessions or request co-taught plans from teams. Emphasize to teachers that this is not a matter of trust; you know that if they are not planning together, they are busy doing other important tasks. However, without your guidance and leadership, those other important tasks will usurp the co-planning time altogether. You are the dance coach, the lead choreographer, or the owner of the ballet; whatever your title, the desired result is the same. You want results. We know that if teams don't plan and practice together, they will never perform to the level that we want and that they are capable of. Remind them that finding them time to plan was the first step and giving them the tools to plan was the second, but this third step is theirs. They need to be doing the actual planning. Unfortunately, we have worked with many schools whose administrators have told us that although they worked hard to create common planning time in the schedule, their teachers weren't using the time effectively. Naturally, the end result was that those administrators saw the common planning time as unnecessary and had it removed. We caution teachers that although there are many distractions that may work to interrupt their planning time, they need to use the time they are given and ensure that their administrators are informed of the impact that planning is having on them as partners and, most importantly, on their students.

Once teachers do sit down to plan together, they may find their interactions stymied by a lack of co-planning skills. We have three suggestions for improving teachers' skills in co-planning. First, we recommend that co-teachers try to observe the co-planning session of another co-teaching team and debrief on what they observed. If the team is a highly successful and effective team, your co-teachers should

---

For Your Bookshelf

Help teachers put their plans on paper to aid with reflection, communication, differentiation & continuity. Get the best-selling *Co-Teaching Lesson Plan Book* by Lisa Dieker by going to www.cec.sped.org/CEC_Store.

---

learn strategies for improving their own planning prowess. On the other hand, if the other team is ineffective and wastes time during planning, that too may be helpful in assisting co-teachers to see what not to do when planning. Strong school leaders may encourage teachers to watch each other teach, but rarely do any encourage teachers to observe one another during planning. This is an option that has been underutilized.

A second option relates to getting professional development on how to co-plan. Teams may be struggling with particular areas that can be identified and strategically addressed. For example, if a team is having a hard time coming up with strategies to engage all learners and provide choice, they may need to attend a conference on Universal Design for Learning (UDL). If a team is disagreeing and having conflict when planning, they may need to attend seminars in communication and problem-solving skills. Some teams may need an overview of the various co-teaching approaches, strategies for finding time for co-planning, and a structure for using co-planning time. All of these topics can be made available to your teams through professional development.

A third option is to provide co-teachers with a structure, format, and steps to guide them in their co-planning. A lesson plan format is provided for you to share with teachers in Appendix 2. Next to that in Appendix 3 you will see a structure overlaid on top of the lesson plan format. This structure is based on an article Wendy published recently which explained the "What/How/Who" approach to co-planning (Murawski, 2012). This What/How/Who approach structures co-planning time for teachers so they can maximize the small amount of time they may have. It is easy for teachers, indeed for us all, to fall into small talk, venting sessions, or personal conversations when we get together with colleagues. Planning time, however, needs to be sacrosanct. We need to help teachers use it wisely. The box, "IN ACTION 5-2" demonstrates the What/How/Who approach used effectively.

For Your Bookshelf

Want consistent professional development (PD) year after year to address teacher turn-over and increase capacity? Buy a training module on topics of interest.

www.2TeachLLC.com offers a PD module with PowerPoint, facilitator's guide, and handouts included called "Co-Planning for Success" (among other titles).
www.csun.edu/ctl offers PD modules on "Creating a Collaborative Culture" and "Towards Truly Collaborative IEP Meetings."

In Action 5-2

Kiernan walked into Oliver's classroom, carrying a box. "Ready for our 20-minute Monday lunch planning meeting?" he asked with a smile. "Only if you brought the pizza," replied Oliver, smiling back. Kiernan handed over the pizza as he asked, "So, what's on the agenda for next week?" As Oliver pulled off a large slice of gooey pepperoni pizza, he replied, "We really need to focus on the concept of checks and balances in government. We need to teach the three branches of government, who is in each branch, what their roles are, how they overlap, and how they differ. I thought that we could teach it by — " "Whoa, man," Kiernan interrupted. "Remember our co-planning structure? Let's make sure we're both good with what we are teaching before we go into how we will teach it." "Oh yeah. Sorry. I jumped the gun," said Oliver sheepishly. "No worries," stated Kiernan, "I'm good with the three branches of government, but I think that talking about checks and balances will be really overwhelming for some of the students in here, so would it be fair to say that the big idea in this lesson is that no one person or group has all the power? And then piggy-backing on that, could our Essential Question for all students to answer be: Why is it important that there are different branches of our government?" "Works for me," said Oliver, "It's simple, but I know we need to break it down to concepts that all students can know before we move on to what most students will know and then what some students will know."

"Great. Now that we're clear on what we are teaching, we can move into the how. So, what was your great idea on how we can teach this lesson?" Kiernan asked. "Well, I love the station teaching approach you taught me a few weeks ago, and I thought this would be a great time to use that again. We could have each branch of government be represented in a station. What do you think?"

Oliver asked. Kiernan replied, "Sounds perfect. Why don't we start the lesson by hooking them with a role-play? We could act as if one of us wants all the power and the other won't let that happen. After our team teaching role play, we could do the stations for most of the class session, and then end by doing alternative teaching with you wrapping up with the large group and giving homework while I work with a small group of any students who appeared lost or confused during the stations. Good?" "Perfect. We can use that same structure for Tuesday and Wednesday's lessons as we reinforce the same concepts. So, who do you think might struggle with this?" Oliver asked.

> ### In Action 5-2 (cont'd)
>
> Kiernan gave his co-teaching friend some positive reinforcement for his obvious use of the planning structure. "Nice segue to the who part of our lesson, buddy. Let's see. Who will need additional consideration? Before we even start the class, I think one of us will need to tell Xavier that we'll be doing stations that day, as that might upset him a bit if he's not expecting that movement. I don't believe we'll have any additional considerations during the role plays, do you?" "Nope," said Oliver, "We should be good there. For stations though, in addition to Xavier, I was thinking that Brandon may struggle working in a small group and Jana might not complete the tasks in time. Do you have ideas for that?" "Sure," replied Kiernan, "How about we make sure Holden is in Brandon's group? They work well together. And for Jana, let's use a timer to help her stay on target and maybe give her fewer questions to answer if needed. Let's also both keep an eye out during stations to see who is struggling so I can pull them to the side of the room to do some review at the end of the lesson as you are going over homework." The bell rang as Oliver wiped pizza off his mouth. "Wow. Yet another productive, pizza-eatin' Monday. I think we're set. How about I prep the judicial and legislative stations and you prep the executive one?" "Cool. Will do. I'll throw it in Dropbox when I'm done," said Kiernan as he headed out of the room.

Notice that Oliver and Kiernan start by talking about what they need to teach. On a lesson plan, this discussion would encompass the common core standards, objectives, big idea, or Essential Question. Too many teachers start planning by coming up with cute activities without first ensuring they are both on the same page in terms of what needs to be accomplished and what would be reasonable expectations for all students. After knowing what needs to be taught, teachers should use the principles of UDL to begin to conceptualize how they will teach that lesson. UDL principles encourage teachers to proactively plan for the whole class by remembering that there will be different learners with different needs, preferences, and interests. UDL emphasizes the use of choice in instruction, especially as it relates to providing multiple means of representation, engagement, and expression (www.cast.org/udl). Last, once co-teachers have a general plan for how they will co-instruct the lesson and what co-teaching approaches they will use during that instruction, they need to consider who might need additional support. Different students may require various accommodations, modifications, or challenges to be built into the lesson plan. Notice how this approach to structuring planning enables teachers to consider the curriculum and common core standards as well as quality instruction for all students before there is any focus on individual students with special needs. The "who" time can also be used to discuss who will do what in terms of bringing in materials, preparing activities, creating adaptions, and so on.

In terms of the time spent planning, this particular approach may take teachers more than 10 minutes to plan, but remember that Lisa's research was with veteran co-teachers — yet another reason for keeping teams together. Rather than re-creating lessons from scratch every year, co-teachers who have history as a team can build off the lessons they designed the year previous. From the 20 minutes it might take using the What/How/Who approach for newer co-teaching teams, veteran teams can easily move to the 10 minutes found in Lisa's research.

When Co-Planning Goes Wrong

Despite the best of intentions and the maximum amount of planning time provided, there will naturally be instances when co-teachers are simply not functioning well as a team. We've identified some of the more common issues we see and paired them with a few strategies you may try in order to help that team move forward.

Issue: Lack of Time Management

In this situation, one of the partners always has an excuse regarding why she can't make the previously agreed-upon planning meeting, or she has to leave early on a regular basis. An absent co-teacher or one who departs early from planning can be extremely frustrating for the partner who is there on time and ready to work.

- Have a regularly scheduled time for planning and make it clear that teachers are expected to be there promptly and stay the entire time. If this time is during the regularly scheduled school day, or if a stipend is attached to the planning, as a leader it is a reasonable expectation to mandate and monitor this time.

- Encourage the partner who is on time to share her concerns with her frequently tardy partner. Remind her to use "I-language" in her communication (e.g., "When I am waiting for you to show up, I feel that my time is wasted and not respected.").

- Provide multiple options for these teachers to meet and plan at a different time of day, perhaps through the use of technology. See if they can be more consistent in their meeting if they are able to Skype some meetings and perhaps reduce their meeting time through the use of Google Docs and Dropbox.

Issue: Lack of Preparation

In this situation, one partner forgets to bring materials, curriculum, examples, student work, and other materials to co-planning meetings, despite agreeing to do so. There appears to be no follow-through on previous planning sessions, which means time is wasted doing work that was supposed to be done outside of the planning session.

- Encourage partners to create a checklist of materials that are supposed to be brought to each planning session. The more organized partner can be asked to e-mail a reminder to the partner who struggles with organization.

- Teach partners about applications they can put on their cell phones to remind them of important tasks. For example, Awesome Note is an application that can be used to organize reminders and set alarms. On a Mac computer, teachers can use the Sticky Notes application to write themselves reminder notes. Of course you can also go back to the old standby of a low-tech whiteboard for making to-do lists.

- Again, remind partners of the need to communicate throughout this process. If one partner is frustrated with the other's lack of follow-through, she needs to communicate that frustration.

- Encourage partners to discuss their own strengths and areas of weakness. If one teacher is a procrastinator or highly disorganized or forgetful, teachers should strategize how they can use one another's strengths to minimize those areas of need. Encourage them to do a strengths assessment to identify and then share their own personal strengths (www.strengthsfinder.com or www.viacharacter.org).

Issue: Lack of Listening or Parity

This issue manifests in a variety of ways. Sometimes we have teachers who are merely distracted during planning, thinking about their own classes and not paying attention while their partner is speaking. In other cases, we have teachers who try to multitask during the planning meeting, which results in a partner who feels that the session isn't as productive as it could be if they were focused solely on the co-taught class. A third manifestation is when one partner doesn't listen because he simply wants his own way and feels the class is his anyway.

- We know this is redundant, but trust us, it's important. Help teachers with communication! If they are unable to talk to one other about their frustrations, they will be running to you constantly to referee. Encourage them to share their feelings and their need to keep the common planning time focused on their particular class.

- Assist teachers in finding a planning space that is not in either classroom, nor in a heavily trafficked area. This suggestion will help reduce distractions and will also help teachers avoid multitasking.

- Clear some time in an upcoming faculty meeting for co-teaching teams to share one of their favorite lessons. Remind the teams in advance when you ask them to present that you would prefer they be explicit in sharing with their colleagues how each of them had an active role in the planning and how they met the Essential Question of co-teaching in the lesson they shared. This public sharing is a subtle way to emphasize the need for parity.

- Set a time after a grading period to review student grades with teachers. During that time, ask how they are planning together for success and be sure to validate that both teachers are responsible for all students and must therefore be co-planning, listening to one another, and adding in ideas. If a student fails, they are both equally responsible; likewise, if students are successful, they both deserve the accolades.

Issue: Lack of Initiative

This situation happens often when one teacher is more motivated or hard-working than another. In this case, one partner just sits back and lets the other do it all. Although this may be acceptable to both partners at times, it should not be acceptable to you as the administrator. Both teachers need to be bringing 100% to their planning if you want to be able to address that Essential Question.

- That pesky Essential Question again. Use it to your advantage. Every once in a while, put a piece of paper in co-teachers' boxes with the Essential Question written on it. Have teachers respond to how they are able to answer that question and then debrief with them on their responses.

- Observe a co-planning lesson and frequently ask the submissive teacher what his opinion is and what he would care to add. If he continues to step back, remind him of the need for both teachers to add their expertise to the lesson.

- Facilitate planning with this team by identifying the lesson objective and then asking each partner to silently come up with ideas for teaching that lesson. Give them each 5 minutes to think of the most creative, universally designed lesson they can and then have them share their ideas. See if you can help facilitate a shared or combined lesson through their ideas.

Issue: Lack of Respect

We have heard this complaint often from special educators. In this situation, one teacher ends up changing the lesson and doesn't do what the co-teachers agreed upon during the planning meeting.

- This issue is often hand in hand with a complaint by special educators that they feel they are being treated as glorified aides. It clearly demonstrates a lack of parity and respect between teachers. One of the first things you might do is have a refresher PD on what co-teaching is and what it is not. If an entire PD session is out of the question, merely recirculate the "Dos and Don'ts of Co-Teaching" page (Murawski, 2002, p. 19) that was provided in Chapter 1.

- This issue also often arises when a general education teacher is teaching the same class or lesson during other periods without the special educator present. Thus, if he does it one way alone for Periods 1 and 2, he tends to want to keep it that way during the co-taught Periods 3 and 4 and the solo-taught Period 5. There are two strategies for this. One is to have the special educator co-teach Period 1 so the day is started in the co-taught version. Because that is often not possible, a second suggestion is to encourage the general education teacher to keep his Periods 1 and 2 a day behind the other periods. That way, he and his co-teacher can teach the lesson together during Periods 3 and 4 and he can determine how to teach the lesson solo for Periods 5, 6, 1 and 2.

- Here comes that need for communication again. Partners need to be able to politely but clearly remind one another that they are both teachers and one does not trump the other. It may be understandable that a teacher found it easier to resort to a previously experienced lesson than implementing the new co-taught one (especially when some classes are not co-taught), but it results in his partner feeling disconnected, frustrated, and irritated that time was taken to plan and create materials that were not ultimately used with students.

- Help make sure both teachers are well versed in all of the different co-instructional approaches. Because three of the five approaches involve regrouping students, there are multiple opportunities for teachers to teach in the style they prefer. Remind them as you debrief of this need to group students in multiple formats with the advantage of having two teachers. Chapter 6 provides an explanation of the various co-instructional approaches as well as suggestions regarding how to use them in the classroom. Become very familiar with these so that you can use them as examples when discussing what you have seen (or what you are not seeing) in their collaborative, co-taught class.

Chapter 6

Creating Your Own Moves

Understanding the Various Approaches to Co-Instruction

As an administrator, you may not be planning to co-teach (though that is not out of the question), but you still need to be very aware of the different approaches to co-instruction. Without knowing how teachers can maximize their instruction in the classroom, you won't be able to provide feedback and suggestions for improvement. You won't know who is a model team or what to tell those teachers who are struggling. Most important, you will lose credibility with your teachers if you say things such as, "when you were doing the activities where you broke into two groups." Teachers will say, "You mean, parallel teaching?" And you may respond, "Uh. Yeah. When you did that, I really enjoyed how it reduced the student-teacher ratio. But then when one of you had the large group, I noticed that the other teacher worked with a small group. I don't think that's allowed in co-teaching." The teachers will respond, "Actually, we were using the alternative teaching approach in order to provide enrichment to students who were high-achieving." We're sure you see where we are going with this. You need to at least speak the same language as your teachers; if your teachers don't know the language yet, now is the perfect time for you to take the lead and instruct them on these different teaching techniques.

Because a variety of co-teaching approaches are described in the literature, we developed the chart, "At-a-Glance: Co-Teaching Approaches to Instruction." Although we will go into more descriptive detail for you on five of these approaches, we still want you to be aware of the others in case your district has embraced a particular model or worked with a particular consultant on co-teaching. As we discuss these approaches, keep in mind the essential question (EQ) of co-teaching. Do the "EQ Test" as you observe your co-teachers in action. Would they pass? Could you answer the following EQ favorably?

> ### Essential Question Reminder
>
> **How is what co-teachers are doing together <u>substantively different and better for kids</u> than what one teacher would do alone?**

One Teach-One Support

One Teach-One Support means exactly what you think it does. One teacher is up front providing direct instruction to students while the other is engaged in a support role. We are often asked why this approach warrants a credentialed special educator when it appears a paraprofessional could do the same tasks. Let's delineate the difference. There are some supporting tasks that can be done by either a credentialed teacher or a paraprofessional. They include: taking roll, passing back or collecting papers, walking around and stamping homework, taking basic data on behavior or individualized education program (IEP) goals, writing a note home to a parent in a home-school notebook, or providing proximity control to a rowdy group of students. These are all typical tasks in a classroom and an appropriate use of One Teach-One Support. However, there are other support activities that require a certified or licensed teacher. These activities include such tasks as as conducting an error analysis of mistakes students are making in the class, adapting or modifying instructional materials, prepping for an upcoming content-heavy activity, talking to an individual student to pre-teach vocabulary, taking specific and more complex behavioral data related to IEP goals, coaching students to become more independent, and providing visual supports such as graphic organizers to enrich instruction. There are also activities that the teacher in the support role should not do: standing to the side and simply watching instruction, sitting at a desk and grading papers or catching up on IEP paperwork, leaving the room for errands, constantly running out of the room to deal with a behavior issue as the school's de facto crisis manager, checking e-mail, updating a Facebook status, or hovering near a student with no particular task or purpose. Although observing students can be an appropriate use of a support teacher's time, note that it must be purposeful observation, not just observation done because it appears there is nothing else to do. We all know that there is not enough time in any educator's day to just stand around; that holds true for co-teachers as well.

At-A-Glance: Co-Teaching Approaches to Instruction			
Co-Teaching Approach (Cook & Friend, 1995)	Class Setup	Names for similar approaches	Quick Definition
One Teach-One Support (OT-OS)	Whole Class	Lead and Support (Hughes & Murawski, 2001); Supportive Teaching or Complementary Instruction (Villa, Thousand, & Nevin, 2008); One Teach, One Observe (Friend & Cook, 2007)	One teacher is in front of the class leading instruction. The other is providing substantive support (e.g., collection or dissemination of papers, setting up labs, classroom management). Both are actively engaged.
Team Teaching	Whole Class	Team Teaching (Villa, Thousand, Nevin, 2008)	Both teachers are in front of the class, working together to provide instruction. This may take the form of debates, modeling information or note-taking, compare/contrast, or role-playing.
Parallel Teaching	Regrouping	Simultaneous Instruction (Hughes & Murawski, 2001); Parallel Teaching (Villa, Thousand & Nevin, 2008)	Both teachers take half of the class in order to reduce student–teacher ratio. Instruction can occur in the same or a different setting. Groups may be doing the same content in the same way, same content in a different way, or different content (Murawski, 2009).
Station Teaching	Regrouping	Rotation Teaching (Hughes & Murawski, 2001); Parallel Teaching (Villa, Thousand & Nevin, 2008)	Students are divided into three or more small, heterogeneous groups to go to stations or centers. Students rotate through multiple centers, though teachers may rotate also. Teachers can facilitate individual stations or circulate among all stations.
Alternative Teaching	Regrouping	Tiered Instruction (Hughes & Murawski, 2001); Parallel Teaching (Villa, Thousand & Nevin, 2008)	One teacher works with a large group of students, while the other works with a smaller group providing re-teaching, pre-teaching, or enrichment as needed. The large group is not receiving new instruction during this time so that the small group can rejoin when finished.

Adapted from: Murawski, W.W., & Spencer, S.A. (2011). *Collaborate, Communicate, and Differentiate! How to Increase Student Learning in Today's Diverse Classrooms.* Thousand Oaks, CA: Corwin.

You now know how One Teach-One Support should and should not look. That's just the first step. You also need to be aware of a few cautions regarding this approach. A major caution with this particular approach to co-instruction is that it is grossly over-used. Weiss and Lloyd (2002) conducted research that indicated that teachers who said they were co-teaching also reported that they used the One Teach-One Support approach 80% to 90% of the time! Given that this approach is the most comfortable and is typical of what happens in many classes (i.e., all students in a whole-group format listening to one teacher at the front of the room), this approach will rarely pass our EQ test. That's not to say we that One Teach-One Support should never be used. It can be a valid approach, but only when used appropriately.

Let us give you two specific examples of where you may see a strong reliance on One Teach-One Support that would still be an appropriate use of the approach. In the first scenario, you may observe a class with students who have more severe needs and who require more direct interaction from the special educator. Teachers of students with severe and profound disabilities may need to work more directly with those students when in the general education setting, but their support enables the student to have access to the general education class and content (Downing, 2008). Due to the student's physical, behavioral, or cognitive needs, the special educator may be limited in his or her ability to lead large group instruction as frequently. We still encourage the use of more small groupings (alternative and stations) when possible, but we recognize that the role of the special educator may vary, depending on a student's unique needs.

The second scenario that may result in a more frequent use of One Teach-One Support is due to teacher need, rather than student need. We often see this model used when there is a large gap in the special education teacher's content knowledge (e.g., in a high school physics class; Dieker & Berg, 2002). Although we respect the additional challenge high level secondary content can present, and we acknowledge the need for a level of comfort prior to taking on a leadership role in a classroom, we want to emphasize the need to promote teachers' strengths. As the school leader, you can let teachers know that so long as both teachers are bringing something to the table (e.g., the special education teacher can be supporting students with severe behavioral challenges if the physics teacher does not possess those skills), you will see value in this relationship. What is not acceptable is for those teachers to remain at the support level for the entire year, neglecting the other approaches altogether. Over time, we would expect co-teachers to become more comfortable with one another and the content, and for this relationship to evolve to one in which more approaches are used with regularity.

Some literature identifies One Teach-One Support as a "Level One" or "complementary" method of co-teaching (Chapman & Hart-Hyatt, 2011; Villa, Thousand, & Nevin, 2008). We caution that by identifying different levels of co-teaching, you may send the message that it is acceptable for co-teachers to use only this one approach so long as they say they are only on level one or supporting one another through the complementary approach. Instead, it would be advisable to acknowledge to teachers that although the One Teach-One Support approach may be the most comfortable and an appropriate beginning step for some co-teachers, you do not want them using this approach to the exclusion of any others.

A question to ask in addition to the EQ is: Are your teachers stuck in One Teach-One Support or another of the instructional approaches? As the instructional leader, it is up to you to analyze the performance of your teams and see what you can do to tweak their co-teaching practices. Figure 6-1 provides some questions to ask those teams who appear stuck in one approach. Remember that if co-teachers are dancers, then their students are their audience. What audience wants to see the same performance day after day? "Mixing it up" is a simplistic but effective definition of differentiation (Tomlinson, 1999) and we strongly recommend exactly that. Effective co-teachers are able and willing to mix it up in the classroom, to the benefit of their students.

How will you know if One Teach-One Support is used effectively? If you see one teacher keeping the students' attention and engaging them in instruction or an activity while the other teacher is actively engaged in a support activity that moves the class forward in a productive way, then it is likely they are using the approach effectively. It is even more effective if you notice that teachers do not seem wed to the

---

Figure 6-1. Reflection Questions for Leaders

What approach does this team appear stuck in? What evidence do you have that they use this approach most frequently?

Do the teachers appear to enjoy one another's company? If not, what gives you the opinion that they are struggling with one another?

Was this team given adequate time before the semester started to work out issues such as behavior, assessment, and grading?

Is this team provided with adequate weekly or monthly planning time?

Are both teachers showing up to plan or is something getting in their way?

Do the teachers on this team have different knowledge bases (e.g., one knows content and the other knows learning strategies)? If so, what professional development could be provided to them individually or as a team?

Are all students making learning gains (both academic and socially) in the co-teaching approach most often used? If not, how might a different approach support those students?

---

front of the room, but rather regularly and comfortably interchange who is doing the lead and who is doing the support.

Again, One Teach-One Support can make tasks that teachers need to do on a regular basis (e.g., taking roll, paperwork management, homework checks) less onerous because there are two teachers present. One can take care of the necessary logistical activities while the other ensures increased academic engaged time for students. We don't have a problem with the use of One Teach-One Support if (and only if) it is used judiciously, efficiently, and purposefully.

Parallel Teaching

In this approach, co-teachers divide the class to achieve three purposes:

- reduce the student-teacher ratio
- enable both teachers to engage with a group of students
- provide an opportunity for more interaction, different types of teaching styles, and differentiated instruction.

There are differing explanations of parallel teaching in the literature. Cook and Friend (1995) defined "parallel teaching" as dividing the class into two equal groups and providing the same instruction to both groups. Thousand, Villa, and Nevin (2006) identify eight variations to parallel teaching that encompass all of the other four approaches first defined by Cook and Friend (1995). Hughes and Murawski (2001) used the term "simultaneous teaching" and applied the concept to working with gifted students. Last, Murawski (2009) describes parallel teaching as having three different uses: for teaching the same content in the same way, *for teaching the same content in different ways, and for teaching different content.*

We have found that teachers who are really comfortable with parallel teaching are able to break classes into two equally sized groups and do what is needed. For some, that is merely doing the same thing with smaller groups, whereas for others it involves a "divide and conquer" technique. Remember that to pass the EQ Test, co-teachers need to be conducting lessons that demonstrate the need for both teachers and emphasizes the value added of having the special service provider in the room. Look not only for smaller groupings, but also for what teachers are doing within those groups. Are they using strategies to engage students and help them retain the content? Are they increasing their interactions with students, or does it feel as though they are merely doing a short lecture with fewer students? You may see some teachers break the group in half and only work with their own half; you may see others break the group in half and then flip-flop groups after a certain amount of time. Both of these approaches are perfectly acceptable if the students are learning and both teachers' expertise is being utilized.

As with the other approaches, there are cautions. What we do not want to see is parallel teaching used as an excuse to group students with disabilities into their own permanent group to be served by the special educator. We have seen this model used inappropriately when teachers are in the same room but do not really want to change their roles or engage with one another. Also, although these smaller groups are fantastic for when teachers need to deliver difficult content, both teachers must have planning time or the two groups could easily learn the material in such different ways that there are problems in the future. For example, we observed two teachers in parallel teaching introducing the procedures for division very differently to their two groups, and not on purpose. You can only imagine the outcome when the students were bought back into a whole group format to debrief and apply their new skill; it was total confusion. As a leader, you not only need to know when parallel teaching may be used appropriately, but you also need to be able to debrief with teachers when you notice a breakdown in effectiveness.

Some of the additional difficulties teachers may have that will warrant support from you relate to space and noise. If the co-teaching team you observe is struggling with this approach, or perhaps even resistant to trying it at all, share some suggestions for parallel teaching success. The following box "At-a-Glance: Tips for Parallel Teaching Success," was written for teachers, so give them their own copy to review and discuss.

Station Teaching

If your leadership is primarily at the elementary school level, station teaching is an approach with which you are likely familiar; if you are primarily at the secondary level, it is less likely you have seen station teaching in action. Regardless of the school level, we are major fans of station teaching and would enjoy seeing it used more often in schools. This type of co-teaching is when students are put in small groups and they then rotate around stations (sometimes called centers) until they have been to each station. Stations may include direct instruction by a teacher seated at that station, guided practice facilitated by a paraprofessional or parent volunteer at the station, or independent work or cooperative learning activities. The options for stations are truly endless. Naturally, stations cannot be used if the lesson must be taught sequentially. However, much of what we do in classes can be taught in different order so teachers who are creative can use station teaching frequently. We especially support this approach as an option to review, enrich, or reinforce concepts.

At-A-Glance: Tips for Parallel Teaching Success

1. If space is available and easily accessible, allow the two groups to have their own space. It's much more manageable that way. Empty classrooms, cafeterias, large hallways, auditoriums, libraries, gymnasiums, and computer labs are a few of the venues that creative teachers have used for parallel teaching.

2. If, however, there is no alternative space to use, don't give up! When doing parallel teaching in the same room, it's imperative that you do not have students facing one another with the teachers' backs to one another. Make sure teachers are able to maintain eye contact so that students in different groups are not facing one another. We recommend the group be in a shape close to the teacher so that the sound is going toward the wall and not toward the other group when the students talk to one another.

3. Don't let seat placement or small rooms dissuade you either. Students can move the chairs and tables, sit on the floor or move outside, or even stand for different activities. Remember, the key to the differentiated class is mixing it up!

4. Discuss the importance of keeping voices low during the use of parallel teaching (for students and adults!). Develop a signal between teachers for when a group or individual is getting too loud. Don't hesitate to ask your partner to ask his group to bring their voices down. The more often you use this approach, the less frequently you'll have to remind one another or the students. You might even consider playing some low level music to demonstrate to students an acceptable sound level. Then, both groups know to keep their voices below or at that level.

5. Remember that while it may take students 2 to 3 minutes to focus on instruction, it will likely take 4 to 5 minutes for you to completely focus on your group and not be a bit distracted by your partner's voice. Just push through those first few minutes, keep your voice low and your eyes focused on your students, and soon enough you will be totally engrossed in your instruction and meeting your students' needs.

6. Don't forget that both of you should watch the time so you end simultaneously. Every teacher knows how frustrating it can be to have one group end before another. Also, if you find timekeeping too difficult a task, assign it to a student; they are happy to use those cell phones for just this activity.

The station teaching approach ensures kinesthetic movement, brain breaks, chunking of content, smaller student-teacher ratios, and an opportunity for more differentiated questions or activities. As with all of the regrouping approaches (i.e., stations, alternative, parallel), station teaching requires organization on the part of teachers, but if they plan proactively, co-teachers will find that stations can accomplish myriad tasks that they may not otherwise have considered. For example, one teacher can take the lead on planning two stations while the other teacher takes the lead on the other two. (There can be as many stations as are deemed necessary for the lesson or unit at hand. Don't forget to encourage technology. We love to see computers being used as a station that is teacher free.) By dividing and conquering, co-teachers can minimize the face time needed for planning and create stations that can be used this year and in future years. It is also helpful to note that the rotation between stations does not have to occur in one day. If teachers plan eight stations, this could be the model used Monday through Thursday, with students going to two stations per day. This approach is also very helpful in addressing issues of students failing or being lost in the larger grouping of other types. We typically encourage teachers who are comfortable in One Teach-One Support to try this approach as their next stage of growth. Because there are small groups of instruction or reinforcement, there is a comfort level for teachers that might not be present in the approaches that include larger groups (i.e., parallel and team).

There are, of course, some tips for ensuring smooth stations. As with parallel teaching, co-teachers need to teach their classes about the appropriate noise level and voices that can be used during these regrouping approaches. They need to review behaviors to include those needed for transitioning between stations. We are personally fine with students talking to one another during the transition time because we feel it allows them to get their personal talking out so they are better able to focus on the task when the station activity begins. Co-teachers need to determine how they will watch the time and let one another and the students know when it is time to transition, begin to wrap up tasks, clean up, and move again to the next station. They may use online or PowerPoint timers, bells, lights, or other signals, but regardless of their choice they need to plan these proactively because timing is critical with stations. One criticism of stations is that some students may not complete the requisite task before the bell sounds for students to move to the next station. If some students are not able to finish on time, teachers should view that as a clear signal that they need to proactively consider ways to include differentiation at each station. For example, if co-teachers are planning a math activity at a station and they know that Sven will not get through the 10 questions in the 10 minutes allocated, they should not try to figure out when they will have extra time for Sven to finish his activity. It is rare that we can truly find extra time anywhere. Instead, they may simply let Sven know in advance that he will be expected to do every other problem at that particular station. Five problems are required for him; if he finishes those, he is expected to go back and begin to complete the other problems.

Academic considerations are necessary for station teaching, but so too are behavioral considerations. Both of us have spoken with teachers who said they "tried stations" but found it was too chaotic. Just between us, we put that on the teacher, not the students! To us, that indicates there was a lack of planning for behavior. What might you do if you are observing or evaluating a lesson and you see or hear issues of chaos in the classroom? There are a few options. You might suggest that a behavior coach come in and help with the structure for stations (especially if teachers fear trying this model). You might have the team in question observe another team using station teaching to learn the tricks of the trade before they try it out. You might ask the team to share with you how they have proactively planned for behavior, and then help them create additional concrete plans. You might also suggest that, if there is a student with extreme behavior challenges, the person with the strongest behavioral background (typically the special educator, but not always) has that student in his or her group first. Then that student could move to other stations as his behavior deems him ready. If his behavior to a new station could upset the entire model, some teams have the student become a leader and help the teacher repeat the content of that station to his peers as they rotate around. Too often, teachers plan for academic adaptations but completely forget the need to address behavioral and social issues proactively. All three are areas you need to look for and support as you lead your co-teaching teams.

Alternative Teaching

Alternative teaching is, unfortunately, the most misused approach in co-instruction. Because alternative teaching calls for a large group of students and a small group of students, many co-teaching teams seem to justify the use of a class within a class (wherein a small group of students with disabilities who used to be pulled out to a special education classroom remains in the room but works at the back of the room with the special education teacher or paraprofessional) by calling it alternative teaching. However, when Cook and Friend (1995) first defined alternative teaching, they stated that it should be used for reteaching, preteaching, or enrichment. Naturally, students with disabilities are not the only group who might benefit from those three activities. Any student might, at any time! In addition, the special service provider does not need to be the instructor for the small group; the general education teacher might actually appreciate an opportunity to work with a smaller group of students in order to go deeper into a concept or to find out why a group of students is struggling with a particular skill. The general education teacher might also have more in-depth knowledge in a content area from years of teaching that grade level concept. How refreshing that this approach provides an opportunity for the general education teacher then to spend some small group time with the students who need it.

As with the other regrouping approaches (parallel and station), if co-teachers have found another space in which to conduct their additional instruction, do not be opposed to this idea. The myth still exists with some leaders that special educators cannot work with all students. Yet the Individuals With Disabilities Education Improvement Act of 2004 (IDEA 2004) supports special education teachers working with all students so long as their primary role is still serving students with disabilities. We have no problem at all with specialized instruction being provided to any student who needs it by either teacher so long as the selection or movement of students does not appear stigmatizing, based solely on labels or caseloads, or always include the same children. Flexible grouping is the key. Students just need to know that they too might be in the group that leaves occasionally to go to the library or the special service provider's room. It needs to be evident that teachers use these varying approaches on a regular basis to lower the student-teacher ratio and to allow them to work more closely with students. When that is the case, not only will the students not mind, they also will have no need to taunt the small group for being different.

Keep in mind, though, one important caveat for using this approach. If a small group is being pulled aside for reteaching or preteaching of a concept, this small group cannot be concurrently missing a brand new lesson or concept. This type of action created the problem the field of special education had with the pull out model. When students were pulled out of classes in order to get remediation, they missed new content and fell further behind. Co-teachers merely need to consider when they will use the alternative teaching approach.

So when do teachers most often use this approach? We often see it being used while one teacher is doing a warm-up activity, introducing or showing a video, facilitating independent work, starting homework, or doing a wrap-up activity. We highly recommend the use of this model for any team that has students in the class who are failing or need specialized instruction. Don't be afraid to provide small-group or one-on-one instruction. That is the whole purpose of the alternative teaching approach. Remember, this model can be used to remediate or enrich the learning of a subgroup of students. If a small group has demonstrated a solid knowledge base about a concept and needs to be taken to the side to be provided more challenging or complex curriculum, this is the way to do it (Hughes & Murawski, 2001). In fact, many schools that have moved to using a response to intervention approach find that having co-teachers in the classroom can make tiered instruction more possible. Clearly, we find significant value in using alternative teaching often as teachers work collaboratively and proactively to ensure all students are getting the differentiated and specialized instruction they deserve.

Critical Connections

Is your school using RTI (Response to Intervention)? If so, check out Murawski, W. W., & Hughes, C. E. (2009). *Response to Intervention, Collaboration, and Co-Teaching: A necessary Combination for Successful Systemic Change. Preventing School Failure, 53*(4), 67–77.

Team Teaching

The fifth and final approach we address is called team teaching. This approach is the one most people have heard of, and some believe the approach indicates the pinnacle of co-teaching success. In 2011, we facilitated a preconvention workshop for the Council for Exceptional Children (CEC) national conference on leadership for co-teaching. One of our participants shared that he had been telling his teachers that they should work through the other co-teaching approaches until they finally reached the ability to use team teaching, at which point they would be able to always function together in the front of the room. Through our workshop he realized this would be as much a disservice to students as the teachers only using One Teach-One Support. Why? Let us explain.

Team teaching is where co-teachers share the stage. They are both up in front of the students, playing off one another, conducting role-plays or debates, modeling communication or skills, or even agreeing to disagree. This model often takes the most trust and respect between teachers. It typically develops over time and rarely happens naturally from the start or occurs in teams without planning time. Because teachers are typically not used to having another adult in the room with them as they instruct students, finding a way to dance together in harmony takes practice, time, and a commitment to one's dance partner. Keep in mind that in all of the other approaches we have discussed thus far, each teacher can still have his or her own set of students or there is a clear determination of who is in charge at a particular time, even if they switched roles often. In the team teaching approach, however, both teachers are up front and parity is a clear necessity for the approach to be effective. During this approach, spotlight dancing or solo performances disappear, and as the equal dance partners emerge we are treated to an award-winning routine that engages all students.

When team teaching is done well, it is an exciting and powerful instructional tool. Seeing teachers interact and communicate with one another in front of students often energizes everyone. The friendly banter that can occur between teachers is interesting and can help keep students' attention and increase motivation. When this model is used effectively, we don't just see two teachers on stage merely talking at the students; instead the teachers have created a synergy that allows students to lead their own learning.

On the flip side, however, when two teachers are supposed to be sharing the stage and instead appear to be fighting for the lead role, it can be an uncomfortable situation. In addition, if teachers only use team teaching as their sole method of co-instruction, they miss out on the opportunity to reduce the student-teacher ratio and increase differentiation for those who need it. The banter can become distracting over time and can actually take away from instructional minutes. Instead of being novel and increasing attention, the two voices constantly speaking can become tedious and overwhelming for some students. What is the answer? Remind your teachers to mix it up! Not every lesson is appropriate for team teaching (just as they are not always appropriate for stations, parallel, etc.). By planning together, teachers can determine what makes the most sense for that lesson, that day, with that group of students. And that is what results in a truly individualized, appropriate, differentiated and universally designed lesson.

Taking Co-Instruction to a Deeper Level

Now that you are familiar with the five most commonly identified approaches to co-instruction, you will be able not only to talk about them with your teaching teams, but also to suggest various configurations for lessons. If teachers come to you complaining that they are having difficulties sharing the stage, suggest to them that they try using approaches that will allow each of them to be the master of their own domain for a while. For example, stations would enable each of them to design their own lessons, and students would still benefit by getting the variety of instruction. If you see two teachers who have clearly mastered these five basic approaches, encourage them to incorporate multiple approaches together. For instance, while one facilitates the majority of the class doing stations, the other might be pulling a small group of students each time they rotate (essentially doing alternative teaching within station teaching). Or teachers can divide the class into parallel groups and then each teacher leads different tasks with half of the class (one teacher can have her group doing stations while the other teacher divides his group yet again so he has two groups doing different activities). There are so many opportunities when co-teachers are ready to embrace new challenges together.

Co-teachers can also be encouraged to look beyond their class for additional supports. After dividing into two groups (parallel), the special service provider can bring half of the class to the library to co-teach a lesson with the librarian on how to do research in a library. Concurrently, the general education teacher can take the other half of the class to the computer lab to co-teach a lesson with the technology teacher on how to do research online. Tomorrow the groups could switch. The only thing holding teachers back from a variety of options for instruction is their imagination. Their imagination and the curriculum guide, strict pacing plans, standardized tests, benchmark objectives, lack of planning time, and lack of administrative support. Take that last barrier out of the equation. Let co-teachers know you encourage

> **Plugged In**
>
> Go online to www. gatesfoundation.org to view the Measures of Effective Teaching study. Share these results with your teachers and create an ongoing dialogue about what effective teaching means to them.
>
>

them to teach in the most effective way they know how. If that means they are going to try new things and will need some flexibility in following a particular instructional guide, let them know they have your support. The ultimate assessment for success is: Are students learning? The assessment should not be: Have teachers followed the pacing plan to the minute? When teachers know you truly believe that, they will be more apt to put in the extra effort to plan lessons that engage, inspire, motivate, and teach their students. If you don't believe us, then take a moment to review a recent finding reported in the Measures of Effective Teaching study by the Bill and Melinda Gates Foundation (2011). That study found that teachers who teach to the test actually had lower value-added scores. That is just a little something to consider as you see co-teachers who appear to be more focused on covering the content by mentioning curriculum, rather than uncovering the content and truly teaching the information.

The goal of this chapter was to ensure that you have the same language as your co-teachers and a vision of how co-teaching could look in the classroom. Ultimately, we are not bogged down in the names of each approach. We often see teachers who are doing amazing things with one another and the kids and yet can't tell us the correct name of the approach. We really don't care. What we do care about is that they know there are multiple ways to work with one another and the students, and that they are willing and able to use whatever would work best for that day, that content, and that group of students. The various co-instructional approaches are merely tools to give to co-teachers to help them meet the needs of their students. Providing a common language saves time in planning by providing a structure for determining who will do what, with whom, when, and how. In our dance metaphor, this is similar to instructing our partners in a variety of dance moves. The more moves they are familiar with and expert in, the easier it will be for them to put those moves together in new and innovative routines. What is most important to us as instructional leaders is that students are being given the most appropriate and effective instruction these two teachers can provide. As the one responsible for leading this co-teaching dance, we know you share that view.

Chapter 7

So You Think You Can Dance

Observation and Feedback for Co-Teaching

Most administrators are painfully familiar with the protocols of observation and evaluation of individual teachers. You know what a strong teacher looks like. You know what he or she should be doing with students. Believe it or not, observing and giving feedback to co-teachers actually is different, and should be significantly so. In keeping with our dance metaphor, this would be akin to knowing all the steps to the Macarena and being asked to judge at a dance contest. You are given a checklist with the Macarena steps on it, and you are ready to go. A pair of dancers doing the Tango comes on stage and you look at your Macarena checklist, wondering how you can effectively evaluate their dance moves. The checklist is based on one dancer, not two, and it's based on how that one dancer performs alone, not how two dancers perform together. (And let's not forget that the Macarena and the Tango look nothing alike!) Clearly that evaluation form is not appropriate for this situation; likewise the majority of the observation or evaluation forms that most schools use are not appropriate for observing and giving feedback to teachers who are co-teaching in an inclusive class. In fact, in her article entitled "This Doesn't Look Familiar! A Supervisor's Guide for Observing Co-Teachers" (2005), Wilson provides a vignette in which a special education supervisor and a general education administrator observe the same pair of co-teachers and come away with very different observations. This chapter provides strategies and techniques for evaluating the co-teaching dance.

What do you want to see? What are you looking for? In the co-teaching classroom scenario, we actually don't want to see a lesson with which we are familiar. Picture this: you walk into a general education classroom and see the general education teacher standing up front, using the document camera to model math problems. In the back of the room, you see the special education teacher working with a student with disabilities and providing on-the-spot modifications by simplifying the problem so that he can understand what is being asked of him. What do you think? Well, if you analyze each teacher's actions individually on a typical teacher evaluation form, it appears they are both doing their jobs. However, to give quality feedback to teachers who are co-teaching, it is critical to reflect back to the essential question of co-teaching.

We know we are repeating ourselves, but we believe that repetition aids retention, and this is worth retaining! So, again, the essential question of co-teaching is:

> **How is what the co-teachers are doing together substantively different and better for kids than what one of them would do alone?**

Thus, it is imperative that what you are seeing in a co-taught class does not mirror what you would see if either of those teachers were teaching alone. Let's face it: in today's economy, if one teacher can be just as effective alone or with a paraprofessional (who costs less than a fully credentialed teacher), why would we promote having two teachers in the room? Simmons and Magiera (2007) encouraged schools and teachers to ask the question "How do we know if we are truly co-teaching?" In the three schools included in their research, one of the teams resulted in a partnership in which the special educator would stand at the side of the room and watch as the general educator lectured; after the lecture, she would walk around and help with activities. How is this beneficial? How is this substantively different and better for kids than what one would do alone? Clearly, these types of situations do not constitute effective partnerships.

So what are you looking for? You are looking for two teachers who are maximizing their own personal areas of strength. You are looking for the "value added" that can occur when two educators work collaboratively. You are looking for two individuals who clearly trust and respect one another's expertise. You are looking for a class in which the students are engaged and learning, one in which you cannot easily determine who the special education teacher is or who the students with identified disabilities are. All you see is a class where the students are receiving differentiated instruction based on their needs, not their labels, and teachers are working together to do what it takes to motivate, instruct, assess, remediate, enrich, and facilitate. That's all. Sounds easy, right?

All right, perhaps it's not that easy. That is ultimately our goal, but what should you do in the meantime as your co-teaching teams are developing? We suggest you share with them Appendix 4, the Co-Teaching Self-Assessment Checklist (CTSS, 2009). Have co-teachers individually self-assess their current standing in relation to the items on the chart. Have each partner give you their self-assessment and put their results on the comparison chart in Appendix 5. Add in the results you came up with during a recent observation. Having this comparison table will serve as an excellent way for you to communicate with your teams.

If both partners provide the same ratings and your observation scores are in congruence with those ratings, you can be relatively assured that the scoring is an accurate reflection of how those teachers are doing on that item. If partners disagree or if your observations differ from their self-reports, this provides an opportunity for conversation with the co-teachers. The form helps remove emotion and judgment. It enables you to talk to co-teachers about the various items and to dialogue about how they might improve in a particular area; it also provides a forum by which you can offer support or guidance and strategies for improvement. You're the dance coach, so coach them!

Co-Teaching Solutions System Observation Tables

The Co-Teaching Solutions System (CTSS, 2009) is co-teaching software that offers an observation system for schools interested in collecting data on co-teaching effectiveness. The CTSS system enables administrators and other observers (e.g., coaches, university faculty, staff developers, data collectors) to walk into a co-taught class and have specific items to look for, listen for, and ask for conveniently loaded onto their laptops, iPads, or personal digital assistants. The results can then be easily formatted, analyzed, and generated into easy-to-share reports through the click of a button. Do you prefer paper over electronics? You can still collect the same data, although the analyses will be up to you. In Appendices 6, 7, and 8, we have reproduced the forms provided by Murawski and Lochner in their 2011 article in *Intervention in School and Clinic* based on the CTSS software.

The CTSS "look fors" (Appendix 6) involve specific criteria that you would want to see happening in a truly successful, co-taught, inclusive classroom. Although some of these items seem straightforward (e.g., both teachers are in the class on time), others require more expertise in being able to observe and assess (e.g., differentiation is well-selected). If you don't know what the five co-teaching approaches are, it will

---

For Your Bookshelf

Support for lesson planning can be hard copy or electronic. Check out the *Co-Teaching Lesson Plan* book at www.knowledge-by-design.com/planbook.html or the CTSS Teachers' Toolkit at www.coteachsolutions.com

be difficult for you to determine if they are being used. Likewise, if you are unfamiliar with differentiation strategies, you may not know if they are being employed accurately or at all. Thus, although having this list is helpful, it does require that observers are knowledgeable about best practice in co-teaching and special education. Consider talking through the list with your co-teaching teams and discussing as a group how you will interpret each item. Coming to consensus about what each item means to you and how it would look in the classroom will help concretize the list for you as the administrator and for your teachers. No one enjoys being observed, especially if they are being evaluated without any clear criteria.

The CTSS "listen fors" form (Appendix 7) can similarly be discussed with co-teachers. This form takes into account what you hear in the inclusive classroom. For example, you might see co-teachers "including" all students by putting them in three groups, but if you consider your "listen fors" you may realize that Bobby never spoke up in class, was made fun of by his peers when he had awkward body motions, didn't know where to put his chair when they moved into groups, and was never asked a question or engaged by either teacher. Consider using the "listen fors" chart as a tool with which you can talk to some or all of your teachers about scaffolding questions, motivating participation, and teaching social skills and tolerance. These discussions certainly do not need to occur only in a co-taught class; they are appropriate skills for all teachers and all students from early childhood to adult education.

Last, the CTSS "ask fors" chart (Appendix 8) is one that can assist you in obtaining what we call permanent product data. Permanent product data is simply hard copy evidence that shows what has occurred or is occurring. In this scenario, you are looking for evidence that your two teachers are meeting the definition of co-teaching: Are they co-planning, co-instructing, and co-assessing? For each of these areas, the "ask for" list provides examples of what you can collect. For example, in the co-planning area you can certainly ask for copies of teachers' lesson plans. Although our preference is that teachers are using Lisa's *Co-Teaching Lesson Plan* book or the CTSS Teachers' Toolkit for their co-planning efforts, we recognize that different districts have their own planning forms, needs, and requirements. All we ask is that teachers do indeed plan. Too often, teachers only plan verbally or on-the-fly and those plans are fleeting; there is no opportunity to learn from mistakes, document for the future, or share with others. We don't care if co-teachers do their planning on lunch napkins so long as they save those napkins as documentation for future reflection and refinement.

Other Co-Teaching Observation Tools

Co-Teacher Relationship Scale

Developed by Noonan, McCormick, and Heck in 2003, the co-teacher relationship scale was validated with a small sample of early childhood teachers in Hawaii. This tool focuses on more personal characteristics of co-teachers, such as attitudes, beliefs, and personal characteristics. Results can be used to help determine co-teaching partnerships, in addition to assessing current partnerships.

Are We Really Co-Teachers Scale?

Villa, Thousand, and Nevin (2004) created this scale to look more at the actions and behaviors of co-teachers in the classroom, as opposed to merely teachers' attitudes and beliefs. The authors of this scale encourage administrators and school leaders to use this tool to observe co-teachers in action and use the results to determine areas in which co-teachers can use support or additional professional development. Cramer and Nevin (2006) validated this scale with a convenience sample of educators from Miami-Dade County Public Schools.

Magiera-Simmons Quality Indicator (QI) Model

Based on collaborative research between university faculty and school districts, Kathleen Magiera and Rhea Simmons developed this model in 2005. Their QI model provides a rating scale and survey to help co-teachers track their progress in becoming an effective team in the classroom. Through observations and responses to survey questions, special and general education teachers who co-teach together can work toward the best use of their skills in the general education classroom in order to meet the needs of a variety of learners. The QI model is available at http://www.excelsior-ed.com.

For Your Bookshelf

Read more about all of these scales:

Noonan, M. J., McCormick, L., & Heck, R. H. (2003). The co-teacher relationship scale: Applications for professional development. *Education and Training in Developmental Disabilities, 38*(1), 113–120.

Villa, R., Thousand, J., & Nevin, A. (2008). *A guide to co-teaching: Practical tips for facilitating student learning* (2nd ed.). Thousand Oaks, CA: Corwin Press.

Magiera, K. A., & Simmons, R. J. (2005). *The Magiera-Simmons quality indicator model of co-teaching.* Fredonia, NY: Excelsior Educational Service.

Identifying Potential Problem Areas

You now have a variety of tools available to you for observing co-teaching in action. Now what? How do you take action based on the information you have collected? We have the fortune of traveling and seeing what is happening in co-taught classes around the nation and even internationally (most recently, Lisa was in Abu Dhabi and Wendy was in Tanzania). These real world visits have provided us with a very good picture of where co-teachers are succeeding and where they often struggle. We pass on that information to you here in the hopes that it will help you determine what you are seeing. Take a few minutes to read the box, "At-a-Glance: Assessing Co-Teaching Levels"; do your teams typically fall in the A, B, C, or D category of co-teaching? Contrary to most report cards, in this case you actually want your co-teachers to be in the D category. Once you identify where teachers are, it's time to figure out how to move them to the next level. How, you ask? Identify their problem areas and create a strategy for addressing them. We provide you here with some of the most common problem areas.

Three major problem areas keep emerging in our observations. Being aware of these three areas will help you in providing feedback to your co-teachers, but more importantly, will help you determine where you, as the educational leader, need to provide supports to your teachers. The three areas that we find ourselves giving feedback on repeatedly are (1) relationship issues, (2) lack of variety in co-instructional approaches being used, and (3) a lack of differentiation or Universal Design for Learning (UDL) principles. Here we take each of these situations and share the issue, tell you what we would want to see instead, and provide you with the feedback we would give to teachers who struggle in one of these areas.

Relationship Issues

One of the first things we often notice about the teams we observe is how the teachers interact with one another. When teachers clearly aren't communicating or are tense with one another, that tension can come across to the students. If you hear a teacher being condescending to another teacher in front of the students, it is time to intervene. When students are not around, set a time to meet with the team and see if you can help them identify ways to address their lack of collaborative behavior. Also couch your discussion in the importance of modeling to students respect for one another so that the students provide the same respect to the teachers. A simple question such as this one might work after you point out what you observed: What do you perceive you are modeling to students with your current co-teaching relationship?

Another relationship issue might relate to a difference in equity. If you walk into the room and hear one teacher asking the other permission to use materials or let a student go to the bathroom, you know that this team lacks parity. It might be that they simply aren't yet comfortable with sharing the stage, and they may need additional support and guidance in identifying how to ensure it is their shared classroom (even if one of the teachers is only in there for an hour or so). On the other hand, it may also be that one teacher is unwilling to share her authority in the classroom and is treating the other as an assistant.

At-A-Glance: Assessing Co-Teaching Levels			
Level Of Co-Teaching	**Dance Level**	**What You See**	**What You Can Do**
A AVOID STAYING HERE FOR LONG	*Elementary School Dancing* (Boys on one side, girls on the other... because of cooties, of course!)	Tension; Negativity Bad environment for students Large group situation most of class Special educator treated as "aide" My kids/Your kids Obvious stigmatization of students with disabilities	Counseling Individual discussions Have them share needs & issues Creation of shared goals Work on changing their hearts before you change their skills Divorce (if it's really bad)
B BABY STEPS	*Middle School Dancing* (Swaying side to side together but not really interacting... or doing the lambada or line dances as whole group)	Attempt at having special educator get "face time" Special educator jumps in or redirects Some use of additional approaches Some use of differentiation strategies Willing to take turns in front of kids	Have them revisit their goals Support external examples of parity (both names on report cards, door, etc) Discuss lesson plans & need for shared ownership Provide professional development on co-teaching, UDL & differentiation Work on improving skills

At-A-Glance: Assessing Co-Teaching Levels			
C **C**OLLABORATIVE	*High School Dancing* (Can barely pry them apart with a crow bar)	Can't tell special educator from general educator Clear but differentiated sharing of roles & responsibilities that are meaningful Use of different approaches to instruction Co-planning & co-assessing regularly	Have teachers document what they are doing, what works & what didn't, so you can build on successes Provide lots of positive reinforcement (technology, resources, kudos, publicity)
D **D**ARN, THEY'RE GOOD!	*Professional Dancing* (Able to show their own skills but equally able to mentor and teach others how to dance)	Can articulate why they do what they do Can model all approaches & use meaningfully based on need of kids Have examples of successful learning (academic, social & behavioral) Have the communication skills to work with others to help develop their skills	Cultivate a co-teaching mentor cadre Keep good teaching teams together as models for others Videotape & collect data Continue to provide professional development on flexible grouping, enrichment, differentiation, etc.

You may also see teams who are somewhere in the middle. One teacher clearly still takes the lead for the most part, but the other teacher seems to have a role and is able to occasionally jump in or lead a small group or part of the lesson without any perceived negativity from the first teacher. These teachers are in a "baby steps" situation, wherein they need to learn how to share the stage and maximize one another's strengths. This is a team who is willing to dance together but they just aren't sure yet how not to step on one another's toes. They may benefit from additional professional development on the use of the different co-teaching approaches to enhance their ability to teach in the same classroom together.

Last, you may be lucky enough to walk in and see teachers who are clearly enjoying one another's company. You hear laughter, you see smiling faces, and you know that this is a team that gets along. "Wonderful," you think. "It's all about the relationships, right? If so, this team is a guaranteed success!" Well, hold on. Although finding the right personalities is definitely a key component to effective co-teaching, you're not home-free yet. The next item to assess is the teachers' use of co-teaching approaches.

Lack of Variety in Co-Teaching Approaches

Laughter is wonderful. Teachers getting along is a great thing. As your sole benchmark of success alone, this is insufficient. We have seen teachers who are in front of the class, talking to one another, engaging with one another, and enjoying one another's company. Unfortunately, that was all they were doing; they weren't talking to the students or engaging the students. The primary purpose of co-teaching is not to develop friendships or have someone in the room who gets your jokes, although those are wonderful side benefits. The primary purpose of co-teaching is to meet the diverse needs of students so that they can all access the general education curriculum. It's about the kids, not about the adults.

If teachers have complementary personalities, co-teaching is more likely to be effective. Another critical component, though, is that the teachers maximize the fact that there are two teachers in the room; they need to use the various co-teaching approaches to lower the student-teacher ratio, engage and motivate students, increase the use of differentiation strategies, and ensure that both teachers get face time with the students. Chapter 6 provided information on the five different approaches to co-instruction made popular by Cook and Friend. How are the teachers using these approaches? This area is your next item of analysis.

As previously reported, Weiss and Lloyd (2002) found that most teachers who say they are co-teaching are actually using the One Teach-One Support strategy. This type is often a crutch for new co-teachers who are not yet used to sharing the stage or regrouping students. Although this may operate as a baby step for some co-teaching teams, the concern is that when teams use this approach often, they stop walking altogether. It becomes their modus operandi. Some teams argue that their selection of One Teach-One Support is a valid one because the teachers swap the chalk often, or take turns leading. The result, however, is a class that looks suspiciously similar to the general education classes of yore: students in one large group sitting in rows and listening to one voice up front while another adult roams the room and helps with behavior management.

Although the research is clear that teachers over-rely on the One Teach-One Support approach (Dieker, 2001; Moorehead, 2010; Weiss & Lloyd, 2002), don't be fooled by teachers who add one more approach to their repertoire and stick with that particular approach. How would that look? Let us show you in the box "In Action 7-1."

In Action 7-1

Ms. Smith looks at the clock as Mr. Jones walks in, right on time. "Great, kids!" she says to the third grade class. "Mr. Jones is here. Let's move to our stations!"

||➡

The bell rings and the seventh graders just barely make it to their seats. Mrs. Blue and Mr. Red are at the front of the room. "Okay guys, you know the drill. My half of the class will stay in here and Mr. Red's half will go with him to his room down the hall."

||➡

The bell rang 3 minutes ago and a few tenth graders are still straggling in. The warm-up is on the board. As the kids work, Ms. Judith and Mr. Joshua stand at the front of the room. After five more minutes, Ms. Judith says, "Okay, today we are going to start learning about slope of a line." "Right," chimes in Mr. Joshua. "How about those of you who work with me join me at the back table today?"

What's wrong with these scenarios? In debriefing with their administrator, the elementary teachers explain that they were using the station teaching approach. The middle school teachers explain that they were using a parallel teaching approach, and the high school teachers explain that they were using an alternative teaching approach. So all is well, right? Wrong.

The problem here is that it doesn't appear that these teachers are utilizing any of the other co-teaching approaches. When teachers become masters of only one approach, students can actually lose out. Not every lesson or day is conducive to the same co-teaching approach, and not all students will appreciate each approach. Although some may love stations because of the small groups, cooperative learning opportunities, interaction with teachers, and kinesthetic movement, that approach might be bothersome to some students for the same reasons. To always use the same approach when Mr. Jones walks in means that some students are going to dread when Mr. Jones arrives. It also falls dangerously close to becoming boring, and that is something we definitely want to avoid in an inclusive co-taught class.

The parallel teaching approach used in the middle school scenario is a great way to reduce the student-teacher ratio and can allow teachers to be quite creative and responsive to students. Teachers can engage in the same content in the same way, teach the same content in a different way, or teach different content. Yet if teachers use this as their de facto approach, students begin to feel as though they are "mine" or "yours" as opposed to "ours." This approach is akin to two parents who decide that their son will always be with Dad and their daughter will always be with Mom. If there is no sharing and interacting with one another, the feeling of a functioning family unit is lost. It certainly can serve to give both teachers face time, but it can also serve to break the class up into two small separate classes. That's not really the intent of inclusion, is it?

Finally, the scenario provided by the high school teachers may seem to you to be highly unlikely, but we see it far too often. We still see teachers who call for their students to go with them, but they seem to think that by staying in physical proximity to the other students, they are including those students. On the contrary, calling them out in this way is possibly worse than the provision of alternative, pull-out, or resource services because it is being done right in front of their grade level peers. Some teachers try to defend their actions by claiming that the daily interactions with the same small group of students at the small table at the back of the room is still inclusive because not all of the students pulled to work with them have identified disabilities. Some students are only at-risk, the teachers argue. Our counter-argument, however, is that it doesn't matter if students have identified labels or not; if one teacher is always pulling a small group to a back table or separate environment for remediation, that group will suffer from the same stigmatization and loss of access to general education curriculum as the pull-out groups we used to see. This practice certainly is the antithesis of the intent of the whole inclusion paradigm shift.

Lack of UDL and Differentiation Strategies

Let's assume we now have teachers who are enjoying one another's company and who are able to effectively use a variety of co-teaching approaches on a regular basis. They have parity, respect, trust, and a willingness to use various regrouping approaches in the classroom to engage students. Are we home-free? We are close (very close), but unfortunately we are not there yet.

The final piece of the puzzle that seems to elude many teachers is the true integration of UDL instruction and differentiation strategies. Although realizing that many students will need smaller groups in order to interact more appropriately or learn more effectively is a step towards universal design, and the use of different grouping arrangements (e.g., stations, parallel groups) will provide an element of differentiation, teachers cannot stop there. This is the time when the "value added" of the special service provider should come into clear focus. The creation of universally designed lessons with appropriate adaptations already embedded should be the mission of every special educator.

Let us step back a moment and make sure we are all on the same page related to what we mean by some of these terms. As an administrator, we are sure you too have experienced the impact and confusion that frequently occurs when assumptions are made and terms are thrown out without a clear understanding by all regarding what they mean. The box "Need to Know!" clarifies our key terms for this section. Please take a moment to read them through and see if our definitions are in sync with your own.

When co-planning a universally designed lesson, co-teachers need to consider how their students learn best. They will keep this in mind as they consider the content they need to co-deliver, while also considering one another's comfort levels with that content. They will use the What/How/Who Approach (Murawski, 2012) to co-planning, as described in Chapter 6. They know what they need to teach, and they know a variety of ways to deliver that content; they are efficient in using a variety of co-teaching approaches effectively to increase the likelihood that students' needs are met. It is the inclusion of differentiation strategies, however, that will be the hallmark of the special education co-teacher; this should be their domain and area of expertise. We say this knowing full well that there are numerous general educators who also have a plethora of differentiation strategies and experience working with students with special needs. This is meant as no disrespect to them; instead, it is meant as a gauntlet we are throwing down to special educators. We want them to be expert strategists, rather than merely generalists.

We now return to that classroom observation. How will you know if you are seeing differentiation in action? To be honest, you may not. If the co-teachers are truly incorporating differentiation strategies seamlessly, it is possible they will pass out three different versions of a worksheet with no one the wiser. It is possible they will give verbal cues to some students to focus on particular problems rather than having them do them all, without anyone even noticing what the teachers are doing.

It is possible that co-teachers will have already crafted multiple levels of questions to ensure concrete questions for some students and higher-order questions for others, and all you observe in the classroom is two teachers lobbying various questions to students throughout the lesson. It is possible that prior to getting into groups, one of the teachers spoke proactively to a student with a behavior issue to remind him of his point card, while the other teacher had quietly talked to a student with autism at the beginning of the class to discuss the change of structure. It is indeed possible that when students open their folders, they each have work individually tailored to their particular needs, strengths, and levels. Students who are gifted are provided with more challenging and conceptual work, whereas those with learning disabilities are provided concrete examples, and students with cognitive impairments have questions that link the content with functional skills on which they are working. All of these things may be happening, and you may not see them. How, then, do you assess if differentiation is truly occurring?

You ask the students what is going on during the class by quietly walking around and seeing what students are doing. You ask how they know what they are supposed

Need to Know!	
Term	**Definition**
Differentiation	The provision of different plans, materials, instruction, or assessments for students based on their need (not their label)
Universal Design for Learning (UDL)	The careful consideration of the variety of potential student needs during the creation of a lesson, in order to ensure access to that lesson's content and instruction proactively, rather than reactively trying to retrofit a lesson to a student's needs after the fact; offers multiple means of representation, engagement, and evaluation
Adaptations	Any accommodations or modifications that may be needed for a student that may be different from his or her peers
Accommodations	Changes to the instruction, curriculum or assessment that do not lower the standard
Modifications	Changes to the instruction, curriculum or assessment that do lower the standard

to be doing, if it appears to be different from what their peers are doing. You ask the teachers before and after observations. You ask for examples of how they addressed the needs of different learners. You ask how teachers consider different cultural backgrounds, learning needs, behavioral concerns, and social issues. Be wary of teachers who state that they "treat everyone the same." That's actually not the intent of the inclusive co-taught class. The intent is to be able to treat everyone differently based on his or her particular interests, strengths, and needs. We know that is a tall order for any teacher; that is why we recommend that two teachers may be needed in the same classroom to accomplish this task.

Let us use the work of Dr. Gloria Lodato Wilson from Hofstra University in New York to boil this down even further. Dr. Wilson provided 18 questions that administrators can ask themselves when trying to determine if a co-taught inclusive class is being taught as effectively as possible. We strongly recommend that leaders interested in observing co-teaching refer to her 2005 article in *Intervention in School and Clinic*. She put these 18 questions into three sections. We have taken each of those sections and created one broad question for each section. Here are the three questions you can ask when observing in a co-taught class, as adapted from Wilson (2005):

1. Are the roles of each teacher meaningful?

2. Are the teachers using strategies to promote success for all students?

3. Is there evidence of student success?

For Your Bookshelf

Learn more about how teachers can value & integrate multiple cultures into a classroom in:

Trumbull, E., Rothstein-Fisch, C., Greenfield, P. M. & Quiroz, B. (2001). *Bridging cultures between home and school: A guide for teachers*. Mahweh, NJ: Lawrence Erlbaum.

Rothstein-Fisch, C. & Trumbull, E. (2008). *Managing diverse classrooms: How to build on students' cultural strengths*. Alexandria, VA: Association for Supervision and Curriculum Development.

At-A-Glance: Co-Teaching Observation Guide

When observing a co-teaching team, both general and special education supervisors should work collaboratively to ensure they are both looking for the same elements. In addition, they should ensure that they share a frame of reference regarding what they are seeing. Too often, administrators or observers with different frames of reference may look at the same classroom interaction and evaluate it completely differently. This is frustrating for teachers and can lead to an inconsistent message.

Here are some guiding elements for observers to look for:

The Basics: Meaningful Roles for Each Teacher

- The lesson clearly warrants the use of two teachers.
- Each of the teachers clearly knew their role in today's lesson.
- Each of the teachers was confident with today's content/curriculum.
- Each of the teachers was able to add his/her expertise to today's lesson.
- Students would not have been able to tell the special educator from the general educator.
- Each of the teachers actively participated in today's lesson.

Strategies to Promote Success for All Students

- The lesson was universally designed to proactively address the diverse needs of learners.
- The lesson also includes differentiation strategies for individual learners.
- The lesson incorporates elements to support behavior, attention, social skills, and school success strategies as appropriate.
- The lesson actively engages learners and incorporates motivation strategies.
- Modifications and accommodations are provided to students as per their IEPs and needs.
- Teachers use the variety of co-teaching approaches (parallel, station, alternative) to regroup students.
- Students are regrouped based on flexible grouping strategies to ensure heterogeneity.

Evidence of Success

- Students are actively engaged in the lesson.
- Students are asking and answering a range of questions.
- A diverse range of assessments demonstrate student achievement and include progress in academics as well as behavior and social skills.
- Teachers work collaboratively to ensure students are assessed appropriately and reevaluate the assignment and instruction if students are unsuccessful.

Note. Based on work from: "This Doesn't Look Familiar! A Supervisor's Guide to Observing Co-Teachers," by G. L. Wilson, 2005, *Intervention in School and Clinic, 40*(5), pp. 271–275. and Murawski, W. W., & Lochner, W. (2011). Observing Co-teaching: What to Ask For, Look For, and Listen for. *Intervention in School and Clinic, 46*(3), 174–183.

Providing Feedback for Improvement

Administrators armed with the CTSS forms, which tell them what to look for, listen for, and ask for, as well as knowledge of the three potential co-teaching problem areas (relationships, lack of co-teaching approaches, and lack of differentiation strategies) are good to go for the observation part of their job. However, research on the use of observations as professional development is clear that pre-observation meetings are important to discuss the goals of the lesson. There needs to be a dialogue before the observation so that teachers know that the observation is intended not merely for evaluation, but, more importantly, to help co-teachers improve. For example, in Wischnowski et al. (2004), administrative leaders met with co-teachers to discuss what they would be seeing in the classroom and what approaches the teachers had identified for use in addressing those issues. This type of conversation helps co-teachers know that the observers are there for support and assistance; knowing this results in a feeling of comfort and willingness to try new things, as opposed to a feeling of insecurity and nervousness at the thought of the impending observation.

You've had the pre-observation conference. You've identified a few items that the co-teachers will be working on, and you've gone in and sat through a whole lesson. Wonderful. You're done, right? Sorry, but no. Simple observation is insufficient; feedback on those observations needs to be provided to the co-teaching teams. Feedback is considered most effective when it is immediate, solicited, direct, and focused (Friend & Cook, 2007).

Plugged In

Can't get to each classroom regularly because you're stuck in your office? Use video cameras and similar technology to view classes from the luxury of your office.

When possible, we recommend meeting with co-teaching teams immediately after the observation to discuss what was observed. Given busy administrative schedules, we know this is not always possible, but work to create a time to debrief when co-teachers have a common planning period or can be released by substitute teachers. The most important thing is that you do debrief; the second most important thing is that this debriefing happens relatively soon after the actual observation. We have had teachers complain to us as university professors that their administrators either (a) don't observe at all, (b) do a fly-by observation that wasn't scheduled and isn't substantive, or (c) conduct an observation but then never discuss what was observed. Being observed as a teacher is nerve-wracking. Being observed as a co-teacher is doubly so. Please make sure your teachers know when they are going to be observed, have a discussion with you proactively about what you will be observing content-wise, and are aware of the co-teaching components on which you will be collecting data. We recommend sharing your actual observation sheet and allowing them to do a pre-assessment of their skills.

For example, having the CTSS Self-Assessment checklist in Appendix 4 in front of you will be helpful in sharing with teachers the different areas you will be considering to document their co-planning, co-instructing, and co-assessing. When you meet to debrief with teachers, we suggest discussing the narrative observations prior to sharing the quantitative (0, 1, 2) scores. Many teachers see the quantitative scores as pass/fail, rather than their intended use, which is merely as a way of documenting progress toward more effective co-teaching.

When giving feedback to teachers after the observation, use the sandwich approach. Start with some positives, provide some areas for growth, and end with more positives. Try to avoid overwhelming teachers with too many areas of concern. Research has found that while sharing two to three focus areas for growth results in future improvement, more than that results in confusion and resentment (Ghorpade, 2000). How might this look? See the box, "In Action 7-2" for an example feedback session with a pair of co-teachers.

In Action 7-2

Dr. Cetulio looked over her notes as the bell rang. She had observed Mr. Gompert and Ms. Messer two hours ago and now they were coming to debrief with her during their common planning time. She considered again how she was going to phrase her comments, then looked up and smiled as Mr. Gompert and Ms. Messer entered her office.

"Let's sit together at this table," welcomed Dr. Cetulio, moving away from her large desk. As the three sat down, Dr. Cetulio began by putting them at ease, saying "I really enjoyed being able to come in and observe today, and I appreciate you both opening your classroom to me. Before I share some of my observations, I'd really enjoy hearing what you two thought. I find that often, by having teachers share first, they answer my questions or validate my own observations before I even say anything." For the next 5 to 10 minutes, Dr. Cetulio listened quietly, occasionally taking notes as the co-teachers shared their reflections on today's class. The teachers identified areas in which they thought were strong as well as a few students and situations that were bothersome. Once it appeared they were finished, Dr. Cetulio moved on to sharing her own observations.

In Action 7-2 (cont'd)

"You know, a lot of what you both shared is consistent with what I saw as well. I actually want to start with how encouraging it is for me to see how you two really seem to trust and respect each other in the classroom. I could see that both of you interacted with all students, not just a few, and that the students seemed to respect both of you also. I enjoyed how you both clearly felt comfortable answering students' questions, whether they were to the class or individually, and that both of you were obviously aware of the content, objective, and state standard for this particular lesson.

The co-teaching approach I observed today was One Teach-One Support, with Mr. Gompert keeping the lead role most of the observation. Ms. Messer actively interacted with the students, walked around and provided proximity control, offered instructional assistance, answered questions, and passed out papers. Now, I don't know how often you both use the other co-teaching approaches, so there is no need to be defensive if you only use this approach rarely, but I do want to share that if this is the approach most often used, there is the potential for Ms. Messer to feel similar to an instructional aide. Given that you have 10 years of teaching experience, Ms. Messer, I'm fairly certain that we don't want to do that to you. Before our next observation, I hope you'll both try a variety of the other co-teaching approaches so that you can ensure that both of you have face time with the students and that you can both bring your different areas of expertise to the classroom. What I typically recommend is to try at least two new approaches each week. As I realize using new approaches takes more planning time, I'd be happy to cover one of your classes or arrange for our in-house substitute teacher to cover two classes over the next month to give you extra time if you would like it to plan these types. My hope would be that once you have had experience with planning and experiencing these new types, future planning will be much easier.

That brings me to the second suggestion I have for ongoing improvement. I noticed that you were both very open to having students ask questions, which both of you answered at times, and I also noticed that you both appeared to be totally fine with the accommodations I saw Ms. Messer give to Tony regarding only having to do the odd numbers on his work. I would love it if you both would talk to each other about universal design during your lesson planning, and see if you can incorporate more differentiation strategies in your proactive planning. I'm happy to give you both additional information and strategies if you'd like, or to connect you with others who have great ideas. What I hope

---

In Action 7-2 (cont'd)

to see at our next observation is some obvious use of strategies to assist student learning embedded within your lesson. This might include grouping strategies, mnemonics, graphic organizers, visuals, or realia. Consider what would be appropriate for that particular lesson, which strategies are appropriate for all learners, and which students will need additional individualized differentiation strategies to help them succeed. I know this idea seems a tall order, but Ms. Messer, I know you have lots of these strategies at your fingertips, and because Mr. Gompert has such a great grasp of the curriculum and the content, I know you two are a team that can make this happen.

As I said earlier, I'm so encouraged by the positive rapport you two have with each other. Given the different strengths you each bring to this relationship, I can see this building into a model co-teaching team for our school. I appreciate the opportunity to share with you feedback that I think will move you to that model team, and I look forward to supporting you in this growth. Is there anything you need from me in order to do that?" Wrapping up with that question and expression of support, Dr. Cetulio encouraged Ms. Messer and Mr. Gompert to respond to her observations and ask additional questions. She guided them to a few reference materials and web sites, took notes as they reported concerns about Ms. Messer being called out of the classroom too frequently, and set a time with them for their next observation. As they walked out the door, she smiled to herself because it was obvious this was a team who would try to make their co-teaching relationship work and who knew that the students were their shared, primary concern; all she had to do was help facilitate their ongoing growth.

Jensen and Reichle (2011) from the Gratten Institute completed a comprehensive assessment of the role of teacher feedback. Although this report is not related directly to co-teaching, the power of principal feedback is evident in his findings. Jensen and Reichle remind us that "School principals are responsible for developing and implementing teacher appraisal and feedback programs. Student performance is the ultimate measure. Principals must therefore be able to make difficult decisions about the viability of their programs if they are not improving student performance" (p. 23). Clearly, any and all feedback must be anchored in your most important job, which is student learning. Putting two teachers in a room together may be your first step, and making sure they are using a variety of co-teaching approaches is your second. The final and most critical step, however, is ensuring that every move your teams make creates a better learning experience for each and every student in the co-taught setting. That is the core of evaluation and feedback of successful co-teaching.

Addressing Conflict

Giving feedback and working with teachers is easy when the going is smooth, but what do you do when two co-teachers simply are not getting along? Wendy once had a principal stand up in a training session and announce to the group that he had had two co-teachers literally come to blows in front of a group of students. Ouch! We certainly think something should have been done along the way before it got to that extreme.

First, let co-teachers know that there will be conflict. It's natural. Any time you have two adults working together to educate a group of students, there is bound to be conflict or at least differences of opinion. Melamed and Reiman (2000) write about the need for collaboration and conflict resolution in schools. Positive and productive outcomes can be the result. Unfortunately, unless situations are well managed and facilitated, some teachers might end up blaming co-teaching, collaboration, or inclusion as the reason they are unhappy, unfulfilled, or just downright upset.

There are many things you can do as an administrator to help teachers address (if not avoid) conflict. Ploessl, Rock, Schoenfeld, and Blanks (2010) offer insights to co-teachers to help address or minimize possible areas of conflict. We have taken those insights and provided them here, with adaptations made to make them more appropriate for the administrative perspective.

- *Respect cultural differences.* The more teachers learn that they come with different cultures and frames of reference and how these differences can actually add to the co-teaching classroom positively, the better (Cozart, Cudahy, Ndunda, & Van Sickle, 2003). Rothstein-Fisch and Trumbull (2008) write about working with diverse cultures in the classroom. Their books are fantastic for helping teachers recognize ways to include students from varying cultures; they may also be a nice way for teachers to recognize their own teaching and personal preferences as well.

For Your Bookshelf

Need strategies on how to address difficult situations?
Check out Pierce, K., & Fields, L. (2003). How to defuse difficult conversations. *Principal Leadership (Middle School ed.),* 4, 36–39.

- *Make opportunities to discuss minor issues before they escalate.* We published the S.H.A.R.E. worksheet as a tool for teachers to communicate with one another their own preferences, pet peeves, expectations, and desires. Administrators can use this type of tool to ensure that teachers talk to one another objectively prior to letting issues develop and escalate. Also, by developing a shared understanding of how the class will run, co-teachers will be less likely to operate on their own personal agendas, which otherwise might result in disagreements and misunderstandings.

- *Think first, act later.* Administrators are often put in the role of marriage counselor (Murawski, 2010). When disagreements occur between co-teachers, it is not uncommon for one teacher to go running to a vice principal for assistance, especially if she feels her partner is acting unreasonably. Although it is the role of the administrator to support teachers and help when crises develop, it is perhaps more important for administrators to help teachers working together to learn strategies for their own conflict management. For example, Ploessl and colleagues (2010) cite literature that refers to teaching internal monitoring techniques, self-talk skills, breathing reminders, ways to distinguish cognitive from affective conflict, healthy actions for personal improvement, and even the need to remain polite with one another. Sometimes we need to remind teachers that "behaving politely communicates caring and consideration, defusing tense interactions and strengthening the co-teaching relationship" (Ploessl et al., 2010, p. 166).

- *Turn differences into learning opportunities.* Garmston (2005) writes about how to turn conflict into an effective learning process. That is much easier said than done for many partners. Administrators may find themselves having to help co-teachers realize that one specific, negative, or difficult interaction is not a good reason to dissolve the whole partnership. Helping teachers learn from one another and respect their different frames of reference is one of the oft-cited benefits of co-teaching (Dieker & Murawski, 2003; Friend & Cook, 2007). Teachers may have difficulties recognizing these benefits when they are in the middle of a heated disagreement, however, so we suggest you remind them that there will be differences of opinion along the way. In addition, work with them proactively to determine how they will address conflict when it arises. Does one partner prefer time alone to process issues while the other wants to talk it out? You may find yourself in the position of counselor, but better that than referee. The more proactive you can be with co-teachers and the more skills and techniques you can give them for addressing their own conflict, the better it will be for the partnership and for you as a school leader.

Let's assume you've observed teachers, you've debriefed with them, and you've even managed to successfully negotiate some potentially difficult interactions. What's next? You are now ready to move on to collecting data to determine how co-teaching as a service delivery option is impacting your students and your schools. In the next chapter we discuss what you can do to help teachers co-assess and grade their students while also finding ways to analyze the effectiveness of your programs at a broader level. Once you've managed the assessment component of co-teaching, you'll be ready to move on to Chapter 9, which focuses on disseminating your findings and making connections to further your progress. Last, in Chapter 10, we'll give you more resources for building, expanding, and improving your co-teaching programs.

Chapter 8

Getting Your Dance Scores

The Importance of Data Collection

IDEA requires that educational professionals monitor and report the academic and behavioral progress of students with identified disabilities. Thus, in addition to co-planning and co-instructing, the co-assessing part is also a critical piece of effective co-teaching. This chapter is designed to help identify ways for co-teachers and administrators to collect data to guide decision-making with students and with the overall co-teaching program. What we don't want is teachers or administrators who make decisions on the fly or based solely on subjective opinions rather than on objective data. Unfortunately, Austin (2001) found that the majority of the co-teachers in his national study did just that. On a personal level, Wendy recently heard from a school district in Texas that they were going to discontinue their co-teaching program because the new superintendent didn't believe in it; this dramatic shift was especially disheartening because they had been engaged in district-wide professional development for 4 years and there was significant data showing that the co-teaching programs at numerous schools were resulting in huge gains for students. How frustrating!

Data collection does not need to be onerous or excessively time-consuming, but it does need to be thoughtful, proactive, and ongoing. Formative assessment should be a core value in an inclusive school (Dieker, 2013), so expecting co-teachers to gather daily assessments in the general education classrooms should be a natural extension of an already established practice. Conderman and Hedin (2012) provide several purposeful assessment practices for co-teachers that stress the co-assessing aspect of co-teaching. They point out that although researchers have investigated co-planning and co-instructing in the classroom, co-assessment is an aspect that is frequently overlooked. Ploessl and colleagues (2010) state that "frequent joint review of repeated and multiple quantitative measures of pupil performance (i.e., test scores, report card grades, curriculum-based measurement data) can help co-teachers make sound judgments about their instruction" (p. 164). In their article, the authors provide an example matrix created by co-teachers collaboratively to identify and coordinate their students' academic and behavioral adaptations and supports. With this kind of matrix, co-teachers can quickly remind themselves of who needs which accommodations, make decisions regarding grouping practices, and collect data on how various adaptations impact the students' success in the class. The box "At-a-Glance: Decision-Making Matrix" provides an adapted example of the decision-making matrix, based on the work of Ploessl and colleagues..

At-A-Glance: Decision-Making Matrix						
Students with Needs	Point Cards	Reading Support	Assignment Length Adaptation	Parent Notes Home	Text to Speech	Number of Supports
Riki	X	X	X	X		4
Rita			X	X	X	3
Shawn	X	X	X	X	X	5
Kwame	X	X	X			3
Claudette				X		1
* of students who share need	3	3	4	4	2	

There is a national call for more research on co-teaching and its outcomes (Murawski & Swanson, 2001; Wischnowski et al., 2004; Zigmond & Magiera, 2001). Administrators need to be especially concerned about outcomes, as they strive to ensure that they are making data-driven decisions and still embracing a more inclusive culture. Consistent and ongoing gathering of this data is much easier said than done. Few research studies are available in the literature that compare co-taught classes to those that involve children with disabilities but are not co-taught (e.g., Moorehead, 2010; Murawski, 2006; Rea, McLaughlin, & Walther-Thomas, 2002). In fact, Wischnowski and colleagues state that

> research that focused on student achievement in co-taught and single teacher models as well as in co-taught and more restrictive environments is needed; however, under current legislation and practice, finding these distinctions in classrooms, especially for students with high-incidence disabilities, is becoming more and more an outmoded exercise. Evaluative approaches to these questions currently provide a practical alternative in lieu of this current and likely persistent lack of empirical data. (2004, pp. 7–8)

Thus, we offer here a variety of possible ways that data can be collected in co-taught classes in order to establish empirically the impact on students with and without special needs. We have organized these suggestions into academic, social/behavioral, and disability-specific categories.

Academic Data Collection

Just as high-stakes exams may not provide a clear picture into the academic achievement of a student, neither will student grades alone be sufficient to demonstrate the effectiveness of co-teaching. In fact, in a CBS interview on national television on July 16, 2012, when asked if there is too much standardized testing in schools, National Teacher of the Year Rebecca Mieliwocki stated that "It's like going for a physical and saying that the temperature that the nurse took is your health profile. That's not it. It's a piece of it and it's an important piece of it ... We do have to have some numbers about whether kids are learning but ... I want an evaluation system that comes and sees the all of me" (www.cbsnews.com). (As a complete aside, Rebecca is a former co-teacher of Wendy's and we are incredibly excited that she is the model for teachers nationally. She is a real person, an inspirational teacher, and a very funny lady.) Grades are certainly an option for data collection, but they should be paired with additional permanent product data that assist co-teachers and administrators in determining the impact of having two teachers in the room. For example, teachers can work collaboratively to identify students' error patterns. These patterns can be used by teachers for data collection as well as for improving instruction. The box, "At-a-Glance: Errors Patterns in the Co-Taught Classroom" describes four different ways co-teachers can use error patterns effectively.

At-A-Glance: Error Patterns in the Co-Taught Classroom

1 Ignore them: Sometimes in instruction that is inquiry-based, allowing students to make mistakes is the purpose of the activity. We suggest that teachers talk about when to have errorless learning and when data on typical error patterns and correction procedures would be most helpful.

2. *Write them down:* Keep an ongoing data system of error patterns. These can be reflected upon by co-teachers after the class and can help prevent misunderstandings the next year by students.

3. *Own the errors and make them your own:* As co-teachers look for patterns and notice more than three students making the same error, they can use that as a teachable moment for the class by role–playing as if that error is their own.

4. *Create probes:* If a number of students are making similar errors, co-teachers can create a one-minute probe. Teachers can then review concepts, and the next day do another probe to see if the error is corrected. When 90% of the students have an error corrected, the teachers can use the alternative teaching approach to get the remaining 10% over the hump, but a probe is no longer needed. This technique is a great way to ensure there are no gaps in students' learning.

There are a variety of additional ways to collect academic progress from students in the co-taught class. These include:

- Grades (quarter, semester, final)
- Curriculum-based assessments
- Pre- and post-academic assessments
- Permanent product data (e.g., portfolios, work samples)
- Writing examples (e.g., quick writes, blogs, journals, prompts)

Social/Behavioral Data Collection

Students with social and behavioral challenges are frequently included in the co-taught setting without ongoing assessments of their changes in behavior or social skills. Because some of the cited benefits for inclusive education are improvements in behavior and social skills, we recommend collecting data on these areas as well. In the first year or two of being included in a general education setting, you may find that some students may not exhibit statistically significant changes in academics, but their teachers are adamant that there have been vast improvements in social or behavioral skills. We consider these very valid areas to consider when determining the impact of co-teaching and inclusion, but better behavior in this time of high-stakes tests and end-of-course exams is not enough. Including students with behavioral challenges in co-taught settings can be frustrating, thus it is essential to provide strategies for your co-teachers in how to collect data on targeted behaviors. When they can see quantitative changes in behavior, their efforts will feel well worth it. The box, "In Action 8-1" demonstrates how behavior data collection can occur.

In Action 8-1

Mrs. Boucher and Mrs. Farrell wanted to collect data on the number of times Sapphire was called out in the classroom (which they wanted to decrease) and initiated conversations with peers (which they wanted to increase), but they were already overwhelmed with all they had to manage in the class. They simply couldn't come up with a simple way to do it. They approached Mr. Rance, the assistant principal. Sapphire was really disrupting the class, though both teachers admitted it appeared she was improving little by little; they just didn't know for sure if it was their imagination or not. Mr. Rance provided the co-teachers the following suggestions for quick and easy ways to collect data on Sapphire's progress. He suggested they select one or two approaches that appealed most to them and collect the data for two weeks before determining whether or not their behavior management strategies were working or not.

- Keep a clipboard available and make tally marks on an index card that can be kept over time. Record the amount in planner at the end of the day.

- Transfer pennies from one pocket to another during the class session, then count the number of pennies.

- Place a strip of masking tape on a desk or elsewhere each time an event occurs.

- Place rubber bands on wrists for each occurrence.

- Move items over (e.g., books on a shelf) each time the behavior occurs.

The co-teachers not only appreciated his suggestions, but they also realized that many of these strategies would work for collecting data on other students' behaviors as well.

Disability-Specific Data Collection

Why is there a second teacher in the classroom? We imagine you chose to embrace co-teaching at your school(s) not because your general education teachers are ineffective (at least we hope not), but rather because there are students with identified disabilities or special needs entering the class who require specialized supports for their academic, behavior, or social skills in order to be successful. These needs should be outlined in the student's IEP. If this document outlines the student's needs, then this document should be what is assessed regularly. Ideally, in a strong co-taught environment, the IEP becomes a living and breathing document for both teachers in the classroom (Dieker, 2006). The IEP comes to life when teachers incorporate strategies and data collection to regularly assess the goals on that document, and when teachers ensure that they remember to maintain what is special about special education (i.e., that it is designed to meet individual student needs).

As teachers work to meet students' needs and address their IEP goals, we also remind you as the instructional leader to ask them to be able to support their decisions, especially regarding specific adaptations (modifications or accommodations) they make. For example, we have often seen students with disabilities be given a calculator without anyone assessing whether that is the tool that is most helpful (e.g., in reducing fractions, maybe a multiplication chart is a better tool than a calculator), or even whether it is an adaptation that is needed. Not every student with an IEP needs extra time or to be pulled out of the class to have a test read to them! As you lead this dance, don't be afraid to ask these two critical questions:

1. Why are you using that adaptation?

2. What data do you have that your use of these techniques is making a difference to students?

If teachers can respond to these questions, then the tools students are using are appropriate. If not, your role will be to help them re-assess or even to determine whether they are providing too much support for students (something we have seen frequently in the field).

Co-Assessing Strategies

As the instructional leaders, you need to have some "look fors" related to evaluating the assessment skills of your co-teachers. The first thing to look for is both formative and summative assessment skills. Co-teaching teams frequently look at how they will grade their students and even how they will provide accommodations on state or local assessments, but rarely do we see teams assessing the learning that should be occurring in the classroom on a daily basis. We encourage the use of a model presented by Dieker and Hines (2012) that suggests that the special education teacher should clearly know, and be prepared to assess, the goal of what the team believes all students should learn. Concurrently, the general education teacher might be assessing the typical skills that most students should learn, as well as an advanced skill that the teachers hope some kids will learn. Naturally, although the teachers are dividing these tasks based on their particular areas of expertise and on what makes the most sense, they are still working collaboratively and are communicating regarding all decision-making.

To make this more manageable and to provide co-teachers with a framework under which to work, all teachers need to have a solid foundation in Universal Design for Learning (UDL). UDL is defined by the Center for Applied Special Technology (CAST) as "a framework for designing educational environments that enable all learners to gain knowledge, skills, and enthusiasm for learning... by simultaneously reducing barriers to the curriculum and providing rich supports for learning" (2007, n.p.). Instead of having a single assessment, UDL principles suggest that there should be multiple ways for students to express what they know (Rose & Meyer, 2000a). In fact, the major premise behind UDL is that lessons need to provide multiple means of expression, representation, and engagement (CAST, 2007). When co-assessing students, co-teachers would have to make sure they have provided multiple means of expression. Including choice and variety into the design of a lesson helps to reduce the need for reactive adaptations or specific modifications for students with special needs.

Formative Assessments

The primary goals of formative assessments are to evaluate learning (Black & Harrison, 2001) and to improve student understanding by giving ongoing feedback (Bell & Cowie, 2001; Duschl, 2003). Formative assessments can be useful for assisting schools in determining the impact of two teachers collaborating in the classroom as well. Formative assessments can be accomplished through a variety of methods for frequently checking content understanding (Shepard, 2006). However, a challenge to formative assessment is balancing students' current levels of understanding while encouraging higher order thinking (Ruiz-Primo & Furtak, 2006). We don't want to see teachers who never challenge students, nor do we want to see students so frustrated that they turn off to learning altogether. Co-teachers need to come to a consensus when working with students regarding what the appropriate methods of assessment will be; this can be easier said than done when co-teachers have different frames of references related to assessment.

Daily assessments are part of formative assessments and should be created using the principles of UDL. Formative assessments can include technology to allow students to express higher order thinking concepts often not measured by summative assessment tools. Remember that using UDL for instruction and for assessment go hand-in-hand. For example, co-teachers who use hands-on lessons, inquiry-based learning, and student directed discussions (Coombs-Richardson, Al-Juraid, & Stuker, 2000; Kimmel, Deek, Farrell, & O'Shea, 1999) create a climate in which students can learn new content using UDL principles and

> **Plugged In**
>
> Learn more about Universal Design for Learning by going to the following web sites:
> www.cast.org
> www.udlcenter.org
> www.cec.sped.org
> www.greatschools.org

teachers can assess students' learning using UDL. Research has found that 96% of questions in the classroom are teacher-generated (Graesser & Person, 1994); we propose that co-teachers remind one another to let the students do the question-asking. Question-asking is another great way to assess what students know, what they want to know, and what they have learned.

Daily assessment of student learning should occur in the general education setting for all students, but it is especially critical for ensuring that students with disabilities are on the right trajectory for meeting lesson goals. In an inclusive classroom, co-teachers should be able to tell you the goal of their lesson each day and the tools they intend to use for daily assessment of student learning, including adapted or alternative formats as needed (Conderman & Hedin, 2012). You should be able to talk to any student in the inclusive, co-taught class and that student should be able to tell you how he or she is being assessed. This daily assessment must also include students with disabilities. Too often, we talk to teachers who tell us that they are giving certain students adapted assessments or using modified grading criteria, but the student has not been informed of these adaptations. The following box "In Action 8-2" provides an example of what you might observe in a team that is clear and strong in their formative assessments.

In Action 8-2

Mr. Joshua, the general educator, starts the planning session with Ms. Stanford, the special educator, by stating that the objective for days one and two of this week are to ensure students can add and subtract positive and negative numbers. Having established what they need to teach, they know the next goal is to discuss how they will teach it. (For more information on the What/How/Who approach, review Chapter 5.) Ms. Stanford offers to start the bell ringer with a 1-minute assessment of these skills and to end the lesson with a five-minute remediation lesson for those who are struggling. Note how the teachers are incorporating assessment right from the beginning of the lesson and clearly tying it to instruction. At the same time, both teachers are also aware that three students in the class have IEP goals that call for them to start tasks independently within three minutes of teacher direction. Because Ms. Stanford is starting the bell ringer, Mr. Joshua will simply record if these three students did or did not meet this goal on the clipboard the teachers use for the purpose of data collection. During the class instruction, both teachers will be using the clipboard to jot down any time they notice Brittany or Vayd participating in class discussions; their IEP goals state that they will do so at least twice a period. When assigning the independent activity to be done during class, Mr. Joshua is able to walk over to Rahm and tell him to do every other problem (this corresponds to Rahm's IEP, which states that he will complete at least 50% of the problems assigned to his same-age peers). After the activity, one of the teachers will note whether or not Rahm was able to meet that objective and to what degree of success.

Summative Assessments

Summative assessments are commonly experienced as any type of standardized testing or state assessment. In summative assessments, instead of measuring a daily learning goal, teachers are looking at the overall learning of students. We suggest that although summative assessments are based upon state and local standards, they need not always be purely paper and pencil assessments. Encourage teachers to find universally designed ways to assess to ensure that they know what students do and do not know, rather than merely gauging whether or not students know how to take a test.

Summative evaluations are extremely powerful in middle and high school. Secondary education is complex and demands higher levels of understanding, reasoning, and organization. In addition to the increased academic levels, students with disabilities are also required to take high-stakes tests that determine whether or not they move to the next grade, graduate high school, or are accepted to college (Dieker & Murawski, 2003). These tests don't just affect students' individual futures though. One of the most common summative assessments that teachers worry about today are state assessments that are often used to put schools on remediation plans or to award teachers with bonus or merit pay. Since the passage of the No Child Left Behind Act of 2001 (NCLB), challenges such as scheduling and time constraints, inconsistency within the collaborative structure, and the accountability demands of teachers on high-stakes tests have contributed to additional barriers plaguing secondary teachers who would otherwise be interested in co-teaching (Dieker, 2001; Dieker & Murawski, 2003; Walther-Thomas, 1997; Zigmond & Baker, 1996). Because high stakes tests are a given in most states, and because most states are moving to mandated end-of-course exams based upon the common core standards, co-teachers should be reminded that their job is to work collaboratively to teach the concepts on these exams in as many ways as possible to meet the needs of the students with disabilities. There are two needs at play here: students need to learn the content on the exams, but they also need to learn skills in how to take those tests. Who better to teach these two disparate but related areas than co-teachers?

Co-Teaching and Grading

How should grades be calculated for students with special needs? This question is a common one and is not just for those teachers who are co-teaching. The trend for grading seems to be moving toward a system that focuses more on learning outcomes than letter grades. In Lisa's visits to schools, she saw several districts (many being very large urban districts) moving from letter grades to standards-based report cards that will reflect the new common core standards. In a recent issue of Educational Leadership (November, 2011), the entire issue was dedicated to effective grading practices. Guskey (2011) described five obstacles to grading that we believe reflect the same issues facing co-teaching teams. We present those here in the box "Need to Know."

Need to Know

Common Misconceptions That Result in Obstacles to Effective Grading Practices

1. Grades should provide the basis for differentiating students.

2. Grade distribution should resemble a normal bell-shaped curve.

3. Grades should be based on students' standing among classmates.

4. Poor grades prompt students to try harder.

5. Students should receive one grade for each subject or course.

Let's face it — the use of grades does not truly differentiate performance when a letter grade of an A in one school means something different than an A in another school. However, with the emergence of common core standards, we see more and more schools moving to some type of product criteria, which is preferred by teachers who want grades to communicate actual learning (O'Connor, 2009). Some teams will want to incorporate a process criteria that mixes what a student can do (product) with how they got there (process). In this case, teams can include a measurement of work habits, attitudes, time spent academically engaged, attempts, and other processes. When working with students with disabilities, process can sometimes demonstrate more change and improvement than actual product.

The debate over grades is and likely will always be one of the great debates in education. We have seen how difficult a disagreement about grades can be for co-teaching teams. As an instructional leader, we suggest you work with your co-teachers proactively to help them consider grading and assessment for their shared classroom. The strongest grading systems we have seen embrace a wide range of learners and learning styles and are beneficial not just to the students with disabilities but to all students (Obiakor, Obi, & Algozzine, 2001; Wormeli, 2006). Figure 8-1 provides a list of questions you might want teachers to consider related to grading in the co-taught environment, followed by a box "At-A-Glance: Tips for Supporting Co-teachers in Grading."

Figure 8-1: Questions to Encourage Co-Teachers to Discuss

What do you believe about retakes on tests?

What is your opinion on demonstrating learning mastery versus giving a letter or number grade?

How do you see grades communicating to students and their families?

What do you want grades to communicate? Product? Process? Both?

Are letter grades necessary or can students be better served by rubrics or portfolios? Why or why not?

How does our grading system align with what students are required to know or not know?

What is your policy related to homework?

What is your policy on classwork completion?

Do both teachers view the grading process the same or differently?

How will co-teachers determine the grading for each student in the class?

How will IEP goals and objectives be measured in the co-taught setting?

At-A-Glance: Tips for Supporting Co-Teachers in Grading

1. Before school even starts, make sure your co-teachers have committed to a process for assessment and for grading. Remind them that whatever grading structures they agree upon, they must communicate those structures and any appropriate adaptations (accommodations or modifications) to the students and their families.

2. Suggest that co-teachers provide separate grades for content knowledge and social/behavioral skills for some students. Combining these grades can be dangerous for students who don't truly understand their skill levels; it can create a false sense of understanding of their mastery of content for parents and students.

3. Ask how students will be empowered in the grading and assessment process to share their thoughts on their own progress. Encourage all teachers, but especially those teaching in inclusive classes, to have students self-evaluate each quarter as to how they think they did and to predict what grades they believe they can achieve in the upcoming quarter.

4. Encourage all of your co-teaching teams to be consistent in how they grade and assess. Talk with teachers to find consistent ways to measure student learning so that the communication structure about grades is clear across the school and/or district.

5. Have teachers watch Rick Wormeli's presentation on YouTube of the impact of the zero on standards-based grading (http://www.youtube.com/watch?v=h-QF9Q4gxVM). This should make for a lively discussion!

Data Collection by Administrators

There are numerous ways to collect data and each inclusive school has its own culture (McLeskey & Waldron, 2002a), so one of the first things you need to do is determine what data might be necessary for collection at your site. After creating objectives that are particular to your own setting (class, school, district, county, state), develop questions to help you ascertain if you are meeting your objectives, as well as tools or methods by which you will collect your data.

From their work with Geneseo Central schools in New York, Wischnowski, Salmon, and Eaton (2004) shared the objectives, evaluation questions, and methods they designed to help determine how successful the co-teaching program in that district was. This information is an excellent example of how bringing together a group of teachers, administrators, and outside experts might help accomplish the task of evaluating co-teaching results.

Critical Connections

Want to start a thought-provoking dialogue with teachers & parents about our expectations of students, especially related to homework? Screen the documentary "Race to Nowhere" (www.racetonowhere.com).

It is obviously important for co-teaching to have a positive impact on students if it is to be continued as a service delivery option in schools. Without data, it is not possible to make that statement. So far, the research outcomes on co-teaching are scattered at best. There are those who tout its positive outcomes, those who find it does not result in increased success for students, and those who feel the jury is still out. In our work nationally, we see many teachers, schools, and districts collecting data that is used internally, but we don't see many educators outside of the university level sharing that data nationally. Ultimately, we as a field need data that is disseminated widely for us to learn from one another. Consider the variety of assessments that can be used for data collection and analysis in determining the effectiveness of co-taught programs. Have you worked with your teachers to collect data? Excellent. Have you used that data to build on your successes? Great. Now we need you to share that data. Read on to get more information about becoming a professional dance leader.

For Your Bookshelf

A practical and worthwhile reading for you and your faculty is Rick Wormeli's *Fair Isn't Always Equal: Assessing and Grading in the Differentiated Classroom* (2006).

Chapter 9

Becoming a Dance Pro

Lessons Learned

We have learned so much from working nationally and internationally with numerous schools, districts, regional service centers, and states. In fact, our thanks to all of our amazing educators and collaborators! This book is a testament to the work that is going on across the world in inclusive education. In addition to the tips we have been providing throughout the text thus far, there are additional lessons that we wanted to be sure to highlight as you begin to set your goals for instituting, or institutionalizing, co-teaching as a model of service delivery in your schools. We offer two major lessons at each of the following levels: the classroom level, the school level, the district level, and the state level.

At the Classroom Level

Two of the lessons that have stood out for us at the classroom level are (a) never forget there are students involved, and (b) never forget the importance of clarifying roles. We address each of these here.

Don't forget to prepare the students.

One of the most common mistakes we see leaders making is that they spend lots of money and time preparing teachers for co-teaching but completely forget about preparing the students and their families. Many students with disabilities will be moving from a small self-contained classroom to a larger co-taught setting. In

Plugged In

To learn more about soft skills, check out the document *Teaching Soft Skills Through Workplace Simulations in Classroom Settings* on the web site of the Office of Disability Employment Policy. For more information, go to http://www.dol.gov/odep/documents/TeachingSoftSkills.pdf

addition to double the number of teachers, there also may be double to triple the number of general education peers with whom the students are expected to interact daily and often double the pace, the homework, and overall interactions in the day. In classes at the secondary level especially, peers can be difficult, to put it mildly. Thus, preparing students for the social changes of a co-taught setting is critical.

Being proactive in preparing students also means addressing the "soft skills" many students with disabilities lack. This preparation may include some instruction in areas that their nondisabled peers may pick up innately. For example, students may need to go to their lockers or on errands more often to release anxiety, bring critical supplies to class, work in cooperative groups, or even be reminded about simple tasks such as raising their hands, starting work on their own, or not calling out. These skills should be a constant and consistent goal in the general education setting, but preparing students for the possible stigma, as well as change of expectations, is also important. Leaders can do this by working with teachers to create class sessions devoted to preparing for this change, by involving school psychologists to work with small groups on related social skills for the inclusive class, or by sending information home to parents to make them aware of potential areas of needed reinforcement. A very practical approach to consider is through video modeling. Ogilvie (2011) in *TEACHING Exceptional Children* provides a step-by-step process to using video-modeling for students with autism in the inclusive setting. The box on the following page lists the steps suggested by Ogilvie to create video models. In her article she suggests that the video model of specific social skills be created either by students' peers or by the student himself so he can refer back to the video example on an iPod or iPad to remind him of critical skills he should be exhibiting in the classroom. Ogilvie even suggests that video modeling with peer mentors can create a strong culture for behavioral and social skill change in any setting.

Don't forget to clarify all roles.

When you walk into the co-taught setting, you should not be able to tell who the general educator is and who the special educator is. However, we do not intend for that to mean that both teachers should appear to be doing the same things in the same way. We do value diversity in instruction. Instead, we are hoping you will see a seamless class, wherein both teachers stand ready to meet the needs of any student. We want to see teachers who can dance together in front of students, but who also realize that each member of the team has an area of expertise, allowing each to take

Figure 9-1. Ten Steps to Creating and Using Video Models
Step 1: Identify the targeted behavior
Step 2: Collect baseline data
Step 3: Choose typical peers to help create the videos
Step 4: Secure parent/guardian permission and student consent
Step 5: Prep the peer models
Step 6: Prepare the environment
Step 7: Create the video
Step 8: Intervention
Step 9: Gather data
Step 10: Assess and reflect
Note. Adapted from "Step by Step Social Skills Instruction for Students with Autism Spectrum Disorder Using Video Models and Peer Mentors," by C. Ogilvie, *TEACHING Exceptional Children*, 43(6), pp. 20–26. Copyright 2011 by the Council for Exceptional Children. Adapted with permission.

the spotlight when appropriate or to dance in his or her own place on the stage if that is most beneficial for kids. We want them to be able to blend their dance steps, but not lose their identities. Too often, we see special education teachers going into the inclusive classroom and becoming de facto general education teachers or general education teachers losing their focus on the general education curriculum and becoming de facto special education teachers. Again, go back to our *Essential Question*: How is what these two are doing together substantively different and better for kids than what one of them would do alone? Two teachers are not in the room to lose their individual identities, but to blend their dance steps to create a new dance that is better for the students. If you find teachers losing their identities, help them in the process. How might you do that? Here are some reminders:

- Have teachers complete the S.H.A.R.E worksheet we provided in Chapter 2. Remind them to complete it separately first, then come together to see where they have similarities and where they have differences.

- Have teachers articulate to you (in front of one another) what their personal areas of strength are and what they see as their primary roles in the classroom. Help facilitate that discussion by having them complete strengths-based assessments.

- Using Lisa's *Co-Planning Lesson Book,* have teachers regularly answer the reflection questions throughout the book. Ask them to share with you how they have identified their separate but equal roles in the class.

- Ask teachers to share a copy of one of their co-teaching lesson plans with you. As you discuss it with them, ask questions geared to assess if they each have taken a clear role in its development. Can you ascertain what the value added is of the special educator? Can they?

At the School Level

At the school level, we identified two lessons that resonate most with us. These include (a) the need to provide professional development (PD) for all stakeholders and (b) the need for high expectations and passing grades.

Provide professional development for all.

The first lesson at the school level relates to the need for PD. We say: Train everyone! When we say everyone, we mean everyone from the custodians to the bus drivers to the parents to the secretaries to the cafeteria staff to the substitutes, and of course, to the general and special education teachers. Although not all of these people will need the same level of preparation and not everyone will be invited to participate in our co-teaching dance party, everyone deserves to know what co-teaching is and why it is a school initiative. Educating parents may occur at a Back to School night and would help them understand what you mean when you talk about co-teaching and how having two teachers in some rooms enables increased differentiation, which is helpful for all kids. We even recommend you share with parents the full range of services provided through different service delivery options as described in Chapter One. On the other hand, the custodian may need to know why two teachers' desks are needed in the same room, the secretary may need to know why she has to order two teachers' guides for a class, the instructional technology support staff member may need to know why he has to create a way in which to put two names on a report card, and the cafeteria staff may need to know why it is important to provide more time, support, or alternative strategies for some students when they go through the lunch line. No matter what level of training you provide (from a week-long institute to an hour-long inservice to a simple handout) or what type of training you provide (from one focused on merely introducing inclusion to one devoted to specific co-teaching skills), it is important to communicate with all faculty, staff, parents, students, and stakeholders why this is a valued, valid, and critical initiative for the school.

Expect passing grades and high expectations.

A bottom-line expectation for all teams is that students need to learn, behave, and pass their courses. It's that simple. If they are not, we want to know what supports co-teachers need to make this happen. We have seen special educators who take on the role of assistant and are too afraid to insist upon the adaptations and accommodations to which certain students are entitled. We have seen general education teachers who have lowered their expectations to get students to pass, effectively lowering the bar for everyone in the class. We have seen teams who, rather than actively brainstorming proactive ways to improve instruction and class management, spend their planning time griping about the fact that the students in their classes are failing or misbehaving. Your role as leader is to help teams identify what is going wrong if students are not learning, behaving, or passing. Do teams need PD in classroom management or instructional strategies? Do they need an outside observer to come in and give them feedback? Do they need assistance during co-planning? Adjusting the bar for each individual student should be at the core of co-teaching, but we need that bar to remain appropriately challenging. We want high expectations that students can meet. We want a well-managed classroom that results in student learning and achievement. The purpose of co-teaching is to enable both teachers to dance whatever dance is necessary for student success. Olé!

At the District Level

We are always so encouraged when we are asked to work with entire districts, to include district level administrators, because we feel this is the place for real systemic change to occur. When teachers feel the district is behind an initiative and is working to implement it across multiple schools, there is an increased level of buy-in that occurs naturally. Don't rely on that, though. The two lessons we learned at this level are (a) the need for consistency in service delivery across the grade levels, and (b) the need to interview and retain teachers strategically and with inclusion in mind.

Consistency in service delivery across the grade levels

When one school or one grade level decides to adopt co-teaching, it is exciting. Unfortunately, however, without a strategic plan in place, it may be an island that is unsustainable. In fact, as much as we are supporters of co-teaching, we have found that sporadic co-teaching often results in a disservice to the student. Imagine a student who has found great success in a general education co-taught class in sixth grade at the elementary school, only to move to the seventh grade at the middle school and be put in a self-contained class because there is no co-teaching available. Likewise, consider the student who struggles in third grade but succeeds because of the support of co-teachers, only to be placed in a general education fourth grade class with no additional supports; this is a failure waiting to happen. Strong districts have district-wide support for co-teaching that ensures all schools provide similar supports and inclusive structures from Grades K–12 so that students do not have to move in and out of service delivery types unless that is what they need. Work to ensure there is sufficient conversation about the service delivery options for students during articulation meetings between schools and levels.

Interviewing/Retaining for Success

New hires, retirees, and substitutes, oh my! As part of the leadership plan to develop a professional dance team across the district, you can't forget that a dancer may sustain injuries, another may become bored with dancing, yet another might move out of the area, and your best dancer may be promoted to lead her own dance studio. The list could go on and on. You need a system created that is not dependent on an individual. We find that strong schools and districts do everything they can to make sure their teachers are happy and supported, but they don't do that haphazardly; they have a plan. If any member of the dance team leaves (in this case, an individual trained in co-teaching), the replacement is merely not left up to a human resources officer.

Part of your strategy at the district level needs to be to create clear roles for each co-teacher on your professional dance team (e.g., one knows high level mathematics while another is your lead co-teacher for fifth grade in the district). With these clear roles in place, if a fifth grade co-teacher retires then you are not just hiring a new special education teacher, you are specifically looking for a special education teacher who can co-teach across fifth grade. That way, although you may have an excellent special education candidate interview, when you realize her primary experience has been teaching students with severe autism in a self-contained kindergarten class, you can help your team discuss the fact that hiring her may take your co-teaching back a few years as she begins to learn the new dance steps. It may also help you realize that although she is not right for the school looking to replace a co-teacher, she would be perfect for another one of your schools. This plan will also help you in creating questions for the job interview process at the district level. These questions may include:

1. It is the expectation that you will co-teach in this role. What have been your experiences co-teaching thus far?

2. What would you do if the person you were co-teaching with did something you disagreed with in front of the students?

3. Can you give us an example of a co-taught lesson that uses multiple approaches you would be excited about teaching and addresses the fifth grade curriculum and common core standards?

Proactive and thoughtful leaders do an equally good job preparing potential understudies for their roles in the co-teaching dance. We know that students in urban settings are taught by substitutes as many as 50 days a year. Thus, substitutes should be taught what the role of a co-teacher is and how they should interact in a co-taught setting, whether they are substituting for the special or general educator. We have each had the experience of walking into a class that we co-taught, only to find the general education teacher absent and a substitute present who told us we "wouldn't be needed today." How galling. In these situations, it is clear that the substitutes really did not understand the role of co-teaching or the fact that the special educator is a credentialed teacher with much to share. Consider including a basic inservice on what co-teaching is and is not when substitutes are trained in school or district policy. For example, Wendy was hired to train all the teachers and administrators in one district in Wyoming on co-teaching practices. The same district had the insight to realize that they had a large pool of substitutes they used regularly, so that group was brought in for half a day of training as well. Think about it. If the philosophy and practice at your school or district is to serve students' needs through a co-teaching model, then being proactive in this manner is critical for the success of the model.

Large Scale Change

Change is especially difficult to accomplish at the large scale level. We applaud those who have done this so effectively. The two major lessons we learned in working with state departments and state-wide organizations who have created change so effectively are (a) to ensure buy-in, and (b) to emphasize that change takes time.

Ensure buy-in.

As we previously stated, buy-in is a major component for large scale change. Although it would be lovely if everyone already bought into the need for co-teaching support, we know that is unlikely. Remember what we said about changing hearts and changing behaviors? Large-scale PD needs to be provided in both areas. Attention needs to be given to those individual schools or school leaders whose hearts are not yet where we want them to be; they don't understand why this is a dance we are dancing or they simply don't want to dance. On the other hand, those who are ready to build their co-teaching skills also need to be provided with PD that will enable them to do so. In this type of large system change, the need for a consistent message cannot be emphasized enough. It is critical that one message is articulated and that the same message is repeated over and over and over again. Educators who hear different definitions, messages, and agendas are far less likely to buy in to the change; they see the writing on the wall indicating that there is little real vision in this area. On the other hand, if the message is consistent, it becomes evident that real thought has gone into ensuring a strong roll-out.

We have both worked with state departments who have done this type of major initiative roll-out. They have created statewide brochures and newsletters, provided statewide inservices for administrators and teachers, posted statewide videos and webinars, offered statewide on-site consultations, and opened a statewide web site for questions and answers. Lisa has had ongoing relationships across the state of Arkansas where an initiative led by Rose Merry Kirkpatrick created a structure at two levels (see Pearl et al., 2012 for a detailed summary of the process and outcomes of this partnership), co-teaching partnership and building level leadership. Each district involved in the Arkansas Department of Education Co-Teaching Project is asked to create a building level leadership team that at a minimum consists of a special educator, general educator and an administrator who meet monthly through webinars to lead the dance across the building. In addition, co-teaching partnerships were brought to a central location for consistent training in each of the nine years of the project. After the training, monthly follow-up webinars were provided to troubleshoot many of the issues we have presented in this book. These webinars included topics such as finding time to plan, using various types of co-teaching, grading, and assessing learners, to name a few. The result of this large-scale systemic training was that it created a consistent structure across schools, districts, and the state and was not a one-shot approach. Initially much of this work was led by a team from the University of Central Florida, but over time the team at the Arkansas Department of Education was as knowledgeable as the team from University of Central Florida; today this initiative is primarily led by the state level team. So the next time you start to consider having district-wide PD, consider how you might create technological follow-up and a systemic foundation for your leading of the co-teaching dance. This type of commitment naturally takes coordination, vision, and support. It takes a clear plan of action. The action plan needs to include the time, resources, staffing, and coordination

---

For Your Bookshelf

In order to support consistency in message, training modules on co-teaching are available so that new teachers can hear the same message year after year. Some available modules are available at:

www.corwin.com
www.2TeachLLC.com
www.nprinc.com
www.cec.sped.org
www.ber.org
www.csun.edu/ctl
www.forumoneducation.org

that will be needed. If this universal plan for change is identified proactively, there is far more likelihood that the project's implementation will be seamless and that the message to teachers and schools will be crystal clear.

Change takes time.

In terms of time, we cannot reiterate enough the importance of respecting the fact that this will not be a quick-fix. To make a change that is broad enough to cover an entire district, county, or state, yet also strong enough to maintain across various institutions, settings, and leaders, you will need to plan for at least a five year implementation project. The field of business emphasizes that real change takes at least five years, so we would never assume that systematic change at the district or state level would take any less time. Unfortunately, in the areas in which we see co-teaching come and go, we can also pinpoint leaders who were quick to change their support or priorities to move on to the next best thing. That said, we have also been encouraged by the districts and states we have seen that had leaders patient enough and committed enough to allow for the five to seven years it took to institutionalize change. Having a strong vision, philosophy, mission statement, and shared goals and benchmark steps were crucial in rolling out these large multiyear initiatives. Doing so, however, also let the teachers and other school personnel realize that there was true commitment to the program and that co-teaching wasn't going to just go away.

Institutionalizing Co-Teaching Through Goal-Setting

As you are developing a core group of teams that work together effectively, make sure you have a long term plan for success. A frequent concern in schools is that the development of effective teams and more inclusive practices happens at either a snail's pace, as a hodgepodge model, or at one grade level and not another. We often talk about students being failed by schools due to fragmentation of service delivery (Dieker, 2001). From our experience with schools, districts, and states, building a synergistic service model around co-teaching takes between three and five years. Unfortunately, we have often witnessed forward movement happening when, without warning, the leadership changes or a core group of teachers changes and then, quickly, so does the initiative.

The districts we have found that have the best long-term changes are the ones that create a 5-year plan from the start that is built around students, teachers and leadership. This type of plan needs to be vetted to such a level that the plan can stand the test of time, teachers, administrators, or even budget cuts. Without such a plan, we have seen schools where co-teaching is being utilized one day and is gone the next, or schools in which co-teaching was practiced ten years ago, given up, and has now returned. This type of constant change in focus for teachers results in a loss of real investment into the philosophy, PD, and vision, not to mention disjointed instruction and service delivery for the students, which is even more distressing.

As a leader, you also know about the bottom line. New initiatives are always more costly in the beginning as you invest in relationships, planning, and PD. A stop/start model costs far more resources than one where you are able to do capacity building and institutionalization. Most important, the lack of a 5-year plan and commitment to change can negatively impact your most important resource, your students.

Creating an Individualized Education Program for Co-Teaching

Critical Connections

Create a Co-Teaching IEP for Success:

Step 1. Identify your present level of co-teaching performance.

Step 2. Identify your short and long term goals.

Step 3. Identify the actions you will take to meet those goals and who will be involved.

Step 4. Celebrate your successes.

Teachers don't always know where administrators or schools are going in their planning. What they see at the classroom level are initiatives coming in and going out on a cyclical basis. There often seems little rhyme or reason to the decisions made. If you are truly interested in adopting co-teaching as more than just a fly-by-night approach, think about creating an IEP for success (Murawski & Spencer, 2011). By that we mean identify your present level of performance related to co-teaching, identify your goals, and then set your benchmarks for meeting those goals. We recommend at a minimum you set a 1-, 3-, and 5-year goal as to how you will move your co-teaching forward. Craft these goals in collaboration with the faculty, staff, and parents. Having their input in creating goals will make them more manageable and ensure more buy-in.

Forgive us as we repeat ourselves, but we feel it is worthwhile: It often takes five years for change to occur (Pearl et al., 2012). That doesn't, however, mean that you should merely wait five years to see what your outcomes are. Each year, clear goals and objectives have to be evaluated, created, and adjusted as needed. For example, if a new obstacle enters the situation (e.g., new curriculum is adopted), your plan may need to be tweaked in terms of benchmarks or specific practice, but your overall goals need to stay the same. If each year your goals for co-teaching change based on the latest budget or leadership, the forward movement will be disjointed and sporadic, ensuring nothing but fragmentation in the outcomes for all students. How do you ensure the goals remain the same? Create a poster of the 1-year, 3-year, and 5-year goals and post it in the teacher work room or somewhere else equally accessible. Keep it visible and have regular check-in sessions with your leadership team to ascertain if you are still on the right path.

In Appendix 9 ("Sample Goals for Action Plans"), we provide some examples of goals that districts have set related to co-teaching and inclusion. Feel free to share these with your teachers and other administrators as a model for what you might create, but also encourage them to identify their own goals based on personal needs. McLeskey and Waldron (2002b) remind us that every site has its own culture for inclusion and that culture needs to be respected, especially as it relates to professional developments. We have provided you some blank forms in Appendix 10 that can be used to support your co-teaching planning for the next five years.

Creating Co-Teaching Leadership Teams

A solid model we have seen that works in capacity building is the creation of leadership teams, inclusion/co-teaching facilitators, or exemplar teams. Leadership teams would be those teams that represent various groups who have a stake in co-teaching. These teams meet to discuss progress, concerns, successes, and next steps. Inclusion/co-teaching facilitators are usually teachers who work across the district as coaches for co-teaching. They can provide specific skill instruction, model co-teaching lessons, and serve as counselors for those teams who are struggling with communication, personality differences, or differences of opinion. Exemplar teams are those teams who have a particular expertise that other teachers can learn from related to co-teaching. These teams do not need to be perfect at all aspects of co-teaching; you may have one team you refer others to in order to observe their obvious rapport with one another in front of the kids, another team you refer for those who want to see strong differentiation practices, another team who has the different instructional approaches down to a science, and yet another team who has worked out various models of co-assessing. Create a list of exemplar teams from a variety of grade levels from whom others can model their practice. We suggest that these teams also be ones who are extremely positive about co-teaching, have high student achievement scores, and have great success with students accepted within the fabric of the class. As you may imagine, it is much less impressive to go in and observe a team who engages in witty banter with one another if you know that, despite their repartee, 90% of their students are failing.

Money is always an issue with new initiatives so the need to institutionalize and build capacity is critical. Outside consultants can be costly and, if used, it is important that there is consistency

> ### Need to Know
>
> *Leadership teams* can include administrators, general and special education teachers, counselors, parents, and even students.
>
> *Inclusion/ co-teaching facilitators* are usually teachers who work across the district as coaches for co-teaching.
>
> *Exemplar teams* are those teams who have a particular expertise that other teachers can learn from related to co-teaching.

in message across the school, district, county, and state. Different messages can impede success as they cause confusion among participants. Although districts always seem to prefer the expert from afar, at some point you will need to move away from outside consultants and begin to rely on your own school and district leaders. The best PD can many times come from within your staff; encourage successful teams to share the nuts and bolts of an effective co-teaching relationship. When possible, have general educators take a strong lead in sharing their benefits and positive outcomes; you don't want there to be a misconception that co-teaching is a special education practice. It's a teaching practice.

Mentoring Others

Have you ever heard the old saying, "Don't hide your light under a bushel?" This holds true in education too. Too often, when things are going wrong, we complain, vent, share, and ask for support. Unfortunately, when things are going right, we don't share as publically. Encourage your co-teaching teams to regularly talk to other teachers about the benefits of co-teaching, to talk to parents about how well the students are doing behaviorally and socially as well as academically, and to you as the administrator about what aspects of co-teaching are going well and need to be continued and supported. A positive climate is so important; it impacts everyone, from the classroom to the school and all the way up to the district, state, and national levels.

We constantly read research or articles about the problems with co-teaching, yet we know of numerous districts across the country that are hitting it out of the park when it comes to teachers working together and impacting the learning and behavioral needs of students in their school. A great leader knows the perfect balance between bragging about his or her success and being humble at the same time. Not letting others know what is working denies the students at the next grade level, in the next school, or in the next district the chance to learn from your successes. If co-teaching is working in one class, at one grade level, or across the entire building or district, shout it from the rooftop and offer to perform for others.

One of our primary suggestions for PD for any school that wants to begin a co-teaching model is to have them visit another successful team, school, or district. There are plenty of benefits to the school being observed. Research is clear that the more teachers perform and mentor others, the more they hone their own craft. Gimbert, Desai, and Kerka (2010) recommend building a community of practice in a district. A community includes parents, teachers, students, administrators, and community members. A community of practice means that those members have (a) mutual engagement in joint activities, (b) shared practices that are constantly under review and revision, and (c) a commitment to development of all members (Murrell, 2001). Think about how that would look for your school or district.

Now might be the time to invite school board members or someone from the state department who is not sure about funding for co-teaching to see your classrooms. As states move to increased alignment of curriculum with common core standards, consider taking your strengths in schoolwide co-teaching and offering to help another school with the agreement that, in return, they will help you with a weakness. Or if you are still struggling in co-teaching, find a neighboring school or district that has been successful and, again, find an area of strength you have and barter shared PD. In these economic times, the trading off of PD between two districts would certainly be well received and cost effective. Both of us have been astonished how often we are asked to come in and speak at neighboring schools or districts, when we would have been just as happy presenting to both together and having them share the cost and begin a true collaboration and dialogue. We need schools and districts ready and willing to perform their best dance for others, while also being willing to get feedback on performance areas that need to be strengthened. No better panel exists to judge your performance than collaborative colleagues who are there to also give and receive feedback.

Think about it. Why not be the one who offers to become the expert site for a national network on co-teaching, or for co-teaching in mathematics, or specifically for how your co-teachers include students with severe and challenging behaviors? We are in a precarious time in education. We hear threats to shut down the Department of Education, the media can't seem to write enough about what we are failing to do, and the budget continues to spiral downward. The only way to change the course is to be ready to share what is working. Someone has to be first in order to get the first followers. Step one: As you are developing your strong co-teaching model, let your teachers know that in three to five years, your goal will be to the open the doors of your school, district, state, and leaders for all to visit and see how co-teaching looks when it works.

Disseminating Success

As university professors and educational consultants, our job not only involves teaching others but also disseminating our findings through publications, research, and presentations. We love our jobs! Unfortunately, however, we frequently hear from teachers or administrators that they have collected powerful data on their success with co-teaching and that they haven't had time to do anything with it. We have seen time and again successful co-teaching; we have been impressed by its positive and powerful impact on student achievement and behavior, and the increased collaboration between faculty at schools engaging in effective co-teaching. Based on what we have seen and the plethora of data we know is out there, we implore you to help your schools disseminate this information. The field is clamoring for research on the impact of co-teaching (Magiera & Zigmond, 2005; Murawski & Swanson, 2001; Scruggs et al., 2007). Teacher educators need to be prepared to model co-teaching, teach about co-teaching, and support co-teaching if they want it to occur in PreK–12 classes (Cramer, Liston, Nevin, & Thousand, 2010). Now is the ideal time to support your budding writers, your action researchers, and your strong presenters. Collect data on your experiences and then disseminate, disseminate, disseminate!

Partnering With Universities

Building and evaluating co-teaching programs

Concerned that your teachers or administrators don't have the skills or experience to create a research proposal, collect data, or disseminate the findings? Fear not. We have an idea for that as well. Both of us work closely with schools in the areas around our own universities and we enjoy the win-win of being able to support their efforts while also getting to observe them as our own research subjects. These types of partnerships don't have to be just for research collection; they are also helpful in the development aspect of your program.

Wischnowski and colleagues (2004) provide an excellent example of how schools can partner with universities to improve and build their co-teaching programs. In their example, Geneseo Central School District in New York approached two local university professors and asked for their assistance in designing an evaluation of their co-teaching program. These administrators had the foresight to (a) develop both formative and summative evaluations for the co-teaching component of their special education reform effort, and (b) seek outside expertise to ensure its successful development and implementation. The goals and objectives of the Geneseo Central School Co-Teaching Program are worth reviewing. Though they kept their focus very clearly on student success and outcomes, the impressions of teachers and parents were still included in the evaluation.

Co-teaching with student teachers

Yet another growing area for co-teaching is in the area of student teaching. St. Cloud State University in Minnesota has been collecting strong data that indicate that when student teachers and master teachers co-teach, the results for students are stronger than when either the student teacher or the master teacher teaches solo (Bacharach, Heck, & Dahlberg, 2008). Think what a powerful statement that is! Teachers often complain that they don't want student teachers in their room because (a) they are more work, (b) instructional time is lost as the student teacher is getting up to speed, and (c) students are provided with substandard instruction by the novice teacher. These are absolutely valid concerns. Co-teaching with the master teacher, however, takes care of all of those possible issues.

Obviously, there is the issue of parity when student and master teachers co-teach. It is critical that university faculty and school administrators meet with all participants and clearly delineate the experience and what the expectations and roles will be. Master teachers need to be willing to accept the student teacher's fresh content knowledge and ideas for current best practices as that person's expertise, essentially what she is bringing to the table in this relationship. They can then approach the relationship as equals (as much as that is possible). The value added of additional educators in the room, even budding ones, is significant to schools that are consistently barraged with issues related to high student-teacher ratios, behavior management, and the need for differentiation. When student teachers co-teach with master teachers, the benefits extend to the K–12 students and school as well as the university partner. In fact, Wendy recently received a grant to replicate a pilot study she did on student teachers co-teaching in schools; her preliminary results mirror the St. Cloud findings. Administrators have actually approached the university and asked for more opportunities to have student teachers because the results included PD for student and master teachers, smaller student-teacher ratios in the classroom, improved desire by veteran teachers to have a student teacher, and most importantly, increased academic achievement by students. Think about how this will impact teacher willingness to co-teach once these students (or teacher candidates) become teachers themselves! The In Action box 9-1 shares an example of how this might play out in a co-taught, student taught classroom.

In Action 9-1

Ms. Judy Novice was excited to start her student teaching and even more excited about co-teaching with her mentor teacher, Mr. Ben Masters. For the very first class together, Ms. Novice began a slow and smooth transition into the class by taking the support role. During this time, Mr. Masters took the lead on instruction as they used the One Teach-One Support approach to co-instruction. After a few days, Ms. Novice was ready to take a small group to do some preteaching of the upcoming assignment as Mr. Masters continued to work with the large group using the alternative teaching approach. Next, both teachers collaborated to co-plan a lesson that they were then able to teach, providing students the same content in the same way through parallel teaching. This approach enabled Ms. Novice to try teaching half of the class, but she felt so much more comfortable knowing she would be able to debrief what worked and what didn't with Mr. Masters after the lesson. After having experience teaching a lesson that was co-planned with Mr. Masters, it was finally time for Ms. Novice to plan a lesson on her own. Again starting small, Ms. Novice was able to teach her lesson through the station teaching approach, which allowed Mr. Masters to work with a group of students concurrently. As the teachers became more comfortable with each other and the students, they were ready to share the stage and use team teaching. The kids loved watching Ms. Novice and Mr. Masters role-play at the front of the room. As Ms. Novice gained confidence, she was able to conduct a whole group lesson herself, with Mr. Masters again present to lend support using the One Teach-One Support approach. Voilá! At the end of just a few weeks, Ms. Novice and Mr. Masters had used all approaches, supported all of their students, and now both have more experience with co-teaching as well. Watching the team in action, the school principal and the university supervisor looked at each other and smiled; this was truly a positive and collaborative experience for all!

Chapter 10

Performing for Others

Creating a Movement

The technology, entertainment, and design (TED) talks (www.tedtalks.com) are some of our favorite resources for motivational speakers and insightful, powerful messages. One of these messages related to creating a movement was presented by Derek Sivers. If you are able, we strongly recommend you watch this video clip yourself on YouTube before you continue reading. It's at http://www.youtube.com/watch?v=fW8amMCVAJQ or you can Google "shirtless dancing guy." Honest.

If you were not able to take a quick reading break, get online, and watch it, you will need to engage in some powerful visualization. Picture this: a shirtless man begins randomly doing dance moves (we promise we didn't just make this up to go with our metaphor!) as he stands on a hill populated with other people who are lounging, picnicking, or just chatting. His dance moves are erratic, wild, and a bit strange, but he is clearly not concerned about appearance. He is having the time of his life, all by himself. A few minutes after others have started gawking at him, another guy just runs up and begins to join him. They both begin to let loose with their free dancing, occasionally even joining hands or doing a combined movement. Shortly thereafter, another three people join and begin to dance. Within minutes, a throng of people has amassed on the hill and is dancing their hearts out, some with shirts, others without (we will add that all without shirts are guys). And, as Mr. Sivers reports, "A movement was created."

We share this beautiful moment with you (and if you watched it, we know you shared a good laugh too) not just because we wanted to do a visualization activity, but because we wanted to share the power in the message. This video from TED Talks reminds us that a movement is not created by the leader, but by nurturing the first followers. The shirtless dancing guy was just that: one guy. When someone followed him, however, he became a leader. Rather than seeking all the glory himself or requiring a certain dance, he embraced his first follower as an equal and immediately welcomed him. He let his follower mirror his steps, but also create his own. The same happened for the next followers. The message in this example is how important it is to nurture those who begin to follow if you want to create a sustainable movement.

If you have done what we have suggested in chapters 1 through 9, then you should have a team of folks following your lead, and you will have created a movement toward co-teaching. If you are into your third through fifth year, we hope this movement is sustained and you are now ready to expand your movement. This chapter is about how to become the example others watch and want to follow. However, keep in mind that, just as described in the shirtless dancing guy video, you have to humbly and proudly accept that it is not your leading others that makes change happen, but instead it is the nurturing of those who are brave enough to follow. We need to acknowledge and reward their willingness to go out on a limb to do something different in order to positively impact the learning of students.

Continuing Your Research

We decided to end this book by providing you with what we see as ways to shout your success from the mountaintops and to share what works with others. We know that sometimes the most helpful support is the personal kind, so we've asked some of our favorite collaborators (and those who have successfully led the co-teaching dance at their schools, districts, or states) if we could include their names and e-mails. They are here for your support should you be interested in contacting them, and we see them as master dance leaders. We offer you a list of some of our favorite resources (articles, books, and web sites) related to effective co-teaching; naturally we have highlighted our own work as we are hoping we've whet your appetite to read more that we have written and referenced throughout this text. Last but not least, we have provided you with some reflective questions to ask yourself and your teachers as you progress throughout the year, as well as a tool to ensure you are keeping a strengths-based perspective during this process. We see this chapter not as the end of your process, but as the beginning of a movement that is spreading as effective practice across the country. The successful continuation of this movement will be partly based upon your ability to lead, and at the same time, your ability to nurture those who follow. That combination is what makes for powerful change.

Let the dance begin!

Figure 10-1. 20 Ways to Share Your Professional Dance Team With Society
1. Write an article for the local paper about your success.
2. Work within your district or with a local university to do a research study for publication.
3. Nominate your co-teachers for local, state, regional, and national awards.
4. Have parents, students, and teachers involved with co-teaching provide a presentation at a local, regional, state, or national conference.
5. Make certain that your superiors know about the success by inviting board members and superintendents to observe co-taught classes. Remember they may need to be educated about the dance too.
6. Provide local, regional, state, and national legislators with stories and testimonies (in one page or less) of your success.
7. Videotape your teachers (with permission, of course) and send to local and regional TV stations to highlight your effective practices.
8. Make a blog about your co-teaching successes. Share the URL with parents, teachers, and other administrators.
9. Create a podcast showcasing your success and explaining what actions you took to create this dynamic team.
10. Make a YouTube video on your effective co-teaching practices. (For a fun video based on our *50 Ways to Keep Your Co-Teacher* article (Murawski & Dieker, 2008), go to www.youtube.com/watch?v=WVffcgVuANM. These creative co-teachers must have had a blast designing and filming this video.)
11. Create a co-teaching wiki or post information on an Edmodo.com community board with your best ideas and invite neighboring schools or districts to add content.
12. Host a mini-co-teaching conference. Have sessions on co-teaching in mathematics, co-teaching for behavior, co-teaching social skills, and so on. Invite other schools to attend and co-present.
13. Ask your co-teachers to create a co-teaching newsletter filled with best practices, tips for addressing common issues, and differentiation strategies. Encourage them to use Microsoft Publisher or other programs that they can then teach to their own students.
14. Have 5 minutes at each faculty meeting devoted to "inclusive successes" that can be shared by any teacher or team.

15. Create a threaded discussion on your school's web site where parents and teachers can dialogue about ideas for inclusive practices and co-teaching. Do have it go through you prior to posting, just to be sure all comments are appropriate for publication. Edmodo (www.edmodo.com) is a wonderful, secure network that would be perfect for this type of sharing of information, ideas, and questions.

16. Invite parents and community members to come in and co-teach specific units or lessons about areas in which they are experts. Demonstrate for them how the focus on collaboration and co-teaching can be used for all students, not just those with disabilities. Using the station teaching approach would enable a visitor to work with a small group of students at a time to present a limited amount of content, while the co-teachers could each be working with their own small groups concurrently.

17. Let local universities and community colleges know that you are engaged in co-teaching practices and that you are willing to open your doors to those who want to engage in research, provided you get copies of all data and findings. In addition, let them know you are willing to partner with them for student teachers, with the caveat that those student teachers will co-teach with your master teachers. That way, students have the best of all worlds, and so do the teachers.

18. Invite individuals from the State Department of Education (e.g., Special Education or Curriculum & Instruction) to come down and visit your school. Show them areas in which you are willing to be a mentor or visit site for schools that need support in an area in which you excel.

19. Get T-shirts or magnets made that say, "Two heads are better than one – Co-Teach!" or "Collaborating for Student Success at [XXX] Elementary School." Whatever works for you and gets the message across.

20. Most importantly, we recommend that you, as the administrator, be willing to "walk the walk." Once every 9 weeks or so, offer to go in and co-teach with a different team. Take the time to co-plan and have a meaningful role in the lesson. Each time you co-teach, try a different co-teaching approach so teachers can see that you are willing to experience what they have to do on a daily basis. Showing that you too are willing to dance will make you a credible, empathetic, and hopefully more effective dance leader.

Figure 10-2. 10 Mentors for Co-Teaching Leadership
These individuals have worked closely with co-teachers and have successfully led co-teaching practices at their respective sites. We appreciate their willingness to have us provide their names and contact information so they can share their own experiences with you and help you as you progress.
1. Lynn Boyer, Ph.D., Superintendent, West Virginia Schools for the Deaf and the Blind, (also former WV State Director of Exceptional Services) Romney, WV 26757; lboyer@access.k12.wv.us
2. Julie Fabrocini, Ed.D., Senior Program Officer, U.S. Program Education, Bill & Melinda Gates Foundation (also former Executive Director of CHIME Institute), Seattle, WA 98102; jfab@chimeinstitute.org
3. Stephanie Free, Executive Director of Schools, San Angelo, TX 76904; sfree@saisd.org
4. Jolly Piersall, Alisa Stovall, & Matt Johnson, Indiana IEP Resource Center, Terre Haute, IN, 47809; jolly.piersall@indstate.edu; indianaieprc.org
5. Michelle Murphy, LRE Resource Teacher, Baltimore County Public Schools, Towson, MD 20214; mmurphy@bcps.org
6. Lisa Dawes, Director of Student Services, Oconomowoc Area School District, Oconomowoc, WI 53066; lisa.dawes@mail.oasd.k12.wi.us
7. Rose Merry Kirkpatrick, Arkansas Co-Teaching Project, Sherwood, AR 72120; rosemerry.kirkpatrick@arkansas.gov
8. David P. Riley, Ph.D., Executive Director Urban Special Education Leadership Collaborative, Education Development Center, Inc., Waltham, MA 02453; driley@edc.org
9. Jane M Quenneville, Ed.D., Director of Special Education Alexandria Public Schools, Alexandria, VA 22311; jane.quenneville@acps.k12.va.us
10. Cara Lucas-Richt, Blair Community Schools, Blair, NE 68008; cara.lucas-rich@blairschools.org

Note. LRE = least restrictive environment.

For Your Bookshelf

Wendy and Lisa's Top 20 Personal Co-Teaching Publications

(in chronological order, and authored by us, of course)

1. Dieker, L. (1998). Co-teaching: A process to support students with special needs in social studies. *Social Studies Review, 37*(2), 62–65.

2. Murawski, W. W., & Swanson, H. L. (2001). A meta-analysis of co-teaching research: Where are the data? *Remedial and Special Education, 22*(5), 258–267.

3. Dieker, L. A. (2001). What are the characteristics of "effective" middle and high school co-taught teams for students with disabilities? *Preventing School Failure, 46*(1), 14–25.

4. Hughes, C. E., & Murawski, W. W. (2001). Lessons from another field: Applying co-teaching strategies to gifted education. *Gifted Child Quarterly, 45*(3), 195–204.

5. Dieker, L. A. (2002). *The co-teaching lesson plan book* (3rd ed.). Whitefish Bay, WI: Knowledge by Design, Inc.

6. Murawski, W. W. (2002). Including co-teaching in a teacher preparation program: A vital addition. *Academic Exchange Quarterly, 6*(2), 113–116.

7. Dieker, L. A., & Murawski, W. (2003). Co-teaching at the secondary level: Unique issues, current trends, and suggestions for success. *The High School Journal, 86*(4), 1–13.

8. Murawski, W. W., & Dieker, L. A. (2004). Tips and strategies for co-teaching at the secondary level. *TEACHING Exceptional Children, 36*(5), 52–58.

9. Murawski, W. W. (2005). Addressing diverse needs through co-teaching: Take baby steps! *Kappa Delta Pi Record, 41*(2), 77–82.

10. Dieker, L. A. (2006). *7 effective strategies for middle and high school inclusion [DVD]*. National Professional Port Chester, NY: Resources, Inc.

11. Murawski, W. W. (2006). Student outcomes in co-taught secondary English classes: How can we improve? *Reading and Writing Quarterly, 22*(3), 227–247.

12. Murawski, W., & Dieker, L. A. (2008). 50 ways to keep your co-teacher. *TEACHING Exceptional Children, 40*(4), 40–48.

13. Dieker, L. A., & Hines, R. A. (2008). *Winning strategies for inclusive classrooms [DVD]*. Port Chester, NY: National Professional Resources, Inc.

14. Murawski, W. W., & Hughes, C. E. (2009). Response to intervention, collaboration, and co-teaching: A necessary combination for successful systemic change. *Preventing School Failure, 53*(4), 67–77.

For Your Bookshelf (cont'd)

15. Murawski, W. W. (2009). *Collaborative teaching in secondary schools: Making the Co-Teaching marriage work!* Thousand Oaks, CA: Corwin Press; and Murawski, W.W. (2010). *Collaborative Teaching in Elementary Schools: Making the Co-Teaching Marriage Work!* Thousand Oaks, CA: Corwin Press.

16. Little, M., & Dieker, L. A. (2009). Co-teaching: Challenges and solutions for administrators. *Principal Leadership, 9*(8), 42–46.

17. Murawski, W. W., & Lochner, W. (2011). Observing co-teaching: What to ask for, look for, and listen for. *Intervention in School and Clinic, 46*(3), 174–183.

18. Murawski, W. W., & Spencer, S. A. (2011). *Collaborate, communicate, and differentiate! How to increase student learning in today's diverse classrooms.* Thousand Oaks, CA: Corwin Press.

19. Murawski, W. W. (2012). 10 tips for using co-planning time more efficiently. *TEACHING Exceptional Children, 44*(4), 8–15.

20. Dieker, L. A. (2013). *Demystifying secondary inclusion (2nd ed.).* Port Chester, NY: National Professional Resources, Inc.

Plugged In

Five Web Sites to Support Your Dancers
1. http://www.2teachllc.com/
2. http://www.coteach.com/
3. http://www.specialconnections.ku.edu/
4. http://arksped.k12.ar.us/sections/spd/CoTeachingProject.htm
5. http://www.cec.sped.org

Figure 10-3. 10 Excellent Co-Teaching Publications in the Field

1. Scruggs, T. E., Mastropieri, M. A., & McDuffie, K. A. (2007). Co-teaching in inclusive classrooms: A metasynthesis of qualitative research. *Exceptional Children, 73*(4), 392–416.

2. Mastropieri, M. A., Scruggs, T. E., Graetz, J., Norland, J., Gardizi, W., & McDuffie, K. (2005). Case studies in co-teaching in the content areas: Successes, failures, and challenges. *Intervention in School and Clinic, 40*(5), 260–270.

3. Wilson, G. (2005). This doesn't look familiar! A supervisor's guide for observing co-teachers. *Intervention in School and Clinic, 40*(5), 271–275.

4. Magiera, K., Smith, C., Zigmond, N., & Gebauer, K. (2005). Benefits of co-teaching in secondary mathematics classes. *TEACHING Exceptional Children, 37*(3), 20–24.

5. Villa, R. A., Thousand, J. S., Nevin, A. I., & Liston, A. (2005). Successful inclusive practices in middle and secondary schools. *American Secondary Education, 33*(3), 33–50.

6. McDuffie, K., Mastropieri, M. A., & Scruggs, T. E. (2009). Differential effects of peer tutoring in co-taught and non-co-taught classes: results for content learning and student-teacher interactions. *Exceptional Children, 75,* 493–510.

7. Kim, A. H., Woodruff, A. L., Klein, C., & Vaughn, S. (2006). Facilitating co-teaching for literacy in general education classrooms through technology: Focus on students with learning disabilities. *Reading and Writing Quarterly, 22*(3), 269–291.

8. Sileo, J. M., & van Garderen, D. (2010). Creating optimal opportunities to learn mathematics: Blending co-teaching structures with research-based practices. *TEACHING Exceptional Children, 42*(3), 14–21.

9. Conderman, G., & Hedin, L. (2012). Purposeful assessment practices for co-teachers. *TEACHING Exceptional Children, 44*(4), 19–27.

10. Nevin, A. I., Cramer, E., Voigt, J., & Salazar, L. (2008). Instructional modifications, adaptations, and accommodations of coteachers who loop: A descriptive case study. *Teacher Education and Special Education, 31*(4), 283–297.

Figure 10-4: Reflective Framework
1. What is your greatest strength related to co-teaching?
2. What will you do to maintain this level of strength?
3. If you were asked to have visitors tomorrow from the U.S. Department of Education, what would you want them to see as your best examples of co-teaching?
4. Although you may be highly successful at this point, what areas related to co-teaching in your school do you think still need to be tweaked, and how might you support strengthening these areas?
5. What neighboring school, district, or state is doing well in the areas you mentioned in question number 4?
6. How might you expand your collaborative dance to include neighboring partners so that you might grow and learn together? (It's time for a dance party!)

Figure 10-5: Keeping a Strengths-Based Perspective		
As a leader, write down the name of each key staff member who reports to you. Identify the strengths of those staff members related to the co-teaching dance. Now decide how you could showcase their strengths and use them to leverage any potential areas of weakness.		
Name	**Strengths**	**Ways to Maximize Strengths in Promoting Co-Teaching and Inclusive Practices**

Dieker, 2008

References

American Youth Policy Forum and Center on Education Policy. (2002). *Twenty-five years of educating children with disabilities: The good news and the work ahead.* Washington, DC: Author.

Austin, V. L. (2001). Teachers' beliefs about co-teaching. *Remedial and Special Education, 22*(4), 245-255.

Bacharach, N., Heck, T., & Dahlberg, K. (2008). Co-teaching in higher education. *Journal of College Teaching & Learning, 5*(3), 9–16.

Bahamonde, B., & Friend, M. (1999). Teaching English language learners: A proposal for effective service delivery through collaboration and co-teaching. *Journal of Educational and Psychological Consultation, 10*(1), 1–24.

Bell, B., & Cowie, B. (2001). The characteristics of formative assessment in science education. *Science Education, 85*(5), 536–553.

Beninghof, A. (2003). *Co-teaching that works: Effective strategies for working together in today's inclusive classrooms.* Bellevue, WA: Bureau of Education and Research.

Bill and Melinda Gates Foundation. (2011). Learning about teaching: Initial findings from the measures of effective teaching project. Seattle, WA: Author.

Black, P., & Harrison, C. (2001). Feedback in questioning and marking: The science teacher's role in formative assessment. *School Science Review, 82*(301), 55–61.

Boe, E. E., Cook, L. H., Bobbitt, S. A., & Terhanian, G. (1998). The shortage of fully certified teachers in special and general education. *Teacher Education and Special Education, 21*(1), 1–21.

Brownell, M. T., Smith, S., Crockett, J., & Griffin, C. (2012). *Inclusive instruction: Evidence-based practices for teaching students with disabilities.* New York, NY: Guilford Press.

CBS News. (2012, July 16). Teacher of the Year on secrets to her success. [Eye on Education]. Retrieved from http://www.cbsnews.com/video/watch/?id=7415046n&tag=mncol;lst;2.

Center for Applied Special Technology. (2007). *Universal design for learning.* Wakefield, MA: Author. Retrieved from *http://www.advocacyinstitute.org/UDL*

Chapman, C. & Hart-Hyatt, C. (2011). *Critical Conversations in Co-Teaching: A Problem Solving Approach.* Bloomington, IN: Solution Tree Press.

Conderman, G., & Hedin, L. (2012). Purposeful assessment practices for co-teachers. *TEACHING Exceptional Children, 44*(4), 19–22.

Cook, L., & Friend, M. P. (1995). Co-teaching: Guidelines for creating effective practices. *Focus on Exceptional Children, 28*(3), 1–16.

Coombs-Richardson, R., Al-Juraid, S., & Stuker, J. (2000). *Supporting general educators' inclusive practices in mathematics and science education.* (Report No. ED449609). Retrieved from http://www.eric.ed.gov/ERICWebPortal/search/detailmini.jsp?_nfpb=true&_&ERICExtSearch_SearchValue_0=ED449609&ERICExtSearch_SearchType_0=no&accno=ED449609

Co-Teaching Solutions System (CTSS). (2009). Teachers' Toolbox and Observation System. Shepherdstown, WV: Author.

Cozart, A. C., Cudahy, D., Ndunda, M., & Van Sickle, M. (2003). The challenges of co-teaching within a multicultural context. *Multicultural Education, 10*, 43–45.

Cramer, E., Liston, A., Nevin, A., & Thousand, J. (2010). Co-teaching in urban secondary school districts to meet the needs of all teachers and learners: Implications for teacher education reform. *International Journal of Whole Schooling, 6*(2), 59–76.

Cramer, E., & Nevin, A. (2006). A mixed methodology analysis of co-teacher assessments. *Teacher Education and Special Education, 29*(4), 261–274.

Damore, S. J., & Murray, C. (2009). Urban elementary school teachers' perspectives regarding collaborative teaching practices. *Remedial and Special Education, 30*(4), 234–244.

Davis, K. E., Dieker, L., Pearl, C., & Kirkpatrick, R. M. (2012). Planning in the middle: Co-Planning between general and special education. *Journal of Educational and Psychological Consultation, 22*(3), DOI:10.1080/10474412.2012.706561

Davies, S. (Ed.). (2007). *Team around the child: Working together in early childhood education.* Wagga Wagga, New South Wales, Australia: Kurrajong Early Intervention Service.

Dieker, L. (1998). Co-teaching: A process to support students with special needs in social studies. *Social Studies Review, 37*(2), 62–65.

Dieker, L. A. (2001). What are the characteristics of "effective" middle and high school co-taught teams for students with disabilities? *Preventing School Failure, 46*(1), 14–23.

Dieker, L. A. (2002). *The co-teaching lesson plan book* (3ʳᵈ ed.). Whitefish Bay, WI: Knowledge by Design, Inc.

Dieker, L. A. (2006). *Demystifying secondary inclusion.* Port Chester, NY: National Professional Resources, Inc.

Dieker, L. A. (2013). *Demystifying secondary inclusion (2ⁿᵈ ed.).* Port Chester, NY: National Professional Resources, Inc.

Dieker, L. A., & Berg, C. A. (2002). Can secondary math, science and special educators really work together? *Teacher Education and Special Education, 25*, 92–99.

Dieker, L. A., & Hines, R. (2012). *Strategies for to teaching all content effectively in the inclusive secondary classroom.* Upper Saddle River, NJ: Pearson.

Dieker, L. A., & Murawski, W. W. (2003). Co-teaching at the secondary level: Unique issues, current trends, and suggestions for success. *The High School Journal, 86*(4), 1–13.

Downing, J. A. (2008). *Including students with severe and multiple disabilities in typical classrooms: Practical strategies for teachers (3ʳᵈ ed.).* Baltimore, MD: Paul H. Brookes.

Duschl, R. A. (2003). Assessment of inquiry. In J. M. Atkin & J. E. Coffey (Eds.), *Everyday assessment in the science classroom* (pp. 41–59). Arlington, VA: National Science Teachers Association Press.

Emery, D. W., & Vandenberg, B. (2010). Special education teacher burnout and act. *International Journal of Special Education, 25*(3), 119–131.

Fabrocini, J.H. (2012). *Impact of school-wide collaboration systems: Planning for differentiation.* Unpublished dissertation. Northridge, CA: California State University Northridge. (http://hdl.handle.net/10211.2/881).

Friend, M., & Cook, L. (1995). Inclusion: What it takes to make it work, why it sometimes fails, and how teachers really feel about it. In K. L. Freiberg (Ed.). Educating exceptional children: Annual editions (8th Ed.) (pp. 6-9). Guilford, CT: McGraw Hill/Dushkin.

Friend, M., & Cook, L. (2000). *Interactions: Collaboration skills for school professionals* (3ʳᵈ ed.). White Plains, NY: Longman.

Friend, M., & Cook, L. (2007). *Interactions: Collaboration skills for school professionals* (5th ed.). Boston, MA: Allyn & Bacon.

Garmston, R. J. (2005). How to turn conflict into an effective learning process. *Journal of Staff Development, 26*(3), 65–66.

Gerlach, K. (2010). *Let's team up! A checklist for paraeducators, teachers, and principals (7ᵗʰ ed.).* Washington, DC: NEA Checklist Series.

Ghorpade, J. (2000). Managing five paradoxes of 360-degree feedback. *The Academy of Management Executive, 14*(1), 140–150.

Giangreco, M., & Broer, S. (2005). Questionable utilization of paraprofessionals in inclusive schools: Are we addressing symptoms or causes? *Focus on Autism and Other Developmental Disabilities, 20*(1), 10–26.

Gimbert, B., Desai, S., & Kerka, S. (2010). The big picture: Focusing urban teacher education on the community. *Phi Delta Kappan, 92*(2), 36–39.

Graesser, A., & Person, N. (1994). Question asking during tutoring. *American Educational Research Journal, 31*(1), 104–137.

Guskey, T. (2011). Five obstacles to grading reform. *Educational Leadership, 69*(3), 16–21.

Hang, Q., & Rabren, K. (2009). An examination of co-teaching: Perspectives and efficacy indicators. *Remedial and Special Education, 30*(5), 259–268.

Hughes, C. E., & Murawski, W. W. (2001). Lessons from another field: Applying co-teaching strategies to gifted education. *Gifted Child Quarterly, 45*(3), 195–204.

Individuals With Disabilities Education Improvement Act, 20 U.S.C. § 1400 *et seq.* (2006).

Jensen, B. and Reichl, J. (2011). *Better teacher appraisal and feedback: Improving performance.* Melbourne, Australia: Grattan Institute.

Keefe, E. B., & Moore, V. (2004). The challenge of co-teaching in inclusive classrooms at the high school level: What the teachers told us. *American Secondary Education, 32*(3), 77–88.

Kim, A. H., Woodruff, A. L., Klein, C., & Vaughn, S. (2006). Facilitating co-teaching for literacy in general education classrooms through technology: Focus on students with learning disabilities. *Reading and Writing Quarterly, 22*(3), 269–291.

Kimmel, H., Deek, F., Farrell, M., & O'Shea, M. (1999). Meeting the needs of diverse student populations: Comprehensive professional development in science, math, and technology for teachers of students with disabilities. *School Science and Mathematics, 99*(5), 241–249.

King, G., Strachan, D., Tucker, M., Duwyn, B., Desserud, S., & Shillington, M. (2009). The application of a transdisciplinary model for early intervention services. *Infants and Young Children, 22*(3), 211–223.

Klein, J. T., Grossenbacher-Mansuy, W., Häberli, R., Bill, A., Scholz, R. W., & Welti, M. (2001). *Transdisciplinarity: Joint problem solving among science, technology, and society.* Basel, Germany: Birkhäuser Verlag.

Kohler-Evans, P. A. (2006). Co-teaching: How to make this marriage work in front of the kids. *Education, 127*(2), 260–264.

Levine, M. (2002). *A mind at a time.* New York, NY: Simon & Schuster.

Limbrick, P. (2005). Team around the child: Principles and practice. In B. Carpenter & J. Egerton (Eds.), *Early childhood intervention. International perspectives, national initiatives and regional practice.* West Midlands, England: SEN Regional Partnership.

Little, M., & Dieker, L. A. (2009). Co-teaching: Challenges and solutions for administrators. *Principal Leadership, 9*(8), 42–46.

Luckner, J. (1999). An examination of the two co-teaching classrooms. *American Annals of the Deaf, 144*(1), 24–34.

Magiera, K., Smith, C., Zigmond, N., & Gebauer, K. (2005). Benefits of co-teaching in secondary mathematics classes. *TEACHING Exceptional Children, 37*(3), 20–24.

Magiera, K., & Zigmond, N. (2005). Co-teaching in middle school classrooms under routine conditions: Does the instructional experience differ for students with disabilities in co-taught and solo-taught classes? *Learning Disabilities Research & Practice, 20*(2), 79–85.

Magiera, K. A., & Simmons, R. J. (2005). *The Magiera-Simmons quality indicator model of co-teaching.* Fredonia, NY: Excelsior Educational Service.

Mahoney, M. (1997). Small victories in an inclusive classroom. *Educational Leadership, 54*(7), 59–62.

Mastropieri, M. A., Scruggs, T. E., Graetz, J., Norland, J., Gardizi, W., & McDuffie, K. (2005). Case studies in co-teaching in the content areas: Successes, failures, and challenges. *Intervention in School and Clinic, 40*(5), 260–270.

McDuffie, K., Mastropieri, M. A., & Scruggs, T. E. (2009). Differential effects of peer tutoring in co-taught and non-co-taught classes: Results for content learning and student-teacher interactions. *Exceptional Children, 75,* 493–510.

McLeskey, J., & Waldron, N. (2002a). Inclusion and school change: Teacher perceptions regarding curricular and instructional adaptations. *Teacher Education and Special Education, 25*(1), 41–54.

McLeskey, J., & Waldron, N. (2002b). Professional development and inclusive schools: Reflections on effective practice. *Teacher Educator, 37*(3), 159–172.

McLeskey, J., & Waldron, N. (2002c). School change and inclusive schools: Lessons learned from practice. *Phi Delta Kappan, 84*(1), 65–72.

Melamed, J. C., & Reiman, J. W. (2000). Collaboration and conflict resolution in education. *High School Magazine, 7*(7), 16–20.

Miller, A., Valasky, W., & Molloy, P. (1998). Learning together: The evolution of an inclusive class. *Active Learner: A Foxfire Journal for Teachers, 3*(2), 14–16.

Moorehead, T. M. (2010). *Role and interactions of general and special education teachers in secondary co-taught teams.* (Unpublished doctoral dissertation). University of Central Florida, Orlando, FL.

Morvant, M., Gersten, R., Gilman, J., Keating, T., & Blake, G. (1995). Attrition/retention of urban special education teachers: Multi-faceted research and strategic action planning. Final performance report, Volume 1. (ERIC Document Reproduction Service No. ED338154).

Murawski, W. W. (2002a). Demystifying co-teaching. *CARS+ Newsletter, 22(3),* 19.

Murawski, W. W. (2002b). Including co-teaching in a teacher preparation program: A vital addition. *Academic Exchange Quarterly, 6(2),* 113-116.

Murawski, W. W. (2003). *Co-teaching in the inclusive classroom.* Bellevue, WA: Bureau of Education & Research.

Murawski, W. W. (2005). Addressing diverse needs through co-teaching: Take baby steps! *Kappa Delta Pi Record, 41(2),* 77–82.

Murawski, W. W. (2006). Student outcomes in co-taught secondary English classes: How can we improve? *Reading and Writing Quarterly, 22(3),* 227–247.

Murawski, W. W. (2008, September). Five keys to co-teaching in inclusive classrooms. *The School Administrator, 27.*

Murawski, W. W. (2009). *Collaborative teaching in secondary schools: Making the co-teaching marriage work!* Thousand Oaks, CA: Corwin Press.

Murawski, W. W. (2010). *Collaborative teaching in elementary schools: Making the co-teaching marriage work!* Thousand Oaks, CA: Corwin Press.

Murawski, W. W. (2012). 10 tips for using co-planning time more efficiently. *TEACHING Exceptional Children, 44(4),* 8–15

Murawski, W. W., Boyer, L., Melchiorre, B., & Atwill, K. (2009, April). *What is happening on co-taught classes? One state knows!* Presentation at American Educational Research Association (AERA), San Diego, CA.

Murawski, W. W., & Dieker, L. A. (2004). Tips and strategies for co-teaching at the secondary level. *TEACHING Exceptional Children, 36(5),* 52–58.

Murawski, W. W., & Dieker, L. A. (2008). 50 ways to keep your co-teacher. *TEACHING Exceptional Children, 40(4),* 40–48.

Murawski, W. W., & Hughes, C. E. (2009). Response to intervention, collaboration, and co-teaching: A necessary combination for successful systemic change. *Preventing School Failure, 53(4),* 67–77.

Murawski, W. W., & Lochner, W. (2011). Observing co-teaching: What to ask for, look for, and listen for. *Intervention in School and Clinic, 46(3),* 174–183.

Murawski, W. W., & Spencer, S. A. (2011). *Collaborate, communicate, and differentiate! How to increase student learning in today's diverse classrooms.* Thousand Oaks, CA: Corwin Press.

Murawski, W. W., & Swanson, H. L. (2001). A meta-analysis of co-teaching research: Where are the data? *Remedial and Special Education, 22*(5), 258–267.

Murrell, P. C. (2001). *The community teacher: A new framework for effective urban teaching.* New York, NY: Teachers College Press.

Nevin, A., Cramer, E., Voigt, J., & Salazar, L. (2008). Instructional modifications, adaptations, and accommodations of coteachers who loop: A descriptive case study. *Teacher Education and Special Education, 31*(4), 283–297.

No Child Left Behind Act of 2001, 20 U.S.C. § 6301 *et seq.* (2006).

Noonan, M. J., McCormick, L., & Heck, R. H. (2003). The co-teacher relationship scale: Applications for professional development. *Education and Training in Developmental Disabilities, 38*(1), 113–120.

Obiakor, F., Obi, S., & Algozzine, B. (2001). Shifting assessment and intervention paradigms for urban learners. *Western Journal of Black Studies, 25*(1), 61–71.

O'Connor, B. (2009). *How to grade for learning, K–12* (3rd ed.). Thousand Oaks, CA: Corwin.

Ogilvie, C. (2011). Step by step social skills instruction for students with autism spectrum disorder using video models and peer mentors. *TEACHING Exceptional Children, 43*(6), 20–26.

Pearl, C., Dieker, L. A., & Kirkpatrick, R. (2012). A five year retrospective on the Arkansas department of education co-teaching project. *Journal of Staff Development, 38*(4), 571-587. DOI: 10.1080/19415257.2012.668858

Pierce, K., & Fields, L. (2003). How to defuse difficult conversations. *Principal Leadership* (Middle School ed.), *4*, 36–39.

Ploessl, D., Rock, M., Schoenfeld, N., & Blanks, B. (2010). On the same page: Practical techniques to enhance co-teaching interactions. *Intervention in School and Clinic, 45*(3), 158–168.

Rainforth, B. (1997). Analysis of physical therapy practice acts: Implications for role release in educational environments. *Pediatric Physical Therapy, 9*(2), 54–61.

Rea, P. J., McLaughlin, V. L., & Walther-Thomas, C. (2002). Outcomes for students with learning disabilities in inclusive and pull-out programs. *Exceptional Children, 72*, 203–222.

Rice, D., & Zigmond, N. (1999). Co-teaching in secondary schools: Teacher reports of developments in Australia and American classrooms. *Resources in Education.* (ERIC Document Reproduction Services No. ED432558).

Rice, N., Drame, E., Owens, L., & Frattura, E. M. (2007). Co-instructing at the secondary level: Strategies for success. *TEACHING Exceptional Children, 39*(6), 12–18.

Rose, D., & Meyer, A. (2000a). Universal design for individual differences. *Educational Leadership, 58*(3), 39–43.

Rose, D., & Meyer, A. (2000b). Universal design for learning: Associate editor column. *Journal of Special Education Technology, 15*(1), 67–70.

Rothstein-Fisch, C., & Trumbull, E. (2008). *Managing diverse classrooms: How to build on students' cultural strengths.* Alexandria, VA: Association for Supervision and Curriculum Development.

Ruiz-Primo, M. A., & Furtak, E. M. (2006). Informal formative assessment and scientific inquiry: Exploring teachers' practices and student learning. *Educational Assessment, 11*(3), 205–235.

Scruggs, T., Mastropieri, M., & McDuffie, K. A. (2007). Co-teaching in inclusive classrooms: A metasynthesis of qualitative research. *Exceptional Children, 73,* 392–416.

Shephard, K. (2006). Supporting all students: The role of school principals in expanding general education capacity using response to intervention teams. *Journal of Special Education Leadership, 19*(2), 30–38.

Sileo, J., & van Garderen, D. (2010). Creating optimal opportunities to learn mathematics: Blending co-teaching structures with research-based practices. *TEACHING Exceptional Children, 42*(3), 14–21.

Simmons, R. J., & Magiera, K. (2007). Evaluation of co-teaching in three high schools within one school district: How do you know when you are TRULY co-teaching? *TEACHING Exceptional Children Plus, 3*(3) Article 4.

Thousand, J., Villa, R., & Nevin, A. (Eds.). (2002). *Creativity and collaborative learning: The practical guide to empowering students, teachers, and families* (2nd ed.). Baltimore, MD: Brookes Publishing Co.

Thousand, J. S., Villa, R. A., & Nevin, A. I. (2006). The many faces of collaborative planning and teaching. *Theory Into Practice, 45*(3), 239-247.

Tomlinson, C. A. (1999). *The differentiated classroom: Responding to the needs of all learners.* Alexandria, VA: ASCD.

Trumbull, E., Rothstein-Fisch, C., Greenfield, P. M., & Quiroz, B. (2001). *Bridging cultures between home and school: A guide for teachers.* Mahwah, NJ: Taylor & Frances.

U.S. Department of Education, Office of Special Education and Rehabilitative Services, Office of Special Education Programs [OSEP] (2009). *28th Annual Report to Congress on the Implementation of the Individuals With Disabilities Education Act, 2006 (vol. 1).* Washington, D.C.

Villa, R., Thousand, J., & Nevin, A. (2004). *A guide to co-teaching: Practical tips for facilitating student learning.* Thousand Oaks, CA: Corwin Press.

Villa, R., Thousand, J., & Nevin, A. (2008). *A guide to co-teaching: Practical tips for facilitating student learning (2ⁿᵈ ed.)*. Thousand Oaks, CA: Corwin Press.

Villa, R. A., Thousand, J. S., Nevin, A. I., & Liston, A. (2005). Successful inclusive practices in middle and secondary schools. *American Secondary Education Journal, 33*(3), 33–50.

Walther-Thomas, C. (1997). Co-teaching experiences: The benefits and problems that teachers and principals report over time. *Journal of Learning Disabilities, 30*(4), 395–407.

Wasburn-Moses, L. (2006). Preparing special educators for secondary positions. *Action in Teacher Education, 27*(3), 26-39.

Weichel, W. A. (2001). An analysis of student outcomes on co-taught settings in comparison to other special education service delivery options for students with learning disabilities. *Dissertation Abstracts International, 62*(07), 2386. (UMI No. 3021407)

Weiss, M. P., & Lloyd, J. (2003). Conditions for co-teaching: Lessons from a case study. *Teacher Education and Special Education, 26*(1), 27–41.

Weiss, M. P., & Lloyd, J. W. (2002). Congruence between roles and actions of secondary special educators in co-taught and special education settings. *The Journal of Special Education, 36*(2), 58–68.

Welch, M. (2000). Descriptive analysis of team teaching in two elementary classrooms: A formative experimental approach. *Remedial and Special Education, 21*(6), 366–376.

Whitaker, S. D. (2000). Mentoring beginning special education teachers and the relationship to attrition. *Exceptional Children, 66*, 546–566.

Wiggins, G., & McTighe, J. (2005). *Understanding by design* (2ⁿᵈ ed.). Alexandria, VA: Association for Supervision and Curriculum Development.

Wilson, G. (2005). This doesn't look familiar! A supervisor's guide for observing co-teachers. *Intervention in School and Clinic, 40*(5), 271–275.

Wischnowski, M. W., Salmon, S. J., & Eaton, K. (2004). Evaluating co-teaching as a means for successful inclusion of students with disabilities in a rural district. *Rural Special Education Quarterly, 23*(3), 3–14.

Wormeli, R. (2006). *Fair isn't always equal: Assessing and grading in the differentiated classroom*. Portland, ME: Stenhouse Publishing.

Zigmond, N., & Baker, J. (1996). Full inclusion for students with learning disabilities: Too much of a good thing? *Theory Into Practice, 35*(1), 26–34.

Zigmond, N., & Magiera, K. (2001). A focus on co-teaching. *Current Practice Alerts.* (6).

Appendices

Appendix 1: Worksheet for Scheduling Co-Teaching: CODES
Student Name: Name of the student receiving special education services
Disability Type: Reason for services Write school-based acronym that would provide the most information, such as RD (reading disability), LD (learning disability), ED (emotional disability), AUT (autism), ASP (Asperger syndrome), HH (hard of hearing), VI (visually impaired), ADHD (attention deficit hyperactivity disorder), OI (orthopedically impaired), etc.
For the following subject areas, select the best support type for that student: 1 = General education class, monitor only 2 = General education class, some in-class or facilitated support (paraprofessional or teacher) 3 = General education class, daily in-class support (co-teaching) 4 = Special education class, but general education curriculum (higher academic level) 5 = Special education class, maximum support needed (lowest academic level; possibly alternative curriculum)
Content areas include: Language arts (can identify reading vs. writing), **math, social studies, science, and other** (can identify PE, art, music, recess, lunch, etc.) **"Weighting" Student Support** helps determine who to cluster where and with whom to reduce teacher burnout and increase parity among classes
For each student in a general education class, select the amount of support needed 1 = Minimal support; similar to typical general education student 2 = Moderate support; identify whether "A" academic or "B" behavioral 3 = Strong support; identify whether "A" academic or "B" behavioral * Try to cluster students to maximize opportunities to support effectively without overwhelming one class or teacher with too many "3s" or "Bs" in the same class.

Note. Adapted from *Collaborative Teaching in Elementary Schools: Making the Co-Teaching Marriage Work!* (p.190), by W. W. Murawski, 2010, Thousand Oaks, CA: Corwin Press. Adapted with permission.

Worksheet for Scheduling Collaboration and Co-Teaching

Name of school:

Administrator in charge of scheduling:

Number of general education teachers in school:

Number of special education teachers in school:

Number of paraprofessionals in school: :

Number of other support providers in school:

Number of general education students:

Number of special education students:

Complete the following table for each grade:

SE Student Name:	Disability Type:	"Weight" (1, 2, 3) (A, B)	Language Arts (1–5)	Math (1–5)	Social studies (1–5)	Science (1–5)	Other (1–5)

For the following subject areas, select the best support type for that student:

1 = General education class, monitor only
2 = General education class, in-class or facilitated support
3 = General education class, daily in-class support (co-teaching)
4 = Special education class, preparing for general education
5 = Special education class, maximum support needed

Note. Adapted from *Collaborative Teaching in Elementary Schools: Making the Co-Teaching Marriage Work!* (p.191), by W. W. Murawski, Thousand Oaks, CA: Corwin Press. Copyright 2009 by Corwin Press. Adapted with permission.

Worksheet for Scheduling Collaboration and Co-Teaching								
SE Student Name:	Disability Type:	"Weight" (1, 2, 3) (A, B)	Language Arts (1–5)	Math (1–5)	Social studies (1–5)	Science (1–5)	Other (1–5)	Other (1–5)

Note. Adapted from *Collaborative Teaching in Secondary Schools: Making the Co-Teaching Marriage Work!* p.192, W. W. Murawski, 2009, Thousand Oaks, CA: Corwin Press. Copyright 2009 by Corwin Press. Adapted with permission.

Appendix 2: Co-Teaching Lesson Plan

General Educator: _____

Special Service Provider: _____

Co-Teaching Lesson Plan

Subject Area: _____

Grade level:: _____

Content Standard: _____

Lesson Objective: _____

Essential Questions: _____

Key Vocabulary:: _____

Pre-Assessment: _____

Materials: _____

Appendix 2: Co-Teaching Lesson Plan *(cont'd)*

General Educator: _____

Special Service Provider: _____

Lesson	Co-Teaching Approach (can select more than one)	Time	General Education Teacher	Special Service Provider	Considerations (may include adaptations, differentiation, accommodations, and student-specific needs)
Beginning: (may include: Opening; Warm Up; Review; Anticipatory Set)	❏ One Teach-One Support ❏ Parallel ❏ Alternative ❏ Station ❏ Team				
Middle: (may include: Instruction; Checking for Understanding; Independent or Group Practice)	❏ One Teach-One Support ❏ Parallel ❏ Alternative ❏ Station ❏ Team				
End: (may include: Closing, Assessments, Extension of the Lesson)	❏ One Teach-One Support ❏ Parallel ❏ Alternative ❏ Station ❏ Team				

Format compliments of: www.2TeachLLC.com

Appendix 3: Co-Teaching Lesson Plan

General Educator: __Rick G.__   Special Service Provider: __Marcia R.__

Step 1: The first section is done during the WHAT part of the lesson (approximately 5 minutes)

Co-Teaching Lesson Plan

Subject Area: __Language Arts__
Grade level: __8th__
Content Standard: __LA.1.2.1. The student understands the common features of a variety of literary forms__
Lesson Objective: __Students will be able to identify & create a haiku and acrostic poem.__
Essential Questions: __Do poems have to rhyme? Big Idea: There are different types of poems.__
Key Vocabulary: __Poem, haiku, acrostic, rhyme__
Pre-Assessment: __Day before – Do Know-Want to Know-Learned (KWL) about poems to see who already knows acrostics/haiku__
Materials: __Model poems of haiku & acrostics; Ticket out the door w/Cloze; large print poems for Brenda; Braille version of poems for Quinn; put poems & homework on web site; powerpoints & handouts; magnetic letters & magnetic cookie sheets; dry erase boards & markers__

Step 2: The middle section is done during the HOW part of the lesson (approximately 7 to 15 minutes)

Step 3: The considerations section is last and is done during the WHO part of the lesson (approximately 5 minutes)

Lesson	Co-Teaching Approach (can select more than one)	Time	General Education Teacher	Special Service Provider	Considerations (may include adaptations, differentiation, accommodations, and student-specific needs)
Beginning: (may include: Opening; Warm Up; Review; Anticipatory Set)	☑ One Teach, One Support ☐ Parallel ☐ Alternative ☐ Station ☐ Team	10 minutes	Take roll Get materials prepared Pass out cards with "Haiku" or "Acrostic" so students know which group to go to first Talk to students who need proactive reminders	Read 2 poems (haiku, acrostic) Lead students in oral discussion of similarities & differences between poems	Remind Javon & Tim about transition & group behavior; Remind Ryan how to ask for help & sit near friend during group work; Have copies of poems available for students to look at (on overhead, Braille, large copy); Ask higher order questions of Oliver
Middle: (may include: Instruction; Checking for Understanding; Independent or Group Practice)	☐ One Teach, One Support ☑ Parallel ☐ Alternative ☐ Station ☐ Team	32 minutes (15 per group + 2 minute switch)	Take ½ class and teach haiku using powerpoint and examples (good for visual/auditory learners); students can use dry erase boards or paper as desired Switch after 15 minutes and repeat	Take ½ class and teach acrostics using magnetic letters & cookie sheets (good for kinesthetic learners) Switch after 15 min and repeat	Let Kiernan write poems about Bionicles to keep interest; Challenge Oliver by asking him to rhyme his acrostics & use multiple adjectives in haiku; Have example poems available for all students to see; Use mnemonics for remembering differences; have dry erase markers and boards available for students like Amy who prefer to write and erase multiple times before committing to paper
End: (may include: Closing, Assessments, Extension of the Lesson)	☐ One Teach, One Support ☐ Parallel ☑ Alternative ☐ Station ☐ Team	10 minutes	Have large group do "Ticket out the Door" by completing poems using Cloze procedure Remind students to write down home-work from board into their planners	Work with small group of students who need more time or assistance in understanding Haiku & Acrostics Remind students to write down homework from board into their planners	During transition to large group, both teachers can decide who needs extra time in small group. Small group can meet at back table. Have multiple copies of Cloze versions of Ticket out the Door to ensure differentiation; Allow Oliver, Kiernan, Amy, and others who want to create poems from scratch if desired; Adapt level of homework based on individual need

Note. Reprinted with permission from "10 Tips for Using Co-Planning Time More Efficiently," by W. W. Murawski, 2012, *TEACHING Exceptional Children, 44*(4), pp. 8–15. Copyright 2012 by the Council for Exceptional Children. Adapted with permission from http://www.2TeachLLC.com/lessons.html. A free co-teaching lesson plan template is available at www.2TeachLLC.com

	Appendix 4: Co-Teaching Checklist: Self-Assessment			

Check your role: ❑ **General Educator** ❑ **Special Service Provider**

	Co-Teaching Items	0 – We don't do it 1 – We try 2 – We have it down		
		0	**1**	**2**
Two or more professionals working together in the same physical space.	0 = only one adult; two adults not communicating at all; class always divided into two rooms 1 = two adults in same room but very little communication or collaborative work 2 = two adults in same room; both engaged in class & each other (even if not perfectly)			
Class environment demonstrates parity and collaboration (both names on board, sharing materials, and space).	0 = no demonstration of parity/collaboration; room appears to belong to one teacher only 1 = some attempt at parity; both adults share materials and space 2 = clear parity; both names on board/report card; two desks or shared space; obvious feeling from teachers that it is "our room"			
Both teachers begin and end class together and remain in the room the entire time.	0 = one adult is absent or late; adults may leave room for time w/o reason related to this class 1 = one adult may be late but for remaining time, they work together 2 = both adults begin and end together, and are with students the entire time *Note – if adults have planned to use a regrouping approach (e.g., "parallel") and one adult takes a group of students out of the room (e.g., to the library), that is perfectly acceptable			

Note. Reprinted with permission from www.coteachsolutions.com, Co-Teaching Solutions Systems, Shepherdstown, WV.

	Co-Teaching Items	0 – We don't do it 1 – We try 2 – We have it down		
		0	**1**	**2**
During instruction, both teachers assist students with and without disabilities.	0 = adults are not helping students or are only helping "their own" students 1 = there is some helping of various students but adults primarily stay with a few of "their own" 2 = it is clear that both adults are willing to help all students & that students are used to this			
The class moves smoothly with evidence of co-planning and communication between co-teachers.	0 = all planning appears to have been done by one adult and/or no planning is evident 1 = minimal planning and communication is evident; most appears to be done by one adult 2 = it is clear that both adults had input in lesson and communicate regularly as class progresses			
Differentiated strategies, to include technology, are used to meet the range of learning needs.	0 = there is no evidence of differentiation of instruction or use of technology in the classroom 1 = there is minimal differentiation and use of technology; most differentiation appears to be focused on groups rather than individuals 2 = it is clear that adults considered individual student needs and differentiation and use of technology is evident where needed to			

Appendix 4: Co-Teaching Checklist: Self-Assessment *(cont'd)*

Check your role: ❏ General Educator   ❏ Special Service Provider

Note. Reprinted with permission from www.coteachsolutions.com, Co-Teaching Solutions Systems, Shepherdstown, WV.

	Appendix 4: Co-Teaching Checklist: Self-Assessment *(cont'd)*			
	Check your role: ❏ General Educator ❏ Special Service Provider			
	Co-Teaching Items	0 – We don't do it 1 – We try 2 – We have it down		
		0	**1**	**2**
A variety of instructional approaches (5 co-teaching approaches) are used, include regrouping students.	0 = Students remain in large class setting; Adults rely solely on One Teach/One Support or Team 1 = Adults regroup students (using Alternative, Parallel, or Station) at least once 2 = Adults use more than one of the 5 approaches (Friend & Cook's One Teach/One Support, Team, Parallel, Station & Alternative); at least one of the approaches involves regrouping students * note – if teachers have been observed using other approaches in the past and only one approach is observed today (e.g., Stations), it is acceptable to recall previous observations and give a 2 for using a variety of approaches as adults have demonstrated competency			
Both teachers engage in appropriate behavior management strategies as needed and are consistent in their approach to behavior management.	0 = there is no obvious plan for behavior management, nor do adults appear to communicate about how they are approaching class management; possibly inappropriate class management 1 = behavior management strategies are utilized but there is very little clear evidence of how adults have communicated about their use 2 = it is evident that adults have discussed how they will approach classroom/behavior management and adults are consistent in their approach; clear communication between adults			

	Appendix 4: Co-Teaching Checklist: SelfF-Assessment *(cont'd)*			
Check your role: ❏ General Educator ❏ Special Service Provider				
	Co-Teaching Items	0 – We don't do it 1 – We try 2 – We have it down		
		0	**1**	**2**
It is difficult to tell the special educator from the general educator.	0 = Observer could easily determine who was the general/ special educator by their language/roles/ lack of parity. 1 = Observer could tell who was the general/special educator but there was a clear attempt at parity between the teachers. 2 = Observer would not be able to tell who was the general/special educator as parity was evident and adults shared the roles and responsibilities in the classroom.			
It is difficult to tell the special education students from the general education students.	0 = Observer could easily determine who were the general/special education students by their lack of integration (e.g., students at back or separated from class). 1 = Observer could tell who were the general/special education students but there was a clear attempt at inclusion of students for most activities. 2 = Observer would not be able to tell who were the general/special education students as parity was evident and adults shared the responsibilities for working with all students.			

Note. Reprinted with permission from www.coteachsolutions.com, Co-Teaching Solutions Systems, Shepherdstown, WV.

Appendix 5: Co-Teaching Checklist: Comparison Chart			
Co-Teaching Items	**0 – We don't do it** **1 – We try** **2 – We have it down**		
	General Educator Scores	**Special Educator Scores**	**Observer Scores**
Two or more professionals working together in the same physical space.			
Class environment demonstrates parity and collaboration (both names on board, sharing materials, and space).			
Both teachers begin and end class together and remain in the room the entire time.			
During instruction, both teachers assist students with and without disabilities.			
The class moves smoothly with evidence of co-planning and communication between co-teachers.			
Differentiated strategies, to include technology, are used to meet the range of learning needs.			
A variety of instructional approaches (5 co-teaching approaches) are used, include regrouping students.			
Both teachers engage in appropriate behavior management strategies as needed and are consistent in their approach to behavior management.			
It is difficult to tell the special educator from the general educator.			
It is difficult to tell the special education students from the general education students.			
NOTES:			

Note. Reprinted with permission from www.coteachsolutions.com, Co-Teaching Solutions Systems, Shepherdstown, WV.

Appendix 6: Co-Teaching Checklist: Look Fors					
General Educator: _____ Special Service Provider: _____					
Observer: _____ Date/Time: _____					

	LOOK FOR ITEMS	**0 – Didn't See It** **1 – Saw an Attempt** **2 – Saw It Done Well**			
			0	**1**	**2**
Two or more professionals working together in the same physical space.	0 = only one adult; two adults not communicating at all; class always divided into two rooms 1 = two adults in same room but very little communication or collaborative work 2 = two adults in same room; both engaged in class & each other (even if not perfectly)				
Class environment demonstrates parity and collaboration (both names on board, sharing materials, and space).	0 = no demonstration of parity/collaboration; room appears to belong to one teacher only 1 = some attempt at parity; both adults share materials and space 2 = clear parity; both names on board/report card; two desks or shared space; obvious feeling from teachers that it is "our room"				
Both teachers begin and end class together and remain in the room the entire time.	0 = one adult is absent or late; adults may leave room for time w/o reason related to this class 1 = one adult may be late but for remaining time, they work together 2 = both adults begin and end together, and are with students the entire time *note – if adults have planned to use a regrouping approach (e.g., "parallel") and one adult takes a group of students out of the room (e.g., to the library), that is perfectly acceptable				

	LOOK FOR ITEMS	0 – Didn't See It 1 – Saw an Attempt 2 – Saw It Done Well		
Appendix 6: Co-Teaching Checklist: Look Fors *(cont'd)*				
		0	1	2
During instruction, both teachers assist students with and without disabilities.	0 = adults are not helping students or are only helping "their own" students 1 = there is some helping of various students but adults primarily stay with a few of "their own" 2 = it is clear that both adults are willing to help all students & that students are used to this			
The class moves smoothly with evidence of co-planning and communication between co-teachers.	0 = all planning appears to have been done by one adult and/or no planning is evident 1 = minimal planning and communication is evident; most appears to be done by one adult 2 = it is clear that both adults had input in lesson and communicate regularly as class progresses			
Differentiated strategies, to include technology, are used to meet the range of learning needs.	0 =t here is no evidence of differentiation of instruction or use of technology in the classroom 1 = there is minimal differentiation and use of technology; most differentiation appears to be focused on groups rather than individuals 2 = it is clear that adults considered individual student needs and differentiation and use of technology is evident where needed			

	LOOK FOR ITEMS	0 – Didn't See It 1 – Saw an Attempt 2 – Saw It Done Well		
		0	1	2
Both teachers engage in appropriate behavior management strategies as needed and are consistent in their approach to behavior management.	0 = there is no obvious plan for behavior management, nor do adults appear to communicate about how they are approaching class management; possibly inappropriate class management 1 = behavior management strategies are utilized but there is very little clear evidence of how adults have communicated about their use 2 = it is evident that adults have discussed how they will approach classroom/behavior management and adults are consistent in their approach; clear communication between adults			
It is difficult to tell the special educator from the general educator.	0 = Observer could easily determine who was the general/special educator by their language/ roles/ lack of parity. 1 = Observer could tell who was the general/special educator but there was a clear attempt at parity between the teachers. 2 = Observer would not be able to tell who was the general/special educator as parity was evident and adults shared the roles and responsibilities in the classroom.			
It is difficult to tell the special education students from the general education students.	0 = Observer could easily determine who were the general/special education students by their lack of integration (e.g., students at back or separated from class). 1 = Observer could tell who were the general/ special education students but there was a clear attempt at inclusion of students for most activities. 2 = Observer would not be able to tell who were the general/special education students as parity was evident and adults shared the responsibilities for working with all students.			
NOTES:				

Appendix 6: Co-Teaching Checklist: Look Fors (cont'd)

Note. Reprinted from "Observing Co-Teaching: What to Ask for, Look for, and Listen for," by W. W. Murawski and W. W. Lochner, 2011, *Intervention in School and Clinic, 46*(3), pp. 174–183. Copyright 2011 by Sage Publications. Reprinted with permission.

Appendix 7: Co-Teaching Checklist: Listen Fors				
General Educator: _____Special Service Provider: _____				
Observer: _____Date/Time: _____				
	LOOK FOR ITEMS	0 – Didn't See It 1 – Saw an Attempt 2 – Saw It Done Well		
		0	**1**	**2**
Co-Teachers use language that ("we"; "our") demonstrates true collaboration and shared responsibility.	0 = adults use "I" language frequently (e.g., "I want you to…" Or "In my class…"), lacking parity. 1 = adults attempt to use "we" language and include each other, but it is clear that one adult is more used to "ruling" the class 2 = adults clearly use "we" language (e.g., "We would like you to…"), showing that they both share the responsibility and students know they are equally in charge.			
Co-Teachers phrase questions and statements so that it is obvious that all students in the class are included	0 = class is very teacher-directed and little involvement by students; questions/statements are general and not inclusive of all students 1 = a few statements/questions are phrased to encourage participation from a variety of students. 2 = a clear attempt is made by both adults to engage all students through the use of a variety of types of questions and statements.			
Students' conversations evidence a sense of community (including peers with and without disabilities).	0 = students do not talk to one another ever during class or specific students are clearly excluded from the student interactions. 1 = most students appear to be included in the majority of student interactions. 2 = it is evident from the students' actions and words that all students are considered an equal part of the class and are included in all student interactions.			

Appendix 7: Co-Teaching Checklist: Listen Fors				
	LOOK FOR ITEMS	**0 – Didn't See It** **1 – Saw an Attempt** **2 – Saw It Done Well**		
		0	**1**	**2**
Co-teachers ask questions at a variety of levels to meet all students' needs (basic recall to higher order thinking).	0 = adults do not use questions or ask questions geared just to one level (to the middle or "watered down") 1 = adults use closed and open questions at a variety of levels in a general manner. 2 = adults used closed and open questions at a variety of levels in a way that demonstrates they are able to differentiate for specific students in order to ensure maximum (appropriate) levels of challenge.			
NOTES:				

Appendix 8: Co-Teaching Checklist: Look Fors				

General Educator: _____ Special Service Provider: _____

Observer: _____ Date/Time: _____

To Demonstrate the Following Aspects of Co-Teaching:	ASK FOR ITEMS	0 – Didn't See It 1 – Saw an Attempt 2 – Saw It Done Well		
CO-PLANNING	**WHAT ITEMS SHOULD INCLUDE**	0	1	2
Lesson Plans	Lesson plans should demonstrate that both teachers have thought about the instruction and will actively engage all students at the appropriate levels. The CTSS Teachers' Toolbox (www.coteachsolutions.com) and the Co-Teaching Lesson Plan book (www.nprinc.com) are excellent resources for co-planning.			
Modified Materials/ Videos	Co-teachers who have planned together proactively will have materials ready prior to the lesson. These may include books on tape, modified assignments, close-captioned video, manipulatives, etc.			
Letters Home/ Syllabi	All materials that are sent home to parents/ guardians can help demonstrate that co-teachers are engaged in co-planning. They should be co-signed and indicate parity between teachers.			
SHARE Worksheets	Co-teachers should have completed the SHARE worksheets recommended by Murawski and Dieker (2004).			
Problem Solving Worksheet	Co-teachers should be able to provide evidence of problem-solving. They can use a variety of formats (notes from planning) to work through major problems together.			

Appendix 8: Co-Teaching Checklist: Look Fors *(cont'd)*				
To Demonstrate the Following Aspects of Co-Teaching:	ASK FOR ITEMS	0 – Didn't See It 1 – Saw an Attempt 2 – Saw It Done Well		
CO-INSTRUCTING	**WHAT ITEMS SHOULD INCLUDE**			
Behavior Documentation	Co-teachers should be able to produce documentation of data they collect while co-teaching. This documentation could include behaviors, homework, tardiness, social skills, classwork and/or participation in data collection.			
Tiered Lessons	Co-teachers should be able to demonstrate how lessons are tiered to provide differentiated instruction to a variety of individual learners. Lessons should address the high, average, and low achievers.	0	1	2
Class Notes	Class notes indicate what was taught during the class & specifically what was emphasized. They also include mnemonics taught and, in some cases, modifications made.			
CO-ASSESSING	**WHAT ITEMS SHOULD INCLUDE**	0	1	2
Grade Book	Administrators can ask co-teachers to provide a copy of their grade books. Even if one teacher does the actual recording of the grades, it should be evident that both teachers had a hand in grading and communicating about assessments.			
Modified Assignments	Assignments and assessments need to be tailored to individual needs. Co-teachers should be able to provide copies of modified tests, examples of accommodations given to student with special needs, and lists of IEP requirements.			
Description of How Students Are Individually Graded	Co-teachers should have proactively discussed grading and how they will accommodate different learners. They may even have documentation of when they called or wrote parents to inform them of how the student with special needs would be graded in the class.			

Note. Adapted from "Observing Co-Teaching: What to Ask for, Look for, and Listen for", by W. W. Murawski and W. Lochner, 2011, *Intervention in School and Clinic 46*(3), 174–183. Copyright 2011. Adapted with permission.

Appendix 9: Sample Goals for Action Plan				
Goals	Current status of data collected in this area	Measurable Objective	Data to be collected	What if...
Inclusion: All teachers will clearly understand the philosophy of inclusion.	Only the special educators seem to know what co-teaching means, based on conversations.	Teachers will write their personal philosophies and we will come up with a common statement for our school.	Individual and collective goal statements	. . . they will not agree on a goal or write a goal? Plan B is that the principal will give teachers a set of statements to agree or disagree with & then discuss
Co-Teaching: We will increase the attendance and graduation rate of students with behavior disorders in our co-taught classes.	Only 50% of students at our school with behavior disorders in co-taught classes graduate. Only 30% passed the state exam in math and reading; Attendance is unknown	We will increase our graduation rate and proficiency rate for this population to at least 60%; we will gather data on attendance rate to see if this correlates with low success on state test	Attendance data; Conduct focus group with students with behavioral disorders who are not set to graduate; Plan to provide concrete supports through co-teaching models	. . . attendance data is not available school-wide or students are not willing to participate in focus groups? Plan B is that special educators will gather attendance data on their individual caseload of students & will meet with representative sample of students
Collaboration: My team will agree to do at least one observation of each other for 15 minutes to assist with ideas for class management.	We currently only observe each other when we co-teach but we do not have anything structured in place for classroom management.	All 5 team members will conduct at least one observation of 15 minutes and will be observed for at least 15 minutes also by another team member.	Observation notes; Plans made as a tem based on the behavioral issues identified in our observations	. . . someone does not agree to the observation or it cannot occur? Plan B is that the team members will spend at least 15 minutes talking about behavioral issues and classroom management

Appendix 10: Blank form for Goal Setting					
School-Wide Goals	Current status of data collected in this area	Measurable Objective	Data to be collected	What if...	Your role/ commitment

	Appendix 11: Data collection on goals

1. How will others who visit your school know that you are a strong inclusive school/classroom?
2. What will they see and hear that demonstrates your philosophy?
3. What data will you have that proves a commitment to your philosophy?

School-Wide Goals	Current status of data collected in this area	Measurable Objective	Data still to be collected	What if...	Your role/ commitment
5 year					
3 year					
1 year					
Personal or Classroom Level Goals	Current status of data collected in this area	Measurable Objective	Data still to be collected	What if...	Your role/ commitment
5 year					
3 year					
1 year					